COMMUNION WITH GOD
STUDENT'S STUDY MANUAL

By

Mark and Patti Virkler

This manual is the result of the united efforts of both authors. The concepts and ideas
are a culmination of cooperative study and revelation. The experiences described
are common to both. The pronoun "I" is used to demonstrate the unity of our thoughts.

Published by
Destiny Image

**Dedicated to
those who will not rest until
spiritual communion is restored
in their hearts.**

Destiny Image Publishers
P.O. Box 351
Shippensburg, PA 17257

"Speaking to the Purposes of God for this Generation"

ISBN 1-56043-012-5

For Worldwide Distribution
Printed in the U.S.A.

Acknowledgments

This book has been ten years in the making. It is probably impossible to thank all who have helped in so many ways. First, I want to thank Pioneer Christian Fellowship, the church I was pastoring when the Lord gave me this message. They offered me the opportunity to devote myself to the study of the Word, which resulted in this revelation. Next Full Gospel Tabernacle, under the leadership of Dr. Thomas Reid, picked up this message and had it more professionally produced. They had me teach this message many times in their church and Bible School and covered the message as it grew and deepened.

I also want to thank the hundreds of churches who taught this course and hosted me as I conducted "Communion With God" seminars worldwide. They have been my sounding board for this message and convinced me that the message can be applied by anyone who wishes to apply it. It will work for anyone. Through conducting seminars, I have watched tens of thousands of Christians move into two-way dialogue with Almighty God and have heard thousands of people read from their journals, thereby convincing me beyond any shadow of doubt that this truly is the voice of Almighty God coming through the heart of man.

I want to thank Claire Hudson for proofing this book several times, and the four pastors I currently submit to, who have covered me in the growth and release of this message to the body of Christ. They are Dr. John Watson from Marion, Ohio, Rev. Mart Vahi from Fredriction, New Brunswick, Canada, Rev. Maurice Fuller from Calgary, Alberta, Canada, and Pastor Roger Miller from Arcade, New York.

Special thanks to Rev. Maurice Fuller who is a theologian and a Greek and Hebrew scholar, for meticulously proofing this manuscript and for offering countless corrections on pointed Greek and Hebrew insights. These have been added and have improved the finished product considerably, as well as keeping us more accurately on the straight and narrow way.

Introduction

Since the beginning of the Christian Church, believers have been exhorted to pray. Yet in spite of those exhortations, most believers live a life of prayerlessness.

Ministers attend their convocations and invariably are challenged to develop a structured prayer life. Yet in serving God, their prayer life is constantly challenged by their busy schedules. The vows they made at the convocation are soon broken due to their relentless schedules.

These same ministers challenge their congregations to a life of prayer. Again the congregants sitting in their pews are challenged to a new commitment, which also is soon broken. The result is simply a feeling of condemnation because so few Christians have a formal prayer life.

The problem, I believe, is not commitment or lack of desire. The problem is rather the monotony of the prayer life itself. One hardly desires to carry on a monologue. It is understandably "boring" to talk to anyone who fails to talk back.

Thus our prayer lives are plagued by an improper understanding of biblical prayer. The Bible is the result of men and women who "heard from God." This God, we believe, still speaks today. Yet in our prayer lives, it seems, He seldom is heard. Rev. Mark Virkler, in his exciting course "Communion With God," presents to us a biblically sound definition of prayer. Prayer, to the author, is not simply a monologue, but a dialogue. He not only exhorts us to pray but also invites us to an exciting dimension of prayer that will make us want to pray on a regular basis. An orthodox definition of prayer that includes not only talking to God but also hearing God, combined with journaling what He has said, makes the prayer closet an exciting place to be.

I commend **Communion With God** to the church today. I believe it will change your life.

Tommy Reid,
Sr. Pastor, Full Gospel Tabernacle
Orchard Park, NY

Recommendation for Group Use

We recommend that those who want to study these principles do so with at least one other spiritually mature person. It is even better for a group to study together under the covering of a local church. See if your pastor will provide spiritual covering for this group and help you by offering this course to your entire church.

The inner way should not be traveled alone. There is too much room for deception. Commitment to a group and to mature shepherds in the body of Christ gives you the protection necessary to safely enter the Spirit world.

Additional Materials Available for This Course

Audio cassettes and video tapes of Mark Virkler teaching this course are available. See the order form in the back of this book. A teacher's guide and overhead transparencies are also available.

Table of Contents

Preface

All of us realize that prayer is our link to God, and therefore, the most important activity we can engage in. We also know that prayer is supposed to be powerful, effective and meaningful in our lives. Yet, many times it is not. That fact needs to be faced. We need to learn how to make prayer what it should be. Of paramount importance is learning to break free from the container of rationalism in which Western culture is locked and relearning how to have spiritual experiences — experiences that come from God's Spirit to my spirit and only secondarily to my brain. We must return to the balance that was so beautifully expressed in Jesus' life.

The following are the things I needed to learn for prayer to become purposeful in my life.

I can experience God through spiritual experiences rather than the dry monologue of simple mental prayer.

The essence of prayer is my love relationship with the King of Kings rather than my simply going to Him to get things.

The principles from the Bible that relate to prayer and the spiritual realm provide direction and understanding as I travel the road of spiritual experiences.

The Holy Spirit will mold my prayer life, instead of me taking the principles of prayer God has shown me and reducing them to legalistic bondage.

Spirit-born specific action and power flow as a natural result of my love relationship, causing the activities of my life to be of the Spirit and not the flesh. This keeps my relationship with the King of Kings from being simply self-indulgent on my part and helps me to realize that many others need to be touched by His love also.

Prayer and the Sovereignty of God

It is a bothersome question at times why one should pray if God is going to accomplish His will anyway. The startling fact is that God **voluntarily limits Himself to man's requests**. Please write out Ezekiel 22:30,31.

My prayer is, "Lord, would You restore prayer in our lives until it becomes what it is supposed to be! Amen. (So be it.)"

The Use and Abuse of Doctrine and Technique

We must receive the caution Jesus gave in John 5:39,40. "You search the Scriptures, because you think that in them you have eternal life; and it is these that bear witness to Me; and you are unwilling to come to Me, that you may have eternal life."

It is quite easy to acquire correct doctrine and head knowledge from Scripture. We can learn what the Word says about Christ and become satisfied with that information. But such intellectual exercise does not profit our spirits at all. We must take a further step of loving trust in Jesus as a person who is alive right now and yearns to be a part of our lives. Only through heart faith can we experience the things that the Scriptures testify about Him.

Finney spoke of three classes of people.

Many, understanding the "Confession of Faith" as summarizing the doctrines of the Bible, very much neglect the Bible and rest in a belief of the articles of faith. Others, more cautious and more in earnest, search the Scriptures to see what they say about Christ, but stop short and rest in the formation of correct theological opinions; while others, and they are the only saved class, love the Scriptures intensely because they testify of Jesus. They search and devour the Scriptures because they tell them who Jesus is and what they may trust Him for. They do not stop short and rest in this testimony; but by an act of loving trust [they] go directly to Him, to His person, thus joining their souls to Him in a union that receives from Him, by a direct divine communication, the things for which they are led to trust Him. This is certainly Christian experience. This is receiving from Christ the eternal life which God has given us in Him. This is saving faith...The error to which I call attention does not consist in laying too much stress in teaching and believing the facts and doctrines of the Gospel: but consists in stopping short of trusting the personal Christ for what those facts and doctrines teach us to trust Him, and satisfying ourselves with believing the testimony about Him, instead of committing our souls to Him by an act of loving trust. (Taken from protected material used by permission of the Christian Literature Crusade, Fort Washington, Pa. 10934.)

Do not stop with the doctrine and techniques taught in this manual or trust in them. Life and power flow only from Jesus. On the other hand, do not discard doctrines or techniques. Recognize that they have been given as channels through which the grace of God flows. May they be used

to lead us into a full encounter with our Lord Jesus Christ, allowing us to fully experience His life.

Memory Verses

Each week share with the group a memory verse that strengthens you in your prayer life.

Writing Out Verses

Many of the references given in this manual are followed by blank spaces. You are to fill in the verses indicated. It is extremely valuable for you to write out Scripture. Many times as I write the Word I see things I have never seen before.

The Prayer Life of Your Group

You would find it very profitable to record the prayer items of your group and the answers to them.

Beginning To Pray

One really learns to pray **when he begins praying.** We do not need people who think about prayer, who learn about prayer, or who preach about prayer. We need people who pray. Your prayer life is the proof of the pudding; it is where the rubber meets the road. Whether or not you have excelled in prayer will be determined by your prayer life and the results that flow from it.

Very Different from the New Age Movement!

Sometimes people ask me what the difference is between what the New Age teaches and what I am teaching here in **Communion With God.** As I demonstrate on the following page, we begin and build from **a totally different foundation** than the New Age movement.

Therefore, the differences are immense. And these are just a few. As we go along I will point out more. I believe it is ludicrous to suggest that people beginning from such totally opposite foundations could end up in the same place. The New Ager will find himself contacting demons, familiar spirits and evil spirits. The Christian who is covered by the blood of Jesus and guided by Jesus will be led into the throne room of God as John was in Revelation.

The Christian who has decided that the Bible is no longer for today, and that the Spiritual experiences found therein are not able to be experienced by the Church of Jesus Christ, will likely relegate all and any spiritual experiences to satan. I, however, believe the Bible is for today and is to be lived in its fullness. Even though for many years I was taught to dispensationalize many parts of it away, I have now rejected that teaching and discovered myself as a Bible-believing Christian — one who believes the Bible is to be lived today!

We believe:	**The New Ager believes:**
The God of the Bible is the God of this universe.	The God of the Bible is not the God of this universe.
Salvation is by the blood of Jesus.	There is no need of salvation.
The Bible is the inerrant Word of God.	The Bible is not the inerrant Word of God.
One should be a student of the Bible.	There is no need to be a student of the Bible.
All Spirit encounter must be tested against the Bible.	Spirit encounter need not be tested against the Bible.
One should be linked to the body of Christ.	There is no need whatsoever to be linked to the body of Christ.
Each one must walk under the spiritual covering of a Christian pastor.	There is no need to walk under the spiritual covering of a Christian pastor.

PART 1

RESTORING THE SPIRITUAL ASPECT OF PRAYER

I will stand at my GUARD POST
And I will keep WATCH and SEE
What He will SPEAK to me.
Then the Lord said,
RECORD THE VISION.
(Habakkuk 2:12)

Chapter 1

Laying the Foundation

Prerequisites for Studying This Text

This course is not for everyone. In this course you are going to learn how to "enter the spiritual realm." There you will find both the Holy Spirit and the evil spirit. Without protective covering, you can easily become entangled and destroyed by the enemy. Therefore, God has laid out some very clear protective guidelines that will keep you safe as you enter the spiritual world. Stated succinctly they are:

- That you be a born-again Christian, having renounced a life of living for self and embraced the saving power of Jesus' cleansing blood on Calvary.

- That you believe the Bible as the inerrant Word of God.

- That you have a basic working knowledge of at least the New Testament and be working on the rest of the Bible.

- That you be submitted to that which God has shown you from the Word.

- That you be linked to a local expression of the body of Christ and submitted to your spiritual overseer(s).

A fairly young Christian can meet all these requirements. It only takes a day and a half to read through the New Testament, and the rest of the requirements can be met upon conversion. It is best if new Christians begin communing with God during the early days of their walk with God. There they will find the rest and peace their souls so eagerly long for.

Establishing a Spiritual Covering

I believe it is absolutely imperative that everyone establish people in positions of authority in their lives. The Bible says we are to submit ourselves to one another (Eph. 5:21). Hebrews 13:17 specifically states, "Obey your leaders, and submit to them; for they watch over your soul, as those who will give an account. Let them do this with joy and not grief, for this would be unprofitable for you."

What is the purpose of submitting ourselves to someone over us in the Lord? "In the multitude of counselors there is safety (Prov. 11:14, KJV)." God has established spiritual authority as an umbrella of protection to keep us from self-deception within our own hearts, as well as from the deception of satan.

This becomes particularly necessary as one begins to walk in the spirit realm, becoming open to visions and God's intuitive voice within. The role of the spiritual authority is to help catch error in one's journaling and, when necessary, to caution him to wait a bit before proceeding with any action. He also provides much needed confirmation for the learner who is just beginning to hear God's voice, offering him encouragement to go on and assuring him that it truly is the voice of God he is hearing.

The center of this relationship is not authority but friendship.

One who can serve effectively as a spiritual shepherd in another's life is one who is:

- A **close friend** — one who knows the sheep and whose sheep recognize his voice.

- He is one who has a **solid biblical orientation.**

- He can sense — Is sensitive to the **voice of the Spirit** of God in his own heart.

- He is one who is willing to **commit himself to the sheep,** who will invest his time and energy, and is willing to lay down his life for the sheep for whom he is responsible.

- He is **himself submitted**.

The sheep, on the other hand, honors the voice of the shepherd. He is willing to follow the shepherd where he leads and submit his own will to the will of the one over him (Heb. 13:17). He has learned to honor the protective covering of the one God has placed over him. He takes major decisions in his life to the one over him in the Lord and submits them to him before acting on them. A major decision is one that calls for a major change in the direction of his life, his ministry, his job, or a major investment that will commit him financially for several years. (Thus, he can be kept from making a mistake that may leave him in financial poverty for a period of his life.) The sheep has also learned to take his initial journaling and prophecy to his shepherd for covering and confirmation, in order to help him gain confidence in discerning the voice of God within his heart.

The sheep also recognizes that God is the authority over all authorities (Rom. 13:1), and that the heart of the king is in the Lord's hand (Prov. 21:1). Therefore, as he prays for the one over him (1 Tim. 2:1-4), he trusts God to work His perfection through man's imperfection.

When asked, the shepherd will seek God for confirmation or adjustment concerning the things the sheep brings before him. He will share with the sheep those things the Lord speaks into his own heart. If there is a discrepancy, the sheep will go back to the Lord, seeing what God has to say to help clear up the disagreement. He will again present to his shepherd what he senses God is saying, in an effort to resolve the difficulty. If the difficulty cannot be solved, the sheep will accept the will of the shepherd, unless it contradicts a clear command of God in Scripture.

More complete teaching on the principle of authority is given in Chapter 13 and in the "Institute of Basic Youth Conflicts" by Bill Gothard.

Can't Find a Covering?

Some people have a hard time finding a spiritual covering. Let me suggest a few helpful hints. First, recognize that there are no perfect people to submit to. Therefore you might as well plan to submit to an imperfect person and trust that God can work His perfection through imperfect people. Also, look at the people God has already placed around you. You will most likely find your spiritual covering among them. Friends, husband, home cell group leaders, elders, deacons and pastors are all eligible candidates.

How many do I submit to?

Every fact is to be confirmed by the testimony of two or three witnesses (2 Cor. 13:1).

It is recommended that each individual be under the covering of two or three others. When major directional moves are being made, there should be a consensus of all three. I have consistently been submitted to at least three individuals since 1976. They have effectively kept me from making any major mistakes in my life during the last 13 years. That is one of the reasons I love submission.

To Whom Should I Submit?

Some of these relationships are already in place. For instance, parents, husbands, employers, home cell group leaders, pastors, elders, etc. all have spheres of authority and influence in your life. A wife should obviously submit to her husband. Husbands should submit to pastors. A wife may also want a second person to submit some of her journaling to. She and her husband should talk over who this woman should be and agree together so they are both comfortable with the choice. It should be a woman rather than a man since it is not wise to build close spiritual relationships with the opposite sex. There is too much danger that they will evolve into physical relationships and cause destructive explosions.

Isn't This Like Shepherding?

Yes and no. Those involved in the shepherding movement were trying to restore the concept of spiritual covering and spiritual authority. It was a valiant effort, however, in some cases it turned into domination, legalism and a spirit of control. Jesus said that we do not rule over others as the heathen do with the use of force, but **in love we serve one another**. The use of domination, intimidation and control is strictly forbidden within the way of love (1 Pet. 5:1-6). Love draws, domination forces. Therefore I will repeat, the center of these relationships is friendship rather than authority.

Furthermore, I believe we are free to change spiritual shepherds as we grow and change. If you change shepherds every six months, this most likely indicates a problem in your life. However, if every five years or so you are changing shepherds, it may be an indication that growth and change are taking place in your life, which is necessitating new people to mentor you. The important thing is that when you leave one covering relationship you enter another; you should not live without adequate covering.

> **Prayer:** *God, we trust you to work through the principle of authority as laid out in Your Word, and to work Your perfection through our imperfection. To God be the glory, Amen.*

An Overview of the Four Keys to Hearing God's Voice

We will close this preliminary chapter with an overview of the four major keys that opened the door for me and thousands of others to hear the Lord's voice. We will discuss them in depth in the chapters that follow. They are as follows:

As exemplified in Habakkuk:	Stated succinctly:
"I will stand on my guardpost ..."	Have a quiet place to quiet yourself before the Lord.
"And I will keep watch to see"	Look for vision as you pray.
"What He will speak to me ..."	Recognize God's voice as thoughts.
"Then the Lord answered me and said, 'Record the vision ...' "	Record God's words in your journal.

(Hab. 2:1,2)

To Be Signed By One's Shepherd/Spiritual Covering

Having understood the role of a spiritual shepherd as explained above, I sense that God has called me to fill this role in the life of _____ at this time, and I pledge myself to faithfulness in this responsibility.

I myself walk in submission to other recognized spiritual men in the Body of Christ. I understand that to lead with authority does not involve domination, but servant leadership, a giving of my life for the sheep.

When asked for counsel in an area in which I do not feel fully qualified, I will recommend other spiritual oversight which is recognized as strong in that area.

I will never ask a person under my covering to do anything forbidden in Scripture. If these principles are not kept on my part, the person indicated above is released from my spiritual covering and encouraged to find another shepherd to whom he can submit.

Date_____

Name_____

Please fill in this form in duplicate so both parties in this relationship may have a copy. This completed form must be shown to the instructor before the fourth week of the course, "Communion With God" if the student is to remain in the course. The above page may be photocopied so the spiritual shepherd may have a copy.

Chapter 2

"Spiritual Encounter" — The Other Half of Life

Christianity Is More Than a Religion!

One basic distinction between Christianity and the many other religions is that Christianity goes beyond a simple code of ethics, a list of rules and laws that one must follow, and offers direct, spiritual experiences with a loving God. We not only **know about** God, we **experience** Him. We not only say the sinner's prayer, we experience His Spirit bearing witness with our spirits that we are the children of God (Rom. 8:16). We not only seek guidance from the laws of the Bible, we also find guidance through the Spirit granting peace in our hearts. We do not simply read the Bible as a lifeless book with black print on white pages, but we experience it as alive (Heb. 4:12). God "illumines" or quickens it to our hearts as we pray for a spirit of revelation (Eph. 1:17). We do not just pray for a list of things; rather, God "burdens" our hearts to pray for things He desires.

God has sent His Holy Spirit into our hearts, crying "Abba Father" (Rom. 8:15), so that we can have a direct on-going love experience with Him. It is a major provision of the New Testamental period that God has come to dwell within the hearts of men. This is taught in many places throughout the Bible. For instance:

> *And I will ask the Father, and He will give you another Helper, that He may be with you forever; that is the Spirit of truth, whom the world cannot receive, because it does not behold Him or know Him, but you know Him because He abides with you, and will be in you. I will not leave you as orphans; I will come to you (John 14:16-18).*

> *Or do you not know that your body is a temple of the Holy Spirit who is in you, whom you have from God, and that you are not your own? (1 Cor. 6:19)*

> *But we have this treasure in earthen vessels, that the surpassing greatness of the power may be of God and not from ourselves ... (2 Cor. 4:7)*

I am sure all Christians have experienced the truth of Philippians 4:13, "I can do all things through Him [Christ] Who strengthens me [fuses His strength to mine, Greek]." Being too weak to handle a problem, we have called upon the indwelling Spirit to help us and have found His strength overcoming our weakness, His joy overcoming our sorrow, or His peace overcoming our anxiety.

Therefore, Christianity is much more than a code of ethics; it is much more than a religion. It is a love relationship with the King of Kings. It is a direct encounter with Him through the indwelling work of His Holy Spirit, which we freely receive as His gift to us.

This, then, causes Christianity to ascend far beyond rationalism into the world of direct spiritual experiences. First Corinthians 2:9,10 tells us:

> *Things which eye has not seen and ear has not heard, and which have not entered the heart of man, all that God has prepared for those who love Him. For to us God revealed them through the Spirit; for the Spirit searches all things, even the depths of God.*

Heart to Heart — Not Head to Head

We come to know truth with our hearts or spirits, rather than with our minds. God reveals things that our natural eyes and ears could never sense through His Spirit speaking directly to our spirits. It is not that our natural eyes, ears and mind have no place in God's glorious revelation, for they are wonders of His creation as much as our hearts and spirits are. However, each part of man (his body, soul and spirit) has a special function in God's plan. God says that there are some things that He "reveals through the Spirit," which we must then take and test against the Bible, using our minds. Through the indwelling Holy Spirit, God has given us direct communion with Himself. We hear His voice within our hearts. We are led by the Spirit (Rom. 8:14). We have inner subjective experiences. Through insight, we receive revelation from Him, and He illumines Scripture to us. Through intuition, we sense the promptings of the Holy Spirit and the voice of God. So, our life in the spirit, our relationship with God, is an inner, intuitive, spiritual, heart experience.

Experiencing Scripture, Not Just Codifying It

I can study the Bible rationally, simply with the mind, and learn many facts about God. For instance, I can learn that God loves me. But since love is an inner heart experience, I cannot fully experience God's love until He touches my heart with His love, heals my hurts, and breaks my hardness. When He fills me to overflowing and brings tears of joy to my eyes, then through an intuitive, spiritual experience, I have fully experienced the love I read about.

However, spirit-to-Spirit encounters with God have become much too rare among Western Christians. Since rationalism has taken over the Western world in the past few hundred years, the Church has also come under its influence and has not given the attention it should have to the work of the Spirit in our lives. Therefore, we are often bound by rationalism and miss the fullness of relationship with our Father that the early Church enjoyed.

Forty-nine percent of the New Testament contains references to spiritual (non-rational) experiences. To be bound by rationalism will effectively cut off half of New Testament Christianity. If one is not relating intuitively to God, but only rationally, he will lose his opportunity to flow in the nine gifts of the Holy Spirit (word of wisdom, word of knowledge, faith, healing, miracles, prophecy, distinguishing of spirits, kinds of tongues and interpretation of tongues); to receive guidance through dreams and visions; to have a fully meaningful and effective prayer life; to commune with the Lord in a dialogue, building an extremely intimate relationship with Him; and to fully experience the inward benefits of true worship.

Through rationalism (an over-emphasis on reason), Christianity and the Western world have ceased to know how to deal with their inner lives (commonly called heart, spirit, subconscious, "unconscious"). Because this whole area of our lives has been cut off and ignored, not only by Western culture but also by the Church, people have not been able to deal successfully with the forces within them (repressed hurts, fears, anxieties, forces of darkness — demons) and have been left more and more to seek out various escapes such as drinking, drugs, sensual fulfillment and suicide. Others become neurotic and psychotic; still others go to the occult and Eastern religions to satisfy the inner desires of the spirit which are not being met in "rational Christianity."

We must rediscover direct spiritual contact with God and once again become open to intuitive, spiritual experiences. We must rediscover our spiritual senses and reinstate them in our lives, thereby allowing the power of God, Jesus Christ, and the Holy Spirit to heal, empower and guide us from within. Therein lies the work of the Church. Direct inner experiences with the Lord bring healing to the spirit, soul and body.

Take your Bible and **prayerfully read and meditate on** First Corinthians 1:18-2:16, asking God to grant you understanding and revelation concerning these verses. In the following blank space, please record the thoughts and revelations you receive. Please do it now.

The following is a brief comparison of rationalism and "Spirit-to-spirit encounters." Take time to consider its truth and your own life in regard to these two philosophies. Where do you stand?

The Mind and the Spirit (I Cor. 1:18-2:16)

To experience spiritual communication, most Westerners will have to do the following:

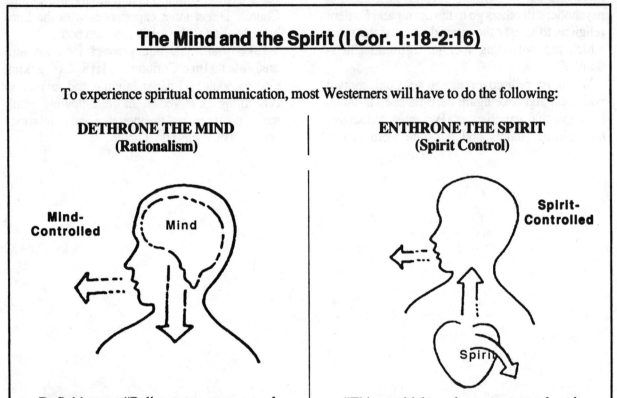

DETHRONE THE MIND (Rationalism)	ENTHRONE THE SPIRIT (Spirit Control)

Definition — "Reliance on reason as the basis for establishment of religious truth ... a theory that reason is in itself a source of knowledge superior to and independent of sense perceptions."
(Webster's New Collegiate Dictionary)

"Things which eye has not seen and ear has not heard, and which have not entered the heart of man, all that God has prepared for those who love Him. For to us God revealed them through the Spirit; for the Spirit searches all things, even the depths of God (1 Cor. 2:9,10)."

Brief historical background: Thomas Aquinas (A.D. 1225-1274), a philosopher and theologian, laid the foundation for rationalism to take over Christian experience. Toward the end of his life, the Lord showed him through dreams, visions AND REVELATION (spiritual experiences) the inability to enclose Christianity within rationalism and, when urged to write about it, he replied, "I can do no more; such things have been revealed to me that all I have written seems as straw, and I now await the end of my life."
(Encyclopedia Britannica)

The men of the Bible believed in and experienced direct communication with God. Fully one-half of the New Testament contains references to spiritual experiences, whether it be with the Holy Spirit, angels, demons, the devil, dreams, visions, or the gifts of the Holy Spirit in operation.

A Brief Examination of the Two Approaches

True reality is the physical world.	True reality is the spiritual world.
Reality is perceived through the mind.	Reality is perceived through the spirit.
My goal is to develop my mind.	My goal is to develop my spirit.
I live out of what my mind is telling me.	I live out of what my spirit is telling me.
My mind directs me through calculated, cognitive and analytical thoughts.	My spirit directs me through spontaneous, flowing thoughts that are placed in it by the Spirit of God.
My mind is cultivated by using it in academic study.	My spirit is cultivated by using it in communication with God.
Direction is received from it by analysis of stored knowledge.	Direction is received from it by waiting quietly upon the Lord allowing Him to spontaneously inject into my heart His thoughts, burdens and visions.
Out of the mind flows *logos* — the written, recorded Word.	Out of the spirit flows *rhema* — what God is speaking to me at that moment.
A Christian who has **only** developed his mind, flows with a knowledge of the *logos*.	A Christian with a developed spirit flows with the power of the Spirit and is grounded in a knowledge of the *logos*.

God is not calling us to use the mind **OR** the spirit, but the mind **AND** the spirit. Biblical meditation **combines the analysis of the mind with the spontaneity of the heart** (or both left and right brain functions).

Jesus joined rationalism and spiritual communion in a perfect balance in His own personal life. Let us seek to do the same. One's life will be fully restored and balanced when it matches the lives of New Testament Christians.

Being a Christian does not mean throwing your mind away. Your mind is highly used as you approach God, but your mind has now found its **proper place**. Although it is the organ that **processes** revelation, it is not the organ through which revelation is **received**. The spirit is. The mind and the spirit work hand-in-hand. Direction in your walk comes by *rhema* through your spirit. Your mind continuously acts as a check and safeguard, comparing all *rhema* to *logos*. Revelation itself is not irrational, but rather **super-rational**. To say it another way, revelation is not foolishness; it has simply taken into account the reality of the spiritual world, and this appears irrational to rationalism, which has limited its scope merely to the physical world.

For example, for Abraham and Sarah to believe they were going to have a baby at 90 years of age is irrational if your framework is limited only to the physical laws. However, if you believe in a God who does inject His supernatural power into the natural, and Who said He was going to give them a child, then it is perfectly rational (or super-rational) to believe for a child.

Contrasting Two Worldviews

The following are two worldviews which are available for you to embrace. Only one of them is right, but let me show you both so you can carefully examine your life and determine your position, and then decide if that is where you want to stand.

One Worldview — Rationalism

In this worldview one believes that man lives in a box. It is a space/time/energy/mass box. This is the totality of the real world. Man touches this world through his five outer senses: touch, taste, sight, hearing and smell. If he were to leave this box and travel toward the spiritual world, he would find that the spiritual world is either non-existent or, if it does exist, it is unknowable.

This is the worldview the Church taught me when I was first saved. They did admit to a spiritual world, but they said it was unknowable in this dispensation. I was told not to expect any direct contact with God during this age because we had been given the Bible and there was no longer a need to encounter God directly. I was also taught not to expect dreams or visions or God's voice or tongues or healing or miracles or any of the gifts of the Holy Spirit to operate. Even though my mind accepted this teaching, my heart hungered for direct spirit encounter with Almighty God, and it would not be satisfied with anything less.

First Worldview

Spiritual World Nonexistant or Unknowable

THE BOX

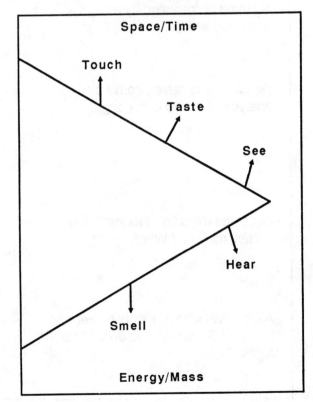

A Second Worldview — Rationalism/Mysticism Combined

Mysticism is not a word I use very often because of the Church's paranoia and inability to separate Eastern mysticism from Christian mysticism. However, here I am using it to mean **a belief in direct spirit encounter.** Surely Christianity as it is portrayed in the Bible involves a lot of direct spirit encounter as God meets with mankind through angels, dreams, visions, His voice and supernatural occurrences of many kinds.

In this worldview one believes that there is both a physical world and a spiritual world. Man is a conscious individual, with five senses that touch the outer world: touch, taste, sight, hearing and smell. However, in this worldview man is recognized as having a heart or a spirit also. Paul called this the "inner man" in Romans 7:22; this part of man also has five senses. These five senses are designed to touch the spiritual world. They are: the eyes of the heart, which see dream and vision; the ears of the heart, which hear God's spoken words (as well as the words of satan, angels and demons); the inner mind, which is able to ponder and meditate deep within (for example, the Bible says in Luke 2:19 that "Mary pondered these things in her heart"); the inner will, where man can make commitments as Paul did when he "purposed in his spirit to go to Jerusalem (Acts 19:21)"; and the emotion of his heart, where man is able to sense and experience the emotions of Almighty God flowing through him. For example, love, joy and peace are all emotions of God that are grown within us as the fruit of the Holy Spirit. The Holy Spirit is joined to our spirits (1 Cor. 6:17), and thus we experience the emotions of God through the emotional capacity of our spirits, which have been designed by God to pick up and incubate the emotions of His Holy Spirit Who lives within us.

In this worldview, instead of having five senses that touch one world, we have ten senses that touch two worlds. Obviously this person will live a much fuller and more complete life than the one who lives rationally only. In this worldview, we recognize that both God and satan are able to communicate to man on both levels, through the

outer world and through the inner spiritual world. For example the Bible says that "the devil ha[d] already **put into the heart** of Judas Iscariot, the son of Simon, to betray Him ... (John 13:2, author's emphasis)."

The following diagram outlines this second worldview.

Second Worldview

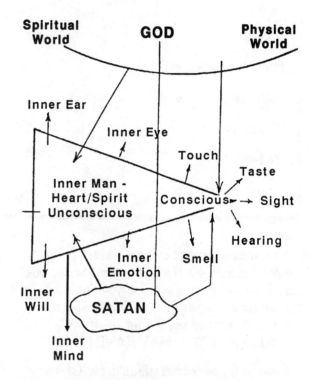

Which Worldview Is Yours?

In which worldview do you live more comfortably? Are you more comfortable responding to your outer senses, or are you more at ease with your inner senses, such as vision and intuition? If you are not living as you want to, you can change. First, acknowledge you are not what you want to be and ask the Lord's forgiveness for allowing yourself to be led astray by the rationalism of our culture. Second, ask the Lord to change you, to heal you, and to restore the eyes and ears of your heart. Then continue reading, and we will give you more specific help in making this transition. I had to make this change ten years ago, so I can promise you it is possible.

Going Beyond Rational Christianity

As I began moving away from rational Christianity toward spiritual Christianity, the Lord gave me the following focuses to help me see the moves I needed to make.

Rational Christianity	Spiritual Christianity
Code of ethics	The power that works within
Laws	Intimacy (Abba Father)
Works	Romance (marriage of the Bride)
Head Knowledge	Illumined Truth
External guidance	Bearing witness
Theology	Spirit encounter
Self-effort	Fused strength
Conscious level only	Dreams, visions, communion

Then the Lord spoke to me a verse of Scripture from John. 5:39,40. He said to me, "Mark, 'you search the Scriptures, because you think that in them you have eternal life; and it is these that bear witness of Me; and you are unwilling to COME TO ME, THAT YOU MAY HAVE LIFE.' "

It was as if a sword went through me. Of course! I had idolized the Bible! In my love for the Scriptures, I had made them God rather than a book that God had written to me about other people's experiences with Him. I had been willing to live out of the Bible, rather than out of God Himself. I was pierced within as I realized that Jesus had initially spoken this verse to the Pharisees of His day. I began to argue with God that I wasn't a Pharisee! But as I told Him everything I did, the Lord told me that the Pharisees also had done those things. I became frightened, realizing that it was very likely I might indeed be a pharisee. I noted that the thing the Pharisees loved most was the Law. They memorized it, spoke it, lived it and taught it to others. That was a perfect description of me. I had been taught to live out of biblical law rather than out of an intimacy with the Holy Spirit. I had not learned how to live out of the truth that Christ had died so we could continuously experience the life of the Holy Spirit within us, and live out of Him, rather than a code.

> *And I will ask the Father, and He will give you another Helper, that He may be with you forever; that is the Spirit of truth, whom the world cannot receive, because it does not behold Him or know Him, but you know Him because He abides with you, and will be in you (John 14:16,17).*

Offering a Prayer of Repentance

I repented, asking the Lord's forgiveness for living like a pharisee and idolizing the Bible. I made a commitment to **come to Him** and to begin trusting the moving of the Holy Spirit within my heart. **It was a new beginning for me!**

If you need to offer a similar prayer, please stop now and spend time with God before continuing.

Discussion of Left and Right Hemisphere Brain Functions *

You may think it strange to be discussing left and right hemisphere brain functions in the middle of a discussion on spirituality and hearing the voice of God. I find it interesting to note studies being undertaken in disciplines other than Christianity that confirm the steps of growth that I am taking in my Christian walk. The discussion on left and right hemisphere brain functions is one of these studies.

In 1981, Roger Sperry won the Nobel Peace Prize for his experimentation on left and right hemisphere brain functions. It has been discovered that although we do use both sides of our brains, most of us tend to lean a bit more heavily on one side or the other. The chart on the following page provides a pictorial overview of the functions carried on by each hemisphere of the brain. Please take a moment and examine it now.

You will note that the left hemisphere of the brain works primarily with analytical functions, while the right hemisphere processes intuitive and visionary functions.

In surveying groups of people in America, I have found that approximately 60% lean toward left brain functions and about 40% toward right brain functions. (In surveying groups of Australians, I noted that the percentages were reversed, an interesting reflection of their more casual approach to life.) Only a few indicate that they have a balance between the two. This imbalance probably exists because our educational system considers reading, writing and arithmetic (required courses which deal with left brain functions) to be more central to effective living than art, music and drama (elective courses which deal with right brain functions).

This idolatry of the left brain functions is so complete in our culture that scientists have discovered that the left half of the brain actually grows slightly heavier than the right side of the brain during the schooling years.

Psychologists tell us that they consider the majority of people in our culture to be neurotic. I suspect that a large contributing factor to this wide spread neurosis is the failure to cultivate both sides of our brains in a balanced way.

Corresponding to this idolization of logic is the demise of creativity, which is more of a right brain function involving vision, intuition and visualization. Statistics show that almost all children rank high in creativity before they enter school at age five. By age seven, only 10% rank high in creativity, and by the time we are adults, only 2% rank high in creativity. Therefore, what we are doing in our current educational system is essentially destroying the creative ability God has placed within man. I believe it is partly because we train the left side of the brain — the logical, analytical part — and stifle the right side of the brain — the intuitive, imaginative side. Where in Scripture do we see God suggesting we do this? I suspect God gave us two sides of our brains so we could use both sides.

Understanding right and left brain functions can help us understand and respect those with gifts different from ours. For instance, when a husband and wife are involved in making a decision, the husband may reason it out (a left brain function) while the wife may intuit the decision (a right brain function). If they have learned to honor the strengths in one another, they will not cut off the other's gift simply because it does not line up with their own decision-making process, but will instead value it as a complement to their own abilities.

When learning to receive revelation from God, those who function in the left brain will find the revelation process flowing through their analytical thoughts. As an example, Luke (Luke 1:1-4) investigated everything carefully, then wrote it out in consecutive order (obviously left brain activity). However, this process resulted in a pure word of revelation that still stands today. May I suggest that he allowed the Holy Spirit's intuitive, spontaneous impressions to flow into his reasoning process, and the end product was pure revelation.

---

* For a well-researched, practical and plain account of left and right brain functions, along with methods of cultivating the less used side of one's brain, read **Whole Brain Thinking** by Jacquelyn Wonder and Priscilla Donovan, published by Ballantine Books, 1984. (Not a Christian Book.)

Left- and Right-Hemisphere Brain Functions

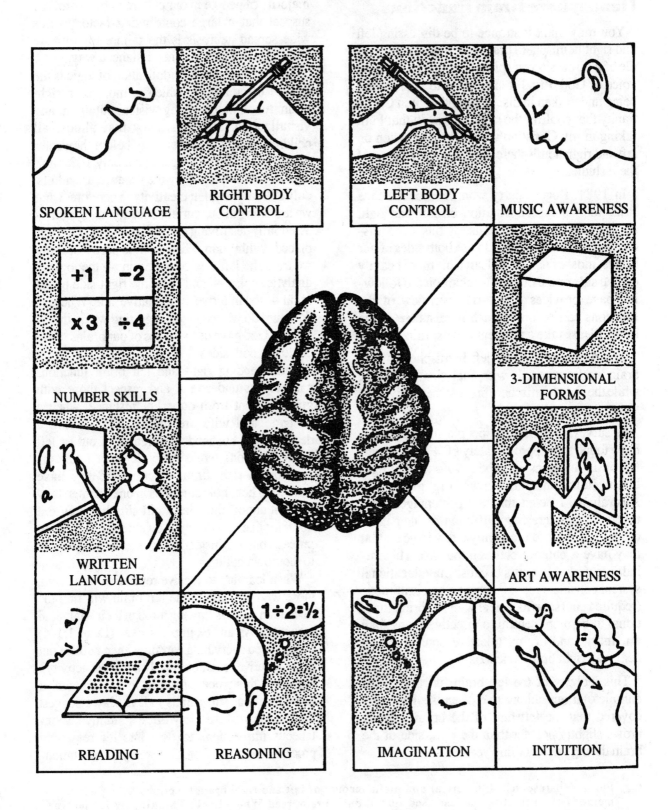

On the other hand, when John wrote Revelation he said, "I was in the Spirit on the Lord's day, and I heard behind me a loud voice ... saying, 'Write in a book what you see ...' (Rev. 1:10-11)." This revelation process involved no left brain functions (except the actual writing). Rather, I believe it flowed through the right side of the brain, coming from the heart. This process also resulted in a pure revelation, one that still stands today. I do not equate the right side of the brain directly with the heart. Rather I would like to **suggest** that the capacities of the heart flow into our consciousness through the right side of the brain.

You can see that there are at least two different approaches one can use when receiving pure revelation: Luke's method and John's method. Both are valid. Both can result in purity. Both are to be honored. It is hard for us to honor the one who is different from us. The left brain person is likely to characterize the right brain person as flaky, impulsive and fly-by-night. The right brain person is likely to characterize the left brain person as being so analytical and academic that there is no possibility that the Holy Spirit could flow through him or her. Let us come to the place where we can honor both Luke's and John's approach to receiving revelation, knowing that the Holy Spirit can flow purely through both.

Let us also consider the approach of Elisha as he sought to hear the voice of the Lord. People often ask, "How can I set aside academic reasoning and experience the inner intuitive flow?" When Elisha wanted to move from academic reasoning (a left brain activity) to hear a word of the Lord spoken intuitively within (flowing through the right side of his brain), he would engage in a right brain activity (i.e. "Bring me a minstrel, so that I might hear the word of the Lord," — paraphrased from 2 Kings 3:15). The music would draw him from the left side of his brain to the right side where he would be perfectly positioned before the presence of the Lord, able to hear the intuitive words that were spoken within. Often people find that the use of vision or enjoying the beauty of nature (both right brain functions) also positions them properly before the

intuitive voice of the Holy Spirit. Therefore, I recommend the use of vision, music and nature when one is seeking to hear the intuitive voice of the Holy Spirit being spoken within. An interesting footnote to this all is made by the studies of Calvin Jeske, from Calgary, Canada. In university studies, he has shown that speaking in tongues stimulates right brain electrical activity, as opposed to normal speech, which stimulates left brain electrical activity.

Intuition — Man's Heart or the Holy Spirit?

I believe both that the voice of intuition is the voice of man's heart, and that it can go beyond this to the voice of the Holy Spirit, Who is fused to the Christian's heart. If man fixes his eyes on himself and tunes to intuition, the intuitive flow is most likely to be the voice of his own heart. If man "fixes his eyes on Jesus the Author and Perfecter of his faith" and tunes to intuition, the intuitive flow will most likely be from Jesus.

In coming to the balance of Jesus of Nazareth, we must learn to be intuitive **and** visionary (John 5:9,20,30) **and** academic. (An example of the latter is Jesus' ability to defeat the scribes and Pharisees in theological debate.) For most of us, that will require stretching and growing, a laying down of what is comfortable, and a willingness to be changed into His likeness. It has taken several years of conscious effort for me to move away from my own marriage to rationalism and come closer to the balance of my Lord and Savior, Jesus Christ.

The test that follows has been scientifically developed and researched; it may be used to help you determine with which side of the brain you currently tend to live most often. You are to check the **one answer that best applies.** Even though you may want to check a couple of answers, if you think about it, you will probably recognize that you lean toward one specific answer most. For questions 8 and 33 you may give more than one answer.

Brain Preference Indicator Test

1.   In a problem-solving situation, do you:
      ____   a.   take a walk and mull solutions over, then discuss them?
      ____   b.   think about, write down all alternatives, arrange them according to priorities, and
                    then pick the best?
      ____   c.   recall past experiences that were successful and implement them?
      ____   d.   wait to see if the situation will right itself?

2.   Daydreaming is:
      ____   a.   a waste of time.
      ____   b.   amusing and relaxing.
      ____   c.   a real help in problem-solving and creative thinking.
      ____   d.   a viable tool for planning my future.

3.   Glance quickly at this picture.

      Was the face smiling?
      ____   a.   yes
      ____   b.   no

4.   Concerning hunches:
      ____   a.   I frequently have strong ones and follow them.
      ____   b.   I occasionally have hunches but don't place much faith in them.
      ____   c.   I occasionally have hunches but don't place much faith in them.
      ____   d.   I would not rely on hunches to help me make important decisions.

5.   In thinking about the activities of your day, which is most typical of your "style"?

_____ a.   I make a list of all the things I need to do ... people to see.

_____ b.   I picture the places I will go, people I'll see, things I'll do.

_____ c.   I just let it happen.

_____ d.   I plan the day's schedule, block out appropriate times for each item or activity.

6.   Do you usually have a place for everything, a system for doing things, and an ability to organize information and materials?

_____ a.   yes

_____ b.   no

7.   Do you like to move your furniture, change the decor of your home or office frequently?

_____ a.   yes

_____ b.   no

8.   Please check which of these activities you enjoy:

_____	swimming	_____	travel
_____	tennis	_____	bicycling
_____	golf	_____	collecting
_____	camping/hiking	_____	writing
_____	skiing	_____	chess
_____	fishing	_____	bridge
_____	singing	_____	roulette
_____	gardening	_____	charades
_____	playing instrument	_____	dancing
_____	home improvements	_____	walking
_____	sewing	_____	running
_____	reading	_____	hugging
_____	arts/crafts	_____	kissing
_____	cooking	_____	touching
_____	photography	_____	chatting
_____	doing nothing	_____	debating

9.   Do you learn athletics and dance better by:

_____ a.   imitation, getting the feel of the music or game?

_____ b.   learning the sequence and repeating the steps mentally?

10.   In sports or performing in public do you often perform better than your training and natural abilities warrant?

_____ a.   yes

_____ b.   no

11.   Do you express yourself well verbally?
       ____   a.   yes
       ____   b.   no

12.   Are you goal-oriented?
       ____   a.   yes
       ____   b.   no

13.   When you want to remember directions, a name, or a news item, do you:
       ____   a.   visualize the information?
       ____   b.   write notes?
       ____   c.   verbalize it (repeat it to yourself or out loud)?
       ____   d.   associate it with previous information?

14.   Do you remember faces easily?
       ____   a.   yes
       ____   b.   no

15.   In the use of language, do you:
       ____   a.   make up words?
       ____   b.   devise rhymes and incorporate metaphors?
       ____   c.   choose exact, precise terms?

16.   In a communication situation, are you more comfortable being the:
       ____   a.   listener
       ____   b.   talker

17.   When you are asked to speak extemporaneously at a meeting, do you:
       ____   a.   make a quick outline?
       ____   b.   just start talking?
       ____   c.   shift the focus to someone else or say as little as possible?
       ____   d.   speak slowly and carefully?

18.   In an argument, do you tend to:
       ____   a.   talk until your point is made?
       ____   b.   find an authority to support your point?
       ____   c.   just become withdrawn?
       ____   d.   push chair or table, pound table, talk louder — yell?

19.   Can you tell fairly accurately how much time has passed without looking at your watch?
       ____   a.   yes
       ____   b.   no

20.   Do you prefer social situations that are:
       ____   a.   planned in advance?
       ____   b.   spontaneous?

21.   In preparing yourself for a new or difficult task, do you:
       ____   a.   visualize yourself accomplishing it effectively?
       ____   b.   recall past successes in similar situations?
       ____   c.   prepare extensive data regarding the task?

22.   Do you prefer working alone or in a group?
       ____   a.   alone
       ____   b.   group

23.   When it comes to "bending the rules" or altering company policy, do you feel:
       ____   a.   rules and policy are to be followed?
       ____   b.   progress comes through challenging the structure?
       ____   c.   rules are made to be broken?

24.   In school, did you prefer:
       ____   a.   algebra
       ____   b.   geometry

25.   Which of these handwriting positions most closely resembles yours?
       ____   a.   regular right-hand position
       ____   b.   hooked right-hand position (fingers pointing toward your chest)
       ____   c.   regular left-hand position
       ____   d.   hooked left-handed position (fingers pointing toward your chest)

26.   In note taking, do you print:
       ____   a.   never
       ____   b.   frequently

27.   Do you use gestures to
       ____   a.   emphasize a point?
       ____   b.   express your feelings?

28.   Do you instinctively feel an issue is right or correct, or do you decide on the basis of information?
        ____   a.   feel
        ____   b.   decide

29.   I enjoy taking risks.
        ____   a.   yes
        ____   b.   no

30.   After attending a musical:
        ____   a.   I can hum many parts of the score.
        ____   b.   I can recall many of the lyrics.

31.   Please hold a pencil perpendicularly to the ground at arm's length, centered in your line of vision and lined up with a frame, board, or door. Holding that position, close your left eye. Did your pencil appear to move?
        ____   a.   yes

        Close your right eye. Did your pencil
        appear to move?
        ____   b.   yes

32.   Sit in a relaxed position and clasp your hands comfortably in your lap.
        Which thumb is on top?
        ____   a.   left
        ____   b.   right
        ____   c.   parallel

33.   Check as many of these items as you feel are true about you:
        ____   I can extract meaning from contracts, instruction manuals, and legal documents.
        ____   I can understand schematics and diagrams.
        ____   I strongly visualize the characters, setting, and plot of reading material.
        ____   I prefer that friends phone in advance of their visits.
        ____   I dislike chatting on the phone.
        ____   I find it satisfying to plan and arrange the details of a trip.
        ____   I postpone making telephone calls.
        ____   I can easily find words in a dictionary, names in a phone book.
        ____   I love puns.
        ____   I take lots of notes at meetings and lectures.
        ____   I freeze when I need to operate mechanical things under stress.
        ____   Ideas frequently come to me out of nowhere.

34. I have:

    ____   a.   frequent mood changes.

    ____   b.   almost no mood changes.

35. I am:

    ____   a.   not very conscious of body language. I prefer to listen to what people say.

    ____   b.   good at interpreting body language.

    ____   c.   good at understanding what people say and also the body language they use.

Scoring Key

Here is the scoring key to the self-test. Enter the numbers of each answer you checked in the right hand column provided. List the sum of the numbers in the two column questions.

1.	a. 7	b. 1	c. 3	d. 9		_____
2.	a. 1	b. 5	c. 7	d. 9		_____
3.	a. 3	b. 7				_____
4.	a. 9	b. 7	c. 3	d. 1		_____
5.	a. 1	b. 7	c. 9	d. 3		_____
6.	a. 1	b. 9				_____
7.	a. 9	b. 1				_____

8.					
	swimming	9	travel	5	_____
	tennis	4	bicycling	8	_____
	golf	4	collecting	1	_____
	camping/hiking	7	writing	2	_____
	skiing	7	chess	2	_____
	fishing	8	bridge	2	_____
	singing	3	roulette	7	_____
	gardening	5	charades	5	_____
	playing instrument	4	dancing	7	_____
	home improvements	3	walking	8	_____
	sewing	3	running	8	_____
	reading	3	hugging	9	_____
	arts/crafts	5	kissing	9	_____
	cooking	5	touching	9	_____
	photography	3	chatting	4	_____
	doing nothing	9	debating	2	_____

9.	a. 9	b. 1	_____
10.	a. 9	b. 1	_____
11.	a. 1	b. 7	_____
12.	a. 1	b. 9	_____

13.   a. 9   b. 1   c. 3   d. 5   _____

14.   a. 7   b. 1   _____

15.   a. 9   b. 5   c. 1   _____

16.   a. 6   b. 3   _____

17.   a. 1   b. 6   c. 9   d. 4   _____

18.   a. 3   b. 1   c. 7   d. 9   _____

19.   a. 1   b. 9   _____

20.   a. 1   b. 9   _____

21.   a. 9   b. 5   c. 1   _____

22.   a. 3   b. 7   _____

23.   a. 1   b. 5   c. 9   _____

24.   a. algebra 1   b. geometry 9   _____

25.   a. 1   b. 7   c. 9   d. 3   _____

26.   a. 1   b. 9   _____

27.   a. 2   b. 8   _____

28.   a. 9   b. 1   _____

29.   a. 7   b. 3   _____

30.   a. 9   b. 1   _____

31.   a. 8   b. 2   _____

32.   a. 1   b. 9   c. 5   _____

33.	contracts	1	postpone	7	_____
	schematics	7	find words	1	_____
	visualize	9	puns	3	_____
	advance	2	notes	1	_____
	chatting	3	freeze	3	_____
	plan trip	1	nowhere	9	_____

| 34. | a. 9 | b. 1 | | _____ |

| 35. | a. 1 | b. 7 | c. 5 | _____ |

Now add the number of points you listed on the right and divide the total by the number of answers you checked. (This latter number will vary among testers, since questions 8 and 33 have a large number of parts.) For example: if your points totaled 300 in 40 answers, your Brain Preference Indicator (BPI) would be 7.5.

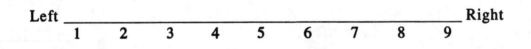

Left _____ Right
         1   2   3   4   5   6   7   8   9

The questions in this self-test cover the most salient differences between dominant rights and lefts.

A score near 5 would indicate that you are using both halves of your brain together quite easily. A score near 1 or 9 would indicate an extreme brain hemisphere preference, and you should work on cultivating a greater ability to use the other hemisphere of your brain. Most scores will range between 3 and 7.

The one who uses **all** the giftedness inherent within him will be more effective in service to the King, especially as he learns to yield these abilities for the Holy Spirit to flow through.

Side note: Having all the members of your family take this test and discussing each family member's score and the resulting differences between each person should help each family member to become more understanding toward the others. It should improve family relationships considerably. Remember, we are not out to try to change others' personalities, but to understand them and come alongside them and support them. I personally am a Luke. I get my revelation in a method similar to Luke's, using a lot of investigation. Others will be more like John. We do not have to turn Lukes into Johns or Johns into Lukes. Honor the differences which God has placed within His body. Don't try to change them.

Personal Application

1.   Write down your thoughts, questions and considerations from this chapter.

2.   Ask God to show you the various kinds of intuitive, spiritual experiences you have had with Him in your life. Record them briefly.

Prayer: "God, may you restore to your Church proper understanding and the full experience of Spirit-to-spirit encounters."

Worksheet for Class Time — Communion: The Desire of God's Heart

Note throughout the covenants the unchanging desire of God.

1. Creation (Gen. 3:8)

2. Nation of Israel (James 2:23; Deut. 5:22-31)

3. David (Acts 13:22)

4. Jesus: the full expression of God's desire (John 17:3)

    (John 17:22)

5. Mary and Martha (Luke 10:38)

6. Paul (Phil. 3:10)

7.   Us (Heb. 12:18-26)

8.   Eternity (Rev. 19:7)

God created us for the supreme purpose of having a love relationship with Him.

A Letter to Your Beloved

Exercise: Write a love letter to Jesus and let Him respond. As you share your heart and love with Jesus you may hear a flow of spontaneous thoughts and impressions coming back to you. God may be telling you of His love for you. If so, begin to write out of the spontaneous flow and allow this to become a two way love letter.

Chapter 3

Rhema — The Spoken Word
(The Spiritual, Super-rational Experience)

Various Ways God Communicates

Our Father desires to share Himself with us in every way possible. Jesus wants to be our Way, our Truth and our Life (John 14:6). He shows us the way to walk through His *logos*, the Word. "Thy word is ... a light to my path" (Ps. 119:105). He also guides us through the counsel of our spiritual overseers (Prov. 11:14). Even circumstances are used to direct our way (i.e. Jonah). Jesus becomes our truth by illuminating Scripture to us, by leading us into truth, and by guiding us through giving us peace or pressing us in our spirits. We may also receive guidance through dreams and visions (Acts 16:9).

Defining *Logos* and *Rhema*

One way Jesus becomes our life is by speaking His words directly into our hearts. The Bible speaks of hearing the voice of God within one's heart. In this chapter we want to examine this experience. Jesus says in John 6:63, "The words that I have spoken to you are spirit and are life." Probably each of us has experienced the breath of life as God's words have come clearly to our

hearts, giving direction for the way before us, encouraging us, or strengthening us.

There are two Greek words in the New Testament that are translated "word:" *logos* and *rhema*. A word can be both *logos* and *rhema* depending on whether you want to emphasize the content of the message or the way the message was received. If you use the word *logos* you indicate that you are emphasizing the content of the message. Use of the word *rhema* demonstrates an emphasis on the way in which the message was received (i.e. through a spoken word).

A Biblical Example

In the seventeenth chapter of John, verses six and eight, Jesus refers to the same word in both verses. In verse six the content is in view, and therefore *logos* is used in the Greek. In verse eight, the fact that it was a spoken word was in view and therefore the word *rhema* is used in the Greek.

Both *Logos* and *Rhema*

The Scriptures can be a *logos* if I view them simply as content. If I view them as a revelation from God, they can be called a *rhema*. If God speaks a Scripture to me, it comes as a *rhema*. If God bids me note the content of the Scripture, I am then treating it as a *logos*. The Scriptures originally came as a *rhema* to the writers (2 Pet. 1:21). Since they had content, they were also a *logos*. The Scriptures are quickened to us by the Spirit and thus become a *rhema* to us in the same way that they were to the original writers. If we ponder the *rhema*, it becomes a *logos*, since we shift from emphasizing its manner of coming to its content.

We Need Both Logos and Rhema

The content of the Bible (*logos*) is necessary because it gives us an absolute standard against which to measure all "truth." It is our safeguard to keep us from error, and our instruction manual for life.

Rhema is also necessary because it emphasizes the way the Bible was initially given — through individuals actively interacting with God. It em-phasizes the fact that God spoke and continues to speak to His children. We need to see that the men and woman throughout the Bible model a way of living which involves ongoing interaction with the God who created them. If the Bible tells us anything from Genesis to Revelation, it tells us that God desires to actively communicate with His children, and that we should expect to hear His voice and see His vision as we walk through life. Before I found God, I lived out of myself. Now that I have found Him, I live out of His spoken word and vision within my heart. We do nothing on our own initiative, only that which we hear and see the Father doing (John 5:19,20,30). We see Jesus as a perfect example, modeling a way of living which we are to emulate.

Therefore, we need both the *logos* and the *rhema* in our lives. The following diagram may help.

1. LOGOS

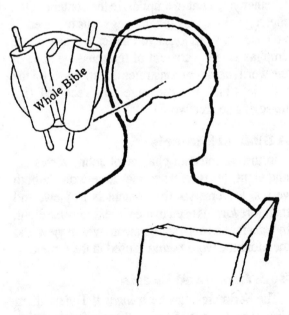

The mind reading and understanding the Bible

2. RHEMA

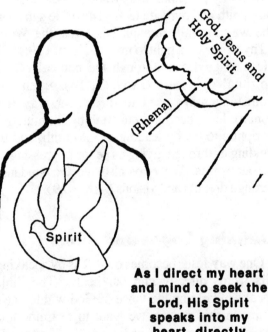

As I direct my heart and mind to seek the Lord, His Spirit speaks into my heart, directly impressing His thoughts and ideas upon it.

Additional Distinctions between Logos and Rhema

	LOGOS	RHEMA	DISTINCTIONS BETWEEN LOGOS AND RHEMA
Used in New Testament	331 Times	70 Times	
Dictionary of New Testament Theology, Volume 3, Colin Brown	Literal Definition "Collect, count, say, intellectual, rational, reasonable, spiritual."	"That which is stated intentionally; a word, an utterance, a matter, event, case."	"Whereas *logos* can often designate the Christian proclamation as a whole in the New Testament, *rhema* usually relates to individual words and utterances: man has to render account for every unjust word (Matt. 27:14); the heavenly ones speak unutterable words (2 Cor. 12:4)."
Vine's Expository Dictionary of New Testament Words, Vine	Literal Definition - "The expression of thought. Not the mere name of an object (a) as embodying a conception or ideal; (b) a saying or a statement."	"Denotes that which is spoken; what is uttered in speech..."	"The significance of *rhema* (as distinct from *logos*) is exemplified in the injunction to take the sword of the Spirit, which is the Word (*rhema*) of God. (Eph. 6:17); here the reference is not to the whole Bible as such, but to the individual Scripture which the Spirit brings to our remembrance for use in time of need, a prerequisite being the regular storing of the mind with Scripture."

I struggled unsuccessfully for years to see a distinction between *logos* and *rhema*. I observed that *logos* was often used for "spoken words," which I had been taught should be *rhema*. Finally, one day I noticed that the opposite was not also true, that *rhema* was never used in the context of "written words." I went through all 70 uses of *rhema* in the New Testament and observed that not once did *rhema* refer to the written word. So there was a uniqueness about *rhema*! As I learned much later in studying the master's thesis by Dr. Font Shultz, *logos* includes all aspects of

Understanding the Power of Rhema: "The Spoken Word"

	KIND OF RHEMA	BIBLICAL EXAMPLES
Most life-giving	I speak that which God is currently speaking with Him (i.e., my *rhema* comes forth from His *rhema*).	"...The words [*rhema*] that I say...I do not speak on My own initiative, but the Father abiding in Me does His works (John 14:10)." "...the words [*rhema*] which Thou gavest Me I have given to them ... (John 17:8)" (See also Luke 1:38, 5:5; John 5:19,20,30; 8:26,28,38; 3:34; 6:63; Acts 10:13; 2 Corinthians 12:4; Ephesians 6:17; Hebrews 11:3; and 12:19.)
Somewhat life-giving	speak the written Word of God.	"... stand and speak to the people in the temple the whole message [*rhema*] of this Life (Acts 5:20)."
Neutral	speak out of myself.	"...by the mouth of two or three witnesses every fact [*rhema*] may be confirmed (Matt. 18:16)."
Somewhat destructive	speak the generalized word of satan, which I have heard in the past.	"...every evil word [*rhema*] that men shall speak, they shall render account for it in the day of judgment (Matt. 12:36)."
Most destructive	speak that which satan is currently speaking within.	"...we have heard him speak blasphemous words [*rhema*] against...God (Acts 6:11)." "The tongue is a fire ... set on fire by hell (James 3:6)."

Our Goal: To produce the maximum amount of life by speaking that which the Father is currently speaking within us, through our fellowship with the Spirit (John 14:10,16).

communication, from the formulation of the ideas to be spoken, to the consideration of the language style, through the actual verbalization and reception by the hearer. *Rhema*, on the other hand, stands specifically for the "uttering" or "actual expressing." You may want to examine each occurrence of *rhema* in the New Testament yourself and note your observations concerning its distinctiveness. The references are as follows:

Rhema is translated "word" in the following 54 passages:

Matt. 4:4	Matt. 12:36
Matt. 18:16	Matt. 26:75
Matt. 27:14	Mark 14:72
Luke 1:38	Luke 2:29
Luke 3:2	Luke 4:4
Luke 5:5	Luke 20:26
Luke 24:8	Luke 24:11
John 3:34	John 5:47
John 6:63	John 6:68
John 8:20	John 8:47
John 10:21	John 12:47
John 12:48	John 14:10
John 15:7	John 17:8
Acts 2:14	Acts 5:20
Acts 6:11	Acts 6:13
Acts 10:22	Acts 10:37
Acts 10:44	Acts 11:14
Acts 11:16	Acts 13:42
Acts 16:38	Acts 26:25
Acts 28:25	Rom. 10:8 (2)
Rom. 10:17	Rom. 10:18
2 Cor. 12:4	2 Cor. 13:1
Eph. 5:26	Eph. 6:17
Heb. 1:3	Heb. 6:5
Heb. 11:3	Heb. 12:19
1 Pet. 1:25 (2)	2 Pet. 3:2
Jude 17	Rev. 17:17

Rhema is translated "saying" in the following eight passages:

Mark 9:32	Luke 1:65
Luke 2:17	Luke 2:50
Luke 2:51	Luke 9:45 (2)
Luke 7:1	Luke 18:34

Rhema is translated "thing" in the following three passages:

Luke 2:15	Luke 2:19	Acts 5:32

Additional verses:

Matthew 5:11: "Shall say all manner of evil [lit., every evil *rhema*] against you falsely..."

Luke 1:37: "with God nothing [lit., not any word] shall be impossible."

Turning *Logos* Into *Rhema*

I cannot turn *logos* into *rhema*. It is done through the movement of the Holy Spirit. However, I can poise myself attentively before the Word and the Spirit, giving myself prime opportunity to hear what the communicating God wants to speak to me. In this way, I can receive revelation consistently as I turn to His Word.

God desires to speak to us through the *logos*. He wants to give us a spirit revelation, to open the eyes of our hearts (Eph. 1:17,18), to cause our hearts to burn within us (Luke 24). He desires for the *logos* to be transformed from simple words to personal heart revelation and conviction as we pray over the Word, allowing the Spirit to cause it to live in our hearts.

How can *logos* become faith-giving *rhema*? How can I precipitate its happening? Primarily by opening all five senses of my spirit to be filled with *logos*. That provides God with the maximum opportunity to grant revelation within my heart. The following steps of action place me in prime position to receive revelation from God.

Ears of my heart — I direct my whole attention to God's Word as I begin to read. I must incline my ear to His words and be in an attentive attitude so that I hear what He is speaking to me from the passage.

Eyes of my heart — I sanctify my imagination, deliberately offering up to Father the eyes of my heart to be filled with visions of the eternal reality that I am reading about in the Word.

Mind of my heart — I constantly keep in the midst of my heart the words and visions I have received. I do not allow the activities of life or doubts or anything else to take away the meditations of my heart from His words.

Will of my heart — I set my will to speak only those words and visions I have received as I have studied the Bible. I will speak nothing to the contrary.

Emotions of my heart — My deep underlying emotions are stirred by what has filled the other senses of my spirit, and I am moved to action. I have a sense of peace and assurance as the witness of the Spirit confirms and deepens the Word into my heart.

As I prayerfully fill all five senses of my spirit with the *logos*, I provide a maximum opportunity for God to move within my heart and grant revelation. The summary diagram on the following page confirms this truth. Fill in the Scripture verses on the lines provided in the diagram. Consider Romans 10:17: "So faith comes from hearing [*akoe*] and hearing by the word [*rhema*] of Christ."

Akoe means "to have audience with, to come to the ears (**Abingdon's Strong's Exhaustive Concordance**)."

Thus, Romans 10:17 expanded and personalized would read:

So faith comes by hearing, that is by having audience with God through the fellowship of the Holy Spirit, and having come to my ears the individual words He is uttering to me.

The master's thesis "A Comparative Study of Logos and Rhema" by Dr. Font Shultz may be ordered from Communion With God Ministries. It offers a scholarly treatment of this subject.

The Effects of *Rhema*

Rhema is **GOD'S** word, spoken with **HIS** mouth, which produces **HIS** results. Consider Isaiah 55:11:

> *So shall My word be which goes forth from My mouth; it shall not return to Me empty, without accomplishing what I desire (emphasis added).*

Logos is the whole Bible. *Rhema* is the word of God spoken by His mouth for the immediate time and situation. We need to understand and experience *rhema* as well as *logos*. *Rhema* is used over 70 times in the New Testament. It occurs in each of the following verses. Note the powerful effects and write down your thoughts and reflections on each of these uses of *rhema*.

1. Productivity

> *But Simon answered and said to Him, "Master, we have toiled all night and caught nothing; nevertheless at Your word [rhema] I will let down the net" (Luke 5:5, NKJ).*

2. Effective ministry

> *For He whom God has sent speaks the words [rhema] of God, for God does not give the Spirit by measure (John 3:34, NKJ).*

3. Life

> *It is the Spirit who gives life; the flesh profits nothing. The words [rhema] that I speak to you are spirit, and they are life (John 6:63, NKJ).*

Turning *Logos* Into *Rhema*

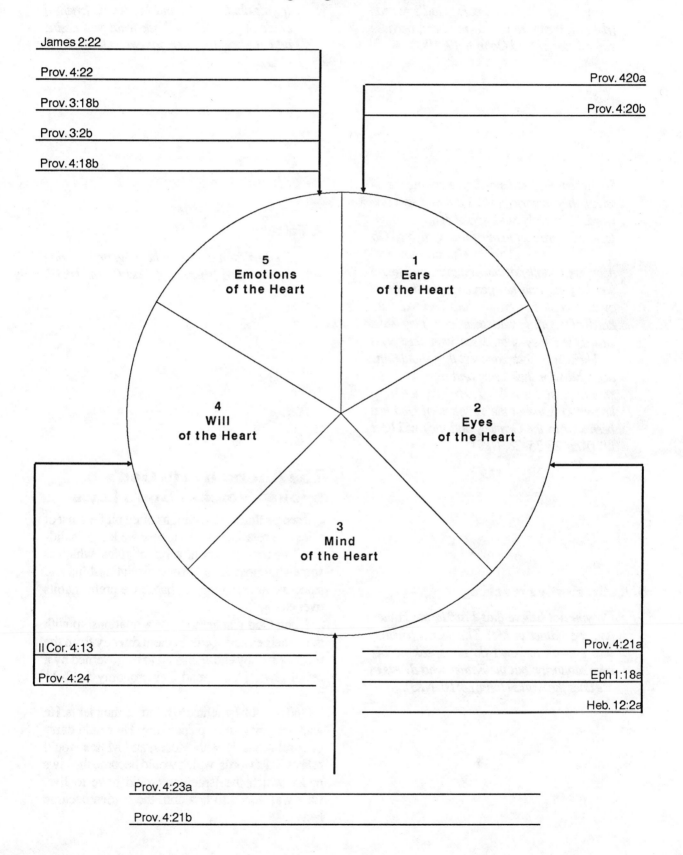

James 2:22

Prov. 4:22

Prov. 3:18b

Prov. 3:2b

Prov. 4:18b

Prov. 420a

Prov. 4:20b

5
Emotions
of the Heart

1
Ears
of the Heart

4
Will
of the Heart

2
Eyes
of the Heart

3
Mind
of the Heart

II Cor. 4:13

Prov. 4:24

Prov. 4:21a

Eph 1:18a

Heb. 12:2a

Prov. 4:23a

Prov. 4:21b

4. Relationship

He who is of God hears God's words [rhema]; therefore you do not hear, because you are not of God (John 8:47, NKJ).

So when they did not agree among themselves, they departed after Paul had said one word: "The Holy Spirit spoke rightly through Isaiah the prophet to our fathers, saying, 'Go to this people and say: "Hearing you will hear, and shall not understand; and seeing you will see, and not perceive; for the heart of this people has grown dull. Their ears are hard of hearing, and their eyes they have closed, lest they should see with their eyes and hear with their ears, lest they should understand with their heart and turn, so that I should heal them." ' Therefore, let it be known to you that the salvation of God has been sent to the Gentiles, and they will hear it!" (Acts 28:25-28, NKJ).

5. Authoritative teaching

Do you not believe that I am in the Father, and the Father in Me? The words [rhema] that I speak to you I do not speak on My own authority; but the Father who dwells in Me does the works (John 14:10, NKJ).

6. Fullness of desire

If you abide in Me, and My words [rhema] abide in you, you will ask what you desire, and it shall be done for you (John 15:7, NKJ).

7. Faith

So then faith comes by hearing, and hearing by the word [rhema] of God (Rom. 10:17, NKJ).

The Alternative to God's Spoken Voice — God's Laws

It seems that we as humans often prefer a list of rules to a relationship. I suppose we feel a "solidness" or security about a list of rules, which is somewhat lost in a growing relationship; and since we are creatures of habit, we prefer habits over change.

When God wanted to have a relationship with the Israelites and speak to them directly from the mountain, they chose instead to be governed by a set of laws. Please read Deuteronomy 5:22-31 now.

God told the Israelites to return to their tents. He was not going to stop speaking. He would carry on a relationship with Moses, and Moses would relay God's words, which would become the laws under which the Israelites would have to live. Law was added to law until the burden became heavy.

The author of Hebrews comments on this situation in Hebrews 12:18-29. Please study it now.

In verse 19, the word *rhema* is used. They did not want to hear the sound of His voice. In verses 22 and 23, we too have come to the Holy Mountain, Mount Zion. In verse 25, He gives us a warning: **"See to it that you do not refuse Him who is speaking."**

Why? Because, if we do, we will forsake the relationship with God that is to characterize Christianity, and we will return to life under the law, even as those in the Old Testament did. Our minister will hear from God and, even as Moses, will give us the laws under which we are to live. How sad that we might not avail ourselves of the living Holy Spirit within our hearts and live in communion with Him, choosing instead to live only out of the New Testament laws and thus become legalists or pharisees.

Anyone who has tried to do this has found out, with me, how burdensome it becomes. The load becomes heavy, instead of being light as Jesus promised. As one grows as a Christian, he simply discovers more laws to obey; eventually the list becomes more than one can handle. The choice often becomes either to stop growing or to abandon Christianity altogether. The Pharisees of Jesus' day had 613 laws they were imposing on Israel. Jesus rebuked them for the heavy load they were laying on the people.

I find that when God's consuming fire is raging and everything that can be shaken is being shaken, the thing most life-giving and strengthening is His inner voice. It (He) keeps me.

Therefore, we, like the Israelites, are faced with a decision: either we hear God speak and live in relationship with Him, or we live under the New Testament laws we discover. I believe it is **imperative** that we learn to discern God's voice and live in it so that our **relationship** is not **reduced** to a **religion**.

How *Rhema* Is Sensed

Probably no question bothers Western Christians more than: "How do I discern God's voice within my heart?" We are now going to try to answer that.

I sought in vain for years to hear God's voice within my heart, but the only thing I found was many different thoughts. I could not hear any voice. This is precisely where many Christians stand frustrated. How can I possibly say "God said" when I am not able to discern His inner voice clearly? Then the Lord finally began bringing the right men, revelation and understanding into my life and allowed me to "see" what I had been missing.

Rhema, or the voice of God, is Spirit-to-spirit communication — where the Holy Spirit, in union with your spirit, speaks directly to you.

> ### *RHEMA* IS SENSED AS:
> ### A SPONTANEOUS THOUGHT, IDEA, WORD, FEELING OR VISION

Thoughts from my mind are **analytical**.
Thoughts from my heart are **spontaneous**.
Biblical meditation combines **analysis and spontaneity**.

Spontaneous Thoughts — The Voice of the Spirit World

Biblical Support

1. All thoughts are not our thoughts.

For the weapons of our warfare are not carnal but mighty in God for pulling down strongholds, casting down arguments and every high thing that exalts itself against the knowledge of God, bringing **every thought** into captivity to the obedience of Christ ... (2 Cor. 10:4,5 NKJ, emphasis added).

Why would we have to bring some thoughts into captivity? Is it not because they originate in satan or an evil spirit? If so, where should we suspect that some of the rest of our thoughts come from? The Holy Spirit, naturally. Then we must come to realize that a lot of the thoughts in our minds are **not our thoughts**. What an incredible idea! I always thought that the thoughts in my mind were **my thoughts**. But in actuality, the Bible makes it clear that many of them are not. They are coming from the spirit world. You see, I am one whom another fills. I am a vessel, a branch grafted into a vine. I do not stand alone but someone else flows through me. I keep forgetting that and think that this is **me living**, when God has made it very clear that I do not live, but Christ lives in me (Gal. 2:20).

Therefore I accept the fact that spontaneous thoughts, ones I did not think up, do not come from my mind. They come either from my heart, the Holy Spirit within my heart, or an evil spirit trying to impress his ideas upon me.

There are many ways of testing whether the spontaneous flow is your heart, the Holy Spirit who is joined to your heart, or an evil spirit who is issuing an attack against you. I will give you an entire chapter later. However, let me offer a couple of easy tests right now that I currently use. One is to line the content of the spontaneous flow up against the names of satan and the names of the Holy Spirit. In the Bible, a person's name depicts his character.

Satan	Holy Spirit
Accuser	Edifier
Adversary	Comforter
Liar	Teacher
Destroyer	Creator
Condemner	Divine Lover
Thief	Healer
Murderer	Giver of Life

Any spontaneous thoughts that have the characteristics in the left column I attribute to satan. Any spontaneous thoughts which have the characteristics of the right column I attribute to the Holy Spirit.

Of course you always test the spontaneous flow against the Bible.

Also, you submit your journaling to your spiritual covering(s) to see if they can confirm that it is from God.

And finally, I observe the principle I have discovered that "the intuitive flow flows out of the vision held before my eyes." Therefore I ask myself if I had my eyes fixed on Jesus while I was tuned to spontaneity. If so, I find that for me the spontaneous flow is from God approximately 95% of the time. We must acknowledge that we will always be vulnerable to mistakes. And that is

okay. We can celebrate our mistakes, laugh at them, and learn from them (Eph. 5:20).

Now let us look at some more biblical support for the concept that spontaneous thoughts are the voice of the spirit world.

2. *Naba* — the Hebrew word for prophet

Naba, the Hebrew word meaning "to prophesy," literally means to "bubble up." Therefore when the prophet would tune to the prophetic flow, he would tune to that which was bubbling up within him. In other words, he would tune to the spontaneous flow which he recognized as the voice of God within him.

Consider the distinctions between true prophesy and false prophesy in the chart on the following page.

3. *Paga* — the chance encounter

The Hebrew word for intercession is *paga*, which literally means "to strike or light upon by chance" or "an accidental intersecting." Genesis 28:11 is an example of the use of *paga* as an accidental intersecting. Please **read it now**. As Jacob was traveling, he "lighted upon" (*paga*) a certain place and spent the night there.

Putting this literal definition of *paga* together with the idea of intercession, we come to a beautiful biblical example of Spirit-to-spirit communication that is familiar to almost every Christian. Can you remember a time when you suddenly had the impression that you should pray for someone? You had not been thinking about them; the thought just came out of nowhere. That was *paga*. You were experiencing *rhema*, God's voice as a "chance idea" that intersects our minds, not flowing from the normal, meditative process, but simply appearing in our hearts. A chance idea. An idea from God lighting upon our hearts and being registered in our minds as a spontaneous idea.

4. The river of the Holy Spirit within the believer's heart

On the last day, that great day of the feast, Jesus stood and cried out, saying, "If anyone thirsts, let him come to Me and drink. He who believes in Me, as the Scripture has said, out of his heart will flow rivers of living water." But this He spoke concerning the Spirit, whom those believing in Him would receive; for the Holy Spirit was not yet given, because Jesus was not yet glorified (John 7:37-39, NKJ).

Now Jesus **is** glorified, and the Holy Spirit **has been** given. Jesus said it would be like a river within us. Therefore, when we tune to the bubbling flow within us, we are tuning to the Holy Spirit within us. **This is more than simply theology. This is an actual experience. There is a river within us,** and we **can** tune to it. This bubbling effortless flow **is** the Holy Spirit. It is so simple that even a child can do it. And that helps prove it is real, because Jesus said we needed to become like children to enter the kingdom. If we make Christianity too difficult for a child to do, we most likely have it wrong.

Other Support

1. The experience of creative flashes

Where do creative flashes come from? I am sure we have all struggled with a difficult situation and then experienced in an instantaneous flash a creative solution to the problem. Where has this flash come from? Was it your own greatness finally coming forth? Or was it the creativity of the Creator who lives within coming forth? I believe that it was the creativity of Almighty God springing forth within the heart of man. I no longer take any credit for these creative insights. I give it to God, the One who lives within.

2. The experience of destructive flashes

Where do destructive and evil thoughts erupt from, when you are not thinking them up but they flash across your mind with a life of their own? I am fully convinced that they come from the destroyer, who is bombarding me with his evil

TRUE AND FALSE PROPHECY

	TRUE PROPHESY	FALSE PROPHESY
Root Hebrew Word	Naba	Ziyd
Literal Definition	"Bubble up"	"Boil up"
Expanded Meaning	His prophecy bubbles up. His prophecy gushes up.	He boils up his prophecy. He cooks up his prophecy.
Inner Poise	Fix eyes on Jesus and tune to spontaneous flow.	Fix eyes on self's desires and devise a word or vision.

thoughts. Therefore I do not accept guilt for the evil thoughts that appear in my mind, nor do I take credit for the creative thoughts that spring up within me. I am one through whom another flows. I give proper credit to whom credit is due, either to satan or to the Holy Ghost.

3. Testimonies of "life after death" encounters

In books on "life after death" encounters, we find a confirming witness of what Spirit-to-spirit communication is. They tell of seeing Jesus or an angel speak; although they had not heard anything audibly, they instantly knew within what had been said. They had received in their spirits the spontaneous, effortless flow of ideas that is Spirit-to-spirit communication (or *rhema*).

4. The example from nature

God often models spiritual truth in the physical world, which is why the whole earth reflects His glory. It is interesting to note that the Jordan river, which flows through the land of Israel, bubbles up from the depths of the earth and simply begins as a full fledged river. As the Holy Spirit bubbles up from our innermost being and simply flows, the Jordan river emerges from the bowels of the earth and flows as a river throughout the land.

Qualities that characterize God's interjected thoughts into your heart

They are like your own thoughts and musings except that you sense them as coming from the heart not the brain; they will be **spontaneous**, not **cognitive** or **analytical**.

- They can come easily as God speaking in the first person.
- They are often light and gentle, and easily cut off by **any** exertion of self (own thoughts, will, etc.).
- They will have an unusual content to them, in that they will be wiser, more loving and more motive oriented than your thoughts.
- They will cause a special reaction within your being, such as a sense of excitement, conviction, faith, life, awe, peace.
- When embraced, they carry with them a fullness of strength to perform them, as well as a joy in doing so.

- Your spiritual senses are trained as time goes on, and you will more easily and frequently experience God speaking in this way.
- Remember: God **is speaking** to you all the time, and you are receiving His injected thoughts. Until you begin distinguishing them from your own, you are simply grouping them all together and assuming they are yours. In learning to distinguish His voice, you are learning how to separate the spontaneous thoughts that are coming from Him, from the analytical thoughts that are coming from your own mind.

To Whom Do We Pray?

I have been asked, and I have asked the Lord, to whom we are to pray. Is it the Father, or is it the Son? Technically, I believe we are to pray to the Father, through the Son, by the working of the Holy Spirit. Therefore, the entire Trinity is involved in prayer.

On the other hand, the fifteenth chapter of John calls us to abide in Christ, or to live in Him. I find for me that a part of living in Jesus involves dialoguing with Him, and that when I look for a vision of the Godhead, He is the image that often appears (Col. 1:15). I find that when I pray with authority, I tend to address the Father, and that when establishing intimacy and friendship, I generally commune with Jesus. When in corporate worship or beginning a class, I often speak to the Holy Spirit, inviting Him to manifest His presence among us.

I have asked the Lord about this, and He has confirmed that it is most proper to pray to Him, through the Son, by the working of the Holy Spirit. However, He has also said that since the Three are One, He will also honor my prayer when it is Jesus and I talking. After all, Jesus only speaks the words the Father has spoken (John 5:19,20).

Actually, in considering First John 1:3 and Second Corinthians 13:14, we find that the Bible tells us we may fellowship with the Father, the Son, or the Holy Spirit.

...and indeed our fellowship is with the Father, and with His Son Jesus Christ (1 John 1:3, emphasis added).

*Let the grace of the Lord Jesus Christ, and the love of God, be with you all through the **fellowship of the Holy Spirit** (2 Cor. 13:14, a paraphrase from the Greek, emphasis added).*

Therefore, I believe our fellowship can be with the Father, the Son and the Holy Spirit.

Praying With an Idol in Your Heart

This section on praying with an idol in your heart will provide a tremendous insight for you in the area of how to purify your journaling. The key is to be aware of where you are fixing your eyes when you are praying. Consider the following.

...any man in the house of Israel who sets up his idols in his heart, puts right before his face the stumbling block of his iniquity, and then comes to the prophet, I the Lord will be brought to give him an answer in the matter in view of the multitude of his idols (Ezekiel 14:4).

This brings into focus a startling truth concerning an inappropriate method of prayer, which I am afraid has been practiced by many.

When I come to the Lord in prayer, I am to be a living sacrifice. I must have laid down my will and be totally sold out to God's will concerning the issue about which I am praying. If that is not my attitude, I am to pray for God to form that spirit within me before I begin praying about the issue at hand. If I pray about the issue while I still have a definite direction about it in my own heart, that "definite direction" of my own will interferes with the signals coming from the throne of God and causes me to believe that God is confirming the direction I felt, whether He actually is or not.

In other words, if I pray about an item and the item is more prominent in my vision or my consciousness than my vision of the Lord, the answer that comes back will be from the item rather than from the Lord. On the other hand, if my vision of the Lord is more prominent in my consciousness than my vision of the issue I am praying about, then the answer will come back from the Lord

and will be pure revelation, not contaminated by my own desires.

The principle is that the intuitive flow comes out of the vision that I am holding before my eyes. That is why I am commanded to fix my eyes on Jesus, the Author and Finisher of my faith. Thus, the vision will be pure.

An example of a seer having his vision clouded and receiving damaging direction can be found in the story of Balaam in the twenty-second chapter of Numbers. Balak had sent messengers to Balaam asking him to come and curse the Israelites. When Balaam sought God about it, God was very clear: "Do not go with them; you shall not curse the people; for they are blessed (Num. 22:12)."

Balak again sent messengers, more distinguished than before, with the offer that Balak would honor him richly and do whatever he asked if he would only come and curse the Israelites. Apparently gold and riches were on Balaam's mind because he said, "Though Balak were to give me his house full of silver and gold, I could not do anything ... (Num. 22:18)" However, he invited them to stay, saying, "I will check with the Lord again." Since he so desperately wanted to receive the honor, gold and riches, he went to the Lord again in prayer, this time with an impure heart. As could be expected, the Lord gave him an answer consistent with the idol in his heart. He said, "Sure! Go ahead!" However, God was angry with Balaam (Num. 22:22) and He sent an angel with a sword to block his path.

There are other examples of Israel praying with an idol in their hearts and receiving the answers to their prayers that eventually brought hurt in their lives. Israel begged God for a king, and even though He didn't want to give it to them, He gave in to their whining. Israel lusted for meat in the wilderness, and God gave it to them, but along with it He sent a wasting disease (Ps. 106:14,15).

In conclusion, when we pray with an idol in our hearts, we may get an affirmative answer from the Lord, but it will bring us to destruction. Therefore, when we pray, we must be certain that our vision is purified, and that we see Jesus as one who is MUCH LARGER than the thing or issue

PRAYING WITH AN IDOL IN YOUR HEART

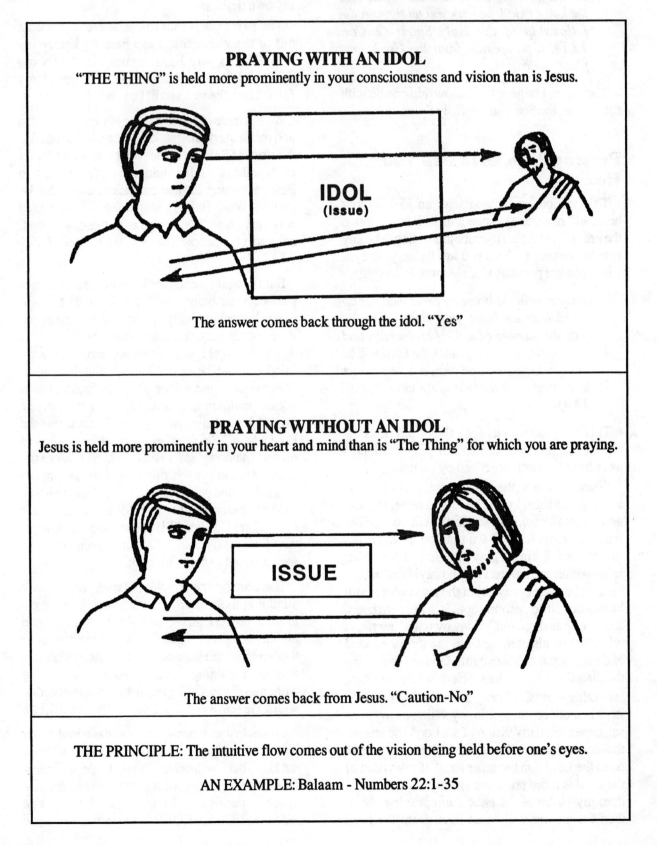

PRAYING WITH AN IDOL
"THE THING" is held more prominently in your consciousness and vision than is Jesus.

IDOL
(Issue)

The answer comes back through the idol. "Yes"

PRAYING WITHOUT AN IDOL
Jesus is held more prominently in your heart and mind than is "The Thing" for which you are praying.

ISSUE

The answer comes back from Jesus. "Caution-No"

THE PRINCIPLE: The intuitive flow comes out of the vision being held before one's eyes.

AN EXAMPLE: Balaam - Numbers 22:1-35

for which we are praying. Only then will our answer be pure and life-giving.

The diagram on the previous page demonstrates these two approaches in prayer.

Personal Application

Complete the journaling exercise below. On this sheet (or another if you prefer) write down a question you would like to ask the Lord. It can be any question that you choose, as long as it is not one of the most traumatic questions of your life. Those issues cause you to become tense; they tend to inhibit you from maintaining the biblical poise of stillness that is commanded as we approach God (Ps. 46:10) — this is especially true when you are just learning the skills of journaling. You may ask Him about His love for you or about a situation you are facing or about what He wants to say concerning the truths of this chapter or whatever. Take a moment, choose a question and write it down.

After you have written down the question, ask Jesus to open the eyes and ears of your heart so that you can receive what He wants to share with you. Then picture Jesus in a comfortable setting. He may be sitting next to you, or walking along the sea of Galilee with you. Become a child. Take His hand. Look into His face. See His joy and expectancy and excitement over sharing this time with you. This is what He longs for more than anything else. See His long robes. See the sandals on His feet. Relax and put a smile on your face. Enjoy being alone with Him. Then as you gaze upon Him, ask Him the question that you have written down.

Tune to spontaneity, fix your gaze upon Him and write what begins to flow within you. Don't test it now. Just write in simple childlike faith. You can test it later. If it is not too private, share it with a spiritual advisor for confirmation.

Chapter 4

Becoming Still

In order for us to hear the still, small voice of God within us, we ourselves must become quiet. God says, "Be still and know that I am God (Ps. 46:10, NKJ)." Other translations of that verse are "cease striving, let go, relax and know that I am God."

Often we miss the importance of quieting ourselves as we approach God. Our lives are such a rush; we just run up to God, blurt out our prayers, and rush away again. I am convinced we will never enter the realm of the Spirit that way.

If we are going to commune with God, first we must become still. Habakkuk went to his guard post to pray (Hab. 2:1). In the early morning when it was still dark, Jesus departed to a lonely place to pray (Mark 1:35). And after a day's ministry, Jesus went to a mountain to pray.

In order for our inner man to commune with God, we must **first** remove external distractions. We must find a place where we can be alone and undisturbed, so that we can center down into our hearts without being distracted by our external circumstances.

Second, we must learn to quiet our inner being, all the voices and thoughts within us that are calling for our attention. Until they are quieted, we most likely will not hear His voice.

Several means can be used to quiet the voices within you. First, you can write them down to be taken care of later. Second, you can quiet your inner members by focusing them on Jesus. You can open your eyes and see in the Spirit the vision that Almighty God wants you to behold. You can lift up your eyes and behold the vision. This will bring your inner attention to the Father and the Son.

You can sense the "cry of your heart" and repeat it over and over. The cry of your heart is that which your heart is seeking to express at any given moment. I often notice it as a song I find myself spontaneously singing in the early morning. Whenever we need to sense our hearts, we can listen for the spontaneous song bubbling within and go with the flow of it.

For example, one day when my life was crumbling around me and God seemed so distant that I could not see Him or sense Him in any way, I found that the spontaneous song that bubbled up from my heart was only two words: "Lord, arise." As I sang those words over and over, I eventually began to sense the Lord rising within me, and His vision and presence being restored in my life. Therefore, we should sing the song on our heart until it realizes its goal.

You may find tension in your body as you become still. That, too, should be released so you are fully open to receive from God, without being distracted or hindered by bodily discomfort. Be in a comfortable, relaxed position as you pray (1 Chron. 17:16). Consciously relax the parts of your body that are tense. Have you noticed how relaxed your breathing is when you awaken? Check your breathing to see how relaxed you are. When I first began public speaking, I would be terrified and my breathing would be short and fast. I found I could calm my body by breathing more deeply and slowly. Check your breathing and use it to help you relax.

Also, biblically speaking, there is a very close connection between breath and spirit. Both breath and spirit come from one word in the Greek, as well as the Hebrew. When our breath is gone from our bodies, our spirit is gone. I do not believe it is an accident that these words are so closely connected in the Bible. I have found I can breathe in the pure Spirit of Christ as I breathe out the contaminated spirit of self.

"Be still and know." Stillness is not a goal in itself. I want to become still in mind and body so my heart can know and sense God moving within. His promptings are gentle, and until my own inner and outer ragings are quieted, I will not sense His inner moving.

In becoming still, I am not trying to **do anything**. I simply want to be **in touch** with the Divine Lover. I am centered on **this moment** of time and experiencing Him in it.

Becoming still cannot be hurried or forced. Rather, it must be allowed to happen. At a point in your stillness, God takes over and you sense His active flow within you. His spontaneous images begin flowing with a life of their own. His voice begins speaking, giving you wisdom and strength. You find that you are "in the Spirit" (Rev. 1:10).

Becoming still is an art to be learned, especially for those of the Western culture who are always on the go. However, our communion with the Lord must begin here. When you come to pray, take the first few minutes to become centered, and proceed **only after** you have become still. Out of your stillness, you will sense God. Then you will be able to commune. You will find that the more you practice becoming still, the easier it becomes and the more quickly it happens. Many also find that being in a group that is seeking to become quiet together helps them quiet down. An atmosphere of quiet engenders quiet.

How Elisha and David Stilled Themselves

It is interesting for me to study the great prophets of the Bible to see what they did when they wanted to touch the Divine flow. Think of Elisha, for instance. In Second Kings 3:15, we find that when Elisha wanted to receive a prophetic word from God, he said: " 'But now bring me a minstrel.' And it came about, when the minstrel played, that the hand of the Lord came upon him. And he said, 'Thus says the Lord ...' "

So we see that Elisha used music to help him tune to the voice of God within and away from outer reasoning. It is interesting to note that outer reasoning is considered left brain by scientists, and that **both** intuition and music are considered right brain.

May I suggest that when one wants to move from reasoning, which flows through the left side of the brain, to intuition, which flows through the right side of the brain, one can do as Elisha did and use music (which also flows through the right side of the brain). This will cause a shift internally from the left hemisphere to the right hemisphere. It is so simple and so thoroughly biblical. Of course David did it as he wrote his psalms. They were set to music, and they record his encounters with God.

I have found it effective for me to sing a quiet love song to the King of Kings and picture the words that I am singing. (Vision also flows through the right side of the brain.) This poises me instantly before the intuitive flow that springs up from my heart, and I begin immediately to record the precious words that flow from my Lord and King.

A side note: For only a few dollars, one may purchase a "Stress Rate Card," which will change colors when you hold your thumb on it for 10 seconds. It will turn black when stressed, red when tense, green when calm and blue when relaxed. It is an excellent tool to help you learn to relax.

The chart below will review some effective ways of quieting yourself.

REMOVING INNER NOISE
(Voices, Thoughts, Pressures)

Problem	Solution
1. Thoughts of things to do.	1. Write them down so you don't forget them.
2. Thoughts of sin-consciousness.	2. Confess your sin and clothe yourself with the robe of righteousness.
3. Mind flitting about.	3. Focus on a vision of Jesus with you.
4. Need to get in touch with your heart.	4. Begin singing and listening to the spontaneous song bubbling up from your heart.
5. Need for additional time to commune when your mind is poised and still.	5. Realize that times when you are doing automatic activities (i.e., driving, bathing, exercising, routine jobs, etc.) are ideal times for hearing from God.

Identifying the State of Being Still

The five key ingredients of the contemplative or meditative state are physical calm, focused attention, letting be, receptivity and spontaneous flow. The opposites of these characteristics are physical tension, distraction, over-control, activity and analytical thought. These could be placed on a continuum as follows:

Physical Tension   Physical Calm
0   1   2   3   4

Distraction   Focused Attention
0   1   2   3   4

Over-control   Letting Be
0   1   2   3   4

Activity   Receptivity
0   1   2   3   4

Analytical Thought   Spontaneous Flow
0   1   2   3   4

Meditation is commanded throughout the Scriptures, and so are each of these elements that make up the meditative pose. Consider the following with me.

The Biblical Exhortation Concerning Physical Calm

There remains therefore a Sabbath rest for the people of God. For the one who has entered His rest has himself also rested from his works, as God did from His. Let us therefore be diligent to enter that rest, lest anyone fall through following the same example of disobedience (Heb. 4:9-11).

And to whom did He swear that they should not enter His rest, but to those who were disobedient? And so we see that they were not able to enter because of unbelief (Heb. 3:18,19).

The Biblical Exhortation Concerning Focused Attention

... let us ... lay aside every encumbrance, and ... sin which so easily entangles us, and let us run ... fixing our eyes on Jesus, the author and perfecter of faith ... (Heb. 12:1,2).

... Truly, truly, I say to you, the Son can do nothing of Himself, unless it is something He

sees the Father doing; for whatever the Father does, these things the Son also does in like manner (John 5:19).

The Biblical Exhortation Concerning Letting Be

Cease striving [marginal reference: let go, relax] and know that I am God (Ps. 46:10).

Be anxious for nothing, but in everything by prayer and supplication with thanksgiving let your requests be made known to God. And the peace of God which surpasses all comprehension, shall guard your hearts and your minds in Christ Jesus (Phil. 4:6,7).

The Biblical Exhortation Concerning Receptivity

Abide in Me, and I in you. As the branch cannot bear fruit of itself, unless it abides in the vine, so neither can you, unless you abide in Me. I am the vine, you are the branches; he who abides in Me, and I in him, he bears much fruit; for apart from Me you can do nothing (John 15:4,5).

The Biblical Exhortation Concerning Spontaneous Flow

He who believes in Me, as the Scripture said, "From his innermost being shall flow rivers of living water." But this He spoke of the Spirit, whom those who believed in Him were to receive ... (John 7:38,39).

On the following lists, check those characteristics that represent your meditative state and your lifestyle, since meditating or abiding is to be a way of living. This will assist you in cultivating the art of stillness before Almighty God.

Physical Calm

_____My heart beats calmly and evenly.

_____My breathing feels calm, easy, even and complete.

_____My muscles don't feel tense, tight or clenched.

_____I don't feel restless and fidgety.

_____I don't feel tense or self-conscious when I say or do something.

_____I don't feel tense, hot and perspiring.

_____I don't feel the need to go to the bathroom when I don't have to.

_____I feel coordinated.

_____My mouth isn't dry.

_____I feel awake and refreshed.

_____I don't have a headache.

_____I don't have a backache.

_____I don't feel unfit or heavy.

_____My shoulders, neck or back is not tense.

_____The condition of my skin is healthy.

_____My eyes are not watery or teary.

_____My stomach feels calm.

_____My appetite is okay.

Focused Attention

_____My thoughts are not scattered.

_____I have little trouble remembering what I am doing.

_____I feel very conscious of things.

_____When disturbed, I find it easy to get back on track.

_____My mind feels clear.

_____I feel centered.

_____I am not indecisive.

_____My goals and priorities are clear.

_____I keep things simple, doing one thing at a time.

_____My mind is steady and focused.

_____I concentrate on what I am doing.

_____I seem to be quite perceptive.

_____My mind is not confused.

_____I don't let interruptions disturb me.

_____I keep my mind on what I want to do.

_____Even if things get hectic, I feel I can work in a calm and orderly manner.

_____I feel quite alert.

_____I devote my full attention to what I decide to do.

_____I feel absorbed.

_____My attention doesn't wander.

_____Things seem lucid and clear.

_____It is fairly easy to keep my mind on my task.

_____I don't feel divided between different courses of action.

____I seem quite aware of things.

____I don't wander from what I set out to do.

____I finish one job before starting something else.

____I live in the present, fully experiencing every moment.

____My mind is like a mirror, clearly reflecting the physical and spiritual worlds without distortion.

Letting Be

____My wants and desires do not drive me.

____I am not hard on myself even though I have some imperfections.

____I don't feel as though I have to urgently push or rush myself.

____I can accept things that cannot be done or understood.

____It feels okay to say "live and let live" about some of my problems.

____I can put things that really matter in perspective.

____I don't get worked up over things that can't be changed.

____I feel I can let go and be myself.

____I feel flexible.

____Some of my wishes seem less important when seen side by side with things that really matter.

____When I have worked enough, I can easily let go and relax.

____I feel patient.

____It feels okay not to worry needlessly about yesterday's or tomorrow's problems.

____It feels okay to let some things be.

____I feel as though I could accept my problems philosophically.

____I don't feel as though everything has to be done at once.

____I feel things aren't so bad even when they don't go the way I want.

____I don't get caught up demanding things I cannot have or that don't really matter.

____I don't feel particularly self-conscious or as though I have to be overly concerned with doing the right thing or making a good impression.

____I don't feel as though I have to have everyone's acceptance and approval.

____I feel part of a larger purpose or scheme of things.

Receptivity

____I am aware of God flowing through me.

____I live in an active dependence upon the Holy Spirit.

____I acknowledge the Holy Spirit's presence.

____I do not tackle projects with a dependence upon my own abilities.

____I offer one word or sentence prayers when in need.

____I am instantly aware when pride or self-dependence encroaches upon me.

____I picture myself as one filled with Another.

____I recognize that my strength comes from God.

____I recognize that my wisdom comes from God.

____I recognize that God is my Source.

____I picture myself as one through whom Another flows.

____I am aware that I can do nothing on my own.

____I am aware that my righteousness is that which is imputed through Christ.

____I see myself as clothed with Christ's righteousness.

____I picture myself as a container filled with Another.

____When I succeed, I am immediately aware that it is Christ's victory.

____When I fail, I am aware that I have not drawn on the One Who lives within.

____I do things without undue strain or effort.

Spontaneous Flow

____I live tuned to spontaneity.

____I recognize that the Holy Spirit's flow is like a river within me.

____I feel willing and comfortable living in flow.

____I feel uncomfortable living in "boxes."

_____ I feel that pure analysis is not as profitable as allowing spontaneity to flow together with analysis.

_____ I am comfortable going with inner promptings.

_____ I feel spontaneous and free.

_____ I feel as though I go with the flow of things.

_____ I can sense when I am in flow.

_____ I purposely relax when working so I can enter the flow experience.

_____ I am aware of creative expression flowing within me.

_____ I seek out quiet, relaxing settings so my creativity can be maximized.

_____ I seek out and enjoy relaxed, spontaneous sessions with others.

_____ I quiet myself, focus myself and relax so the flow can begin.

_____ When in flow, I seek to continue with what I am working on until it is completed.

_____ I do not begin working until I sense the flow experience.

_____ I tackle projects when I sense them flowing within me.

_____ As I practice living in the flow experience, I sense it operating more readily and easily within me.

_____ I understand that all that lasts comes out of the flow experience.

Brain-wave Activity Levels

Some of the research being done in sleep laboratories is interesting as it relates to our quieting ourselves and becoming still. It has been discovered that when we are wide awake and alert, beta level waves go through our minds. However, when we relax or enter sleep, these waves slow down and become alpha level waves. This is a measurable physiological effect of stilling ourselves as God commanded.

I share this because it helps me, a left brain, logical Westerner, to realize that quieting myself before God is not just a nebulous experience. I actually enter a different state of being (i.e. — heart awareness), and the physical manifestations of this state can be measured through tools such as biofeedback. Such tools could possibly help one in learning how to quickly enter this state of rest, which the Bible calls stillness. They did me.

Another pastor on staff at the church where I worked and I purchased a $49 biofeedback system that measured galvanic skin response. I used it for a week or two as I was learning to quiet myself in the Lord's presence. I found it very helpful since it measured the state of relaxation within me. I could quickly discover which things relaxed me and which things didn't. For instance, I discovered that singing rowdy praise songs did not relax me. Neither did singing quiet praise songs, if I was lunging emotionally at God, telling Him how much I loved Him. However, if I quietly spoke the words "I love you" as I sang quiet worship songs, I found that I had entered the stage of relaxed stillness that the Lord had commanded.

The chart on the following page gives an overview of brain wave activity levels.

Similarity to Eastern Religions?

Some have wondered about the similarity of what I have described above to Eastern religions. Well, for starters, I expect satan's counterfeit to be similar to the real. Satan is not an originator. He is a counterfeiter. Therefore, he can never come up with anything original. Consequently, if I see the counterfeit doing something, I ask myself the following question: "I wonder what the real thing is that I am supposed to be doing?" Now that is not the question some people ask. Some people say, "We better stay away from this thing because satan can use it," and as a result they give everything over to satan. All satan has to do to take something away from the Church is to counterfeit it. This makes many within the Church so fearful of even getting close to it that they back away from the real thing entirely. Satan accordingly ends up with everything and the Church has nothing. Just look around you and see if this isn't true. We as the Church have backed away from and given largely over to satan the following: government, politics, television, theater, dance, pageantry, radio, education, money and computers.

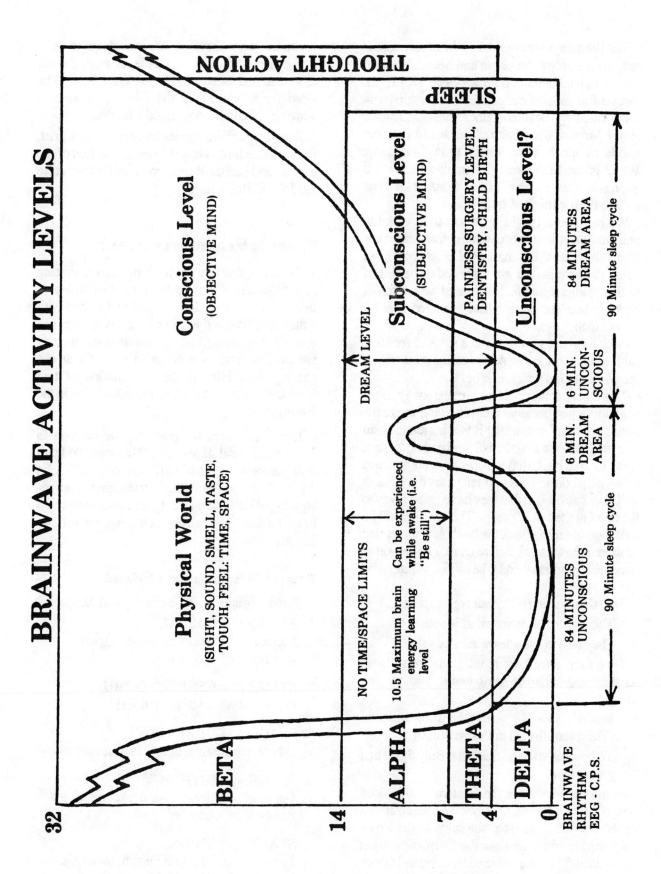

The Bible says we are to be the head and not the tail, we are only to be above and not underneath, we are to lend and not borrow (Deut. 28:12,13). Yet we find most of our political leadership positions filled by heathen rather than Christians. Why? Most of the wealth of the world is in the hands of the heathen rather than Christians. Why? Is the Bible wrong? I think not! We are wrong in that **we live under a spirit of fear rather than a spirit of faith**.

We have been taught to be so afraid of satan and his wiles that we cower in fear and back away from anything that could be perceived as being dangerous. We are supposed to be full of faith and abundant life. But instead we are full of neurotic fear and poverty and are ruled over by the heathen.

God, forgive us for living in a spirit of fear (i.e. faith in the working of satan) rather than "doing the work of God which is to believe ..."

Therefore, I think that to back away from something just because satan is trying to get his hands on it and counterfeit it is a horrendous sin of giving in to the kingdom of darkness. I, for one, want to take back that which satan has stolen. I believe that during the next ten years the Church will take back much that they have given away to the devil in the last 40 years. The nineties will be a decade of taking back the land. And this is one of those areas that we will redeem. I invite you to become a conqueror and take back this land with me.

Two things stand out about counterfeiters:

- They only counterfeit what is real.
- They only counterfeit what has value.

Therefore, since Eastern religions use stillness as they approach the spirit world, I know two things:

- We, too, should probably be using stillness. (This is confirmed in Psalm 46:10).
- To become still and touch the Holy Spirit has great value.

In my opinion, since the Eastern mystic does not go through Jesus Christ, he becomes ensnared by the evil one as he enters the spirit world. However, some of the **paths into** the fourth dimension are neutral. They may be used by either cultists or Christians. Conversely, some paths are not neutral. A non-Christian may use drugs to enter the spirit world. This is an illegal entry for the Christian and strictly forbidden in the Bible. The word for witchcraft in the Bible is *pharmecea* which is, of course, connected with drugs.

Since the Christian goes through Jesus Christ, Jesus guides him safely through the snares of the trapper and into the throne-room of God — as He did John in Revelation.

What is Prayer, Anyway?

I have decided that prayer is two lovers sharing love together. If you go back to the Garden of Eden and see how God walked and talked with Adam and Eve in the cool of the day and realize that God is described as manifesting incomprehensible love, you begin to realize that our sharing with Him is the communion of two lovers. You can find many examples of this in the Psalms.

Therefore, when we pray, we are coming to Jesus, our Friend. Jesus said, "No longer do I call you servants, I now call you friends (John 15:15)." We are building a friendship relationship together. I have found that the development of friendships generally goes through the following steps.

Prayer Is Becoming a Friend

(Not doing something, but being with Someone)

1. STAGE 1 — CASUAL
   I speak of the world outside me (sports, weather).

2. STAGE 2 — BEGINNING TRUST
   I speak of what I think and feel.

3. STAGE 3 — DEEP TRUST
   I share my dreams, mistakes, frustrations.

4. STAGE 4 — INTIMACY
   I sit quietly with my Friend, experiencing a Presence beyond words.

5. STAGE 5 — UNION
   I become one with that Person, speaking, feeling and acting with His reactions.

> *Prayer Is Not Doing Something*
> *But Being With Someone*
> *Until I Become One With Him,*
> *Until I Become The Expression Of Jesus.*

We do not intrinsically become Jesus. But when we have gazed upon Him (Heb. 12:2) with loving affection for so long, we become a reflection of His glory (2 Cor. 3:18), taking on His character (Gal. 5:22-23) and His power (1 Cor. 12:7-11). A union has taken place in our spirits (1 Cor. 6:17), and "I have been crucified with Christ; and it is no longer I who live but Christ lives in me ... (Gal. 2:20)" See also the sixth chapter of Romans.

A Poem About the Present Tense God

A key to living with God is to live in the present tense. As I was learning this art, I discovered this beautiful poem which may be a blessing to you also.

> I was regretting the past
> And fearing the future.
> Suddenly my Lord was speaking:
>
> "My name is I Am." He paused.
> I waited. He continued,
> "When you live in the past,
> With its mistakes and regrets,
> It is hard. I am not there.
> My name is not I Was.
>
> "When you live in the future,
> With its problems and fears,
> It is hard. I am not there.
> My name is not I Will Be.
>
> "When you live in this moment,
> It is not hard. I am here.
> My name is I Am."
>
> Helen Mallicoat

Prayer: "Lord, may we become still so that we may sense Your Spirit."

Personal Application

Ask the Lord to show you the means you have used to still yourself. Ask Him what methods He wants you to cultivate.

Write your personalized form of the above questions in the space that follows. Then relax. Picture yourself with Jesus in a comfortable gospel setting — maybe walking along the Sea of Galilee or strolling through the fields of Judea. Turn to Him. See His love and compassion, and joy and excitement at being able to spend this time with you. Smile! Become a child and take His hand. Let the scene just happen as He wants it to. Ask Him the question on your heart. Tune to spontaneity and write down the answer He gives you. Do not test it while you are receiving it. Stay in simple childlike faith. You will have plenty of time to test it after the flow is finished.

Chapter 5

Dream and Vision — Focusing the Inner Man on God

The Place and Value of Dream and Vision

I will pour forth of My Spirit ... and your young men shall see visions, and your old men shall dream dreams (Acts 2:17, emphasis added).

Daniel **looked** toward Jerusalem as he prayed (Dan. 6:10).

Habakkuk kept **watch** to see what God would speak (Hab. 2:1-3).

John looked inwardly for a **vision** and heard a voice say, "Come up here, and I will show you what must take place after these things," and immediately he **saw a vision** (Rev. 4:1,2).

Jesus spoke forth the things He had seen in the presence of His Father (John 8:38).

God reveals Himself to man through the eyes of his heart by giving him dreams and visions. Furthermore, our inner eyes are used to speak to us about the condition of our hearts every night through dreams or visions of the night. Therefore, we see that inner seeing is a faculty of the heart and is used to express the things of the heart.

Since Christianity is a heart-to-heart, or Spirit-to-spirit relationship, we would expect this facul-

ty to be used a lot in our relationship with God. Unfortunately, it often is not used as much as it should be among Western Christians, because we have been trained to live out of our head rather than our heart. We tend to live more in the world of logical concepts and rational thinking than in the world of heart impressions, dreams and visions. If we are going to allow our hearts to be released, we must learn to live in the world of the dream and the vision (John 5:19,20; 8:38).

God wants to communicate through the eyes of our heart, giving us dreams, visions and an inner flow of images, but first we must recognize this faculty within us and the importance it can have as we present it to Him to be used by Him. For ten years as a Christian, it never occurred to me to use the eyes of my heart and look for vision. Therefore, I never received any visions. Now that I've learned to look, I find vision readily appears to me.

Obviously, the "eyes of our hearts" (Eph. 1:17,18) is a sense located in our hearts. It is one of the ways man's heart communicates — possibly one of the primary ways. I have found that the key that unlocks the door to the inner world is the use of vision. Many spiritual leaders agree with this. Dr. Paul Yonggi Cho, pastor of the world's largest church with over 600,000 members declares, "The language of the Holy Spirit is the dream and vision (**Fourth Dimension 1**)." Watchman Nee, pastor and writer, states that, "the picture is the Holy Spirit memory (**Anointed Preaching**)." These statements are **astounding** in the value they put on seeing in the spirit.

I have come to the conclusion that the ability to think in terms of images is **extremely important** in the Christian's life. I believe that maturity involves both the ability to think logically and rationally, and the ability to be intuitive and visionary. Or, another way of expressing it: maturity involves the ability to use both your head and your heart. In our Western culture, we have put logic on a pedestal and neglected the value of vision. This was not always so. If we look at Scripture or Church history, we see that dreams and visions have been prevalent throughout.

References to Dream, Vision and "Seer" in the Bible

Following is the printout of a study using **CompuBible**, a computer program designed to help Bible students make complete concordance studies on any topic they choose. I commanded the program to find every reference in the Bible that contained the words dream, vision, seer, look and eyes. Obviously, some of the references located referred to natural sight, not spiritual. All of these have been carefully weeded out so that the references listed below refer only to spiritual vision.

I encourage you to take a week or two of your devotional time to study these verses, praying over them and asking God to show you insights and revelations from them which you have not seen before. Keep a paper and pencil nearby and record what you discover. This will form a biblical foundation in your life upon which you can begin building a theology of how God uses dream and vision.

Title: The place of dream and vision in one's spiritual life.

Range: Genesis 1:1 to Revelation 22:21

Subject -	1. dream	2. vision
3. seer	4. look	5. eyes

Gen 3:5	Exo 3:6
Gen 3:6	Exo 16:9
Gen 3:7	Exo 16:10
Gen 15:1	Exo 16:11
Gen 18:2	Exo 24:15
Gen 20:3	Exo 24:16
Gen 20:6	Exo 24:17
Gen 21:19	Exo 24:18
Gen 28:12	Exo 25:1
Gen 31:10	Num 12:6
Gen 31:11	Num 21:8
Gen 31:12	Num 22:31
Gen 31:24	Num 24:2
Gen 37:5	Num 24:3
Gen 37:6	Num 24:4
Gen 37:8	Num 24:15
Gen 37:9	Num 24:16
Gen 37:10	Deu 6:8
Gen 37:19	Deu 11:18
Gen 37:20	Deu 13:1
Gen 40:5	Deu 13:2
Gen 40:6	Deu 13:3
Gen 40:7	Deu 13:4
Gen 40:8	Deu 13:5
Gen 40:9	Deu 29:2
Gen 40:16	Deu 29:3
Gen 41:1	Deu 29:4
Gen 41:5	Jos 5:13
Gen 41:7	Jos 5:14
Gen 41:8	Jos 5:15
Gen 41:11	Jdg 6:12
Gen 41:12	Jdg 6:13
Gen 41:15	Jdg 6:14
Gen 41:17	Jdg 7:13
Gen 41:22	Jdg 7:14
Gen 41:25	Jdg 7:15
Gen 41:26	Jdg 13:16
Gen 41:32	Jdg 13:17
Gen 42:9	Jdg 13:18
Gen 46:2	Jdg 13:19
Gen 46:4	Jdg 13:20
Exo 3:1	1Sa 3:1
Exo 3:2	1Sa 3:2
Exo 3:3	1Sa 3:3
Exo 3:4	1Sa 3:4
Exo 3:5	1Sa 3:5
Exo 3:6	1Sa 3:6

1Sa 3:7	1Ch 25:6	Isa 6:8	Eze 12:23
1Sa 3:8	1Ch 25:7	Isa 6:9	Eze 12:24
1Sa 3:9	1Ch 26:28	Isa 6:10	Eze 12:25
1Sa 3:10	1Ch 29:29	Isa 8:17	Eze 12:26
1Sa 3:15	2Ch 9:29	Isa 17:7	Eze 12:27
1Sa 9:9	2Ch 12:15	Isa 17:8	Eze 13:7
1Sa 9:10	2Ch 16:7	Isa 21:2	Eze 13:16
1Sa 9:11	2Ch 16:8	Isa 22:1	Eze 40:2
1Sa 9:15	2Ch 16:9	Isa 22:5	Eze 40:4
1Sa 9:16	2Ch 16:10	Isa 28:7	Eze 40:6
1Sa 9:17	2Ch 19:2	Isa 29:8	Eze 43:1
1Sa 9:18	2Ch 26:5	Isa 29:10	Eze 43:2
1Sa 9:19	2Ch 29:25	Isa 29:11	Eze 43:3
1Sa 28:6	2Ch 29:26	Isa 30:10	Eze 43:4
1Sa 28:15	2Ch 29:30	Isa 33:17	Eze 43:5
2Sa 7:4	2Ch 32:32	Isa 40:26	Eze 43:6
2Sa 7:5	2Ch 33:18	Isa 42:18	Eze 44:1
2Sa 7:6	2Ch 33:19	Isa 42:19	Eze 44:4
2Sa 7:7	2Ch 35:15	Isa 42:20	Eze 44:5
2Sa 7:8	Job 4:13	Isa 44:18	Eze 46:19
2Sa 7:9	Job 4:14	Jer 5:21	Eze 47:2
Sa 7:10	Job 4:15	Jer 8:15	Dan 1:17
2Sa 7:17	Job 4:16	Jer 14:14	Dan 2:1
2Sa 15:27	Job 7:13	Jer 23:16	Dan 2:2
2Sa 24:11	Job 7:14	Jer 23:18	Dan 2:3
2Sa 24:12	Job 20:8	Jer 23:27	Dan 2:4
1Ki 3:5	Job 33:15	Jer 23:28	Dan 2:5
1Ki 3:6	Job 33:16	Jer 23:32	Dan 2:6
1Ki 3:7	Psa 5:3	Jer 27:9	Dan 2:7
1Ki 3:8	Psa 13:3	Jer 29:8	Dan 2:8
1Ki 3:9	Psa 25:15	Jer 29:21	Dan 2:9
1Ki 3:10	Psa 89:19	Lam 2:9	Dan 2:19
1Ki 3:11	Psa 119:18	Eze 1:1	Dan 2:26
1Ki 3:12	Psa 123:1	Eze 1:4	Dan 2:28
1Ki 3:13	Psa 123:2	Eze 2:9	Dan 2:36
1Ki 3:14	Psa 141:8	Eze 7:13	Dan 4:5
1Ki 3:15	Pro 29:18	Eze 7:26	Dan 4:6
1Ki 6:15	Ecc 5:3	Eze 8:3	Dan 4:7
1Ki 6:16	Ecc 5:7	Eze 8:4	Dan 4:8
1Ki 6:17	Isa 1:1	Eze 8:5	Dan 4:9
2Ki 17:13	Isa 6:1	Eze 8:7	Dan 4:10
1Ch 9:22	Isa 6:2	Eze 10:1	Dan 4:13
1Ch 17:15	Isa 6:3	Eze 10:9	Dan 4:18
1Ch 21:9	Isa 6:4	Eze 11:1	Dan 4:19
1Ch 21:10	Isa 6:5	Eze 11:24	Dan 5:12
1Ch 21:16	Isa 6:6	Eze 12:2	Dan 7:1
1Ch 25:5	Isa 6:7	Eze 12:22	Dan 7:2

Dan 7:7	Zec 6:1	Rev 4:3	Rev 14:1
Dan 7:13	Zec 10:2	Rev 5:6	Rev 14:14
Dan 7:15	Zec 13:4	Rev 6:8	Rev 15:5
Dan 8:1	Mat 1:20	Rev 9:17	
Dan 8:2	Mat 2:12		
Dan 8:3	Mat 2:13		
Dan 8:13	Mat 2:19		
Dan 8:15	Mat 2:22		
Dan 8:16	Mat 13:15		
Dan 8:17	Mat 13:16		
Dan 8:18	Mat 24:23		
Dan 8:26	Mat 27:19		
Dan 8:27	Mar 8:18		
Dan 9:21	Mar 9:8		
Dan 9:22	Luk 1:22		
Dan 9:23	Luk 24:23		
Dan 9:24	Luk 24:31		
Dan 10:1	Joh 12:40		
Dan 10:5	Act 1:10		
Dan 10:6	Act 2:17		
Dan 10:7	Act 7:55		
Dan 10:8	Act 9:10		
Dan 10:9	Act 9:11		
Dan 10:10	Act 9:12		
Dan 10:11	Act 10:3		
Dan 10:12	Act 10:4		
Dan 10:13	Act 10:17		
Dan 10:14	Act 10:19		
Dan 10:15	Act 11:5		
Dan 10:16	Act 11:6		
Dan 11:14	Act 12:9		
Dan 12:5	Act 16:9		
Hos 12:10	Act 16:10		
Joe 2:28	Act 18:9		
Amo 7:12	Act 26:18		
Oba 1:1	Act 26:19		
Mic 3:6	Act 28:27		
Mic 3:7	Rom 11:8		
Nah 1:1	Rom 11:10		
Hab 2:2	2Co 4:18		
Hab 2:3	2Co 12:1		
Zec 1:18	Eph 1:18		
Zec 2:1	Heb 11:10		
Zec 4:2	Rev 1:10		
Zec 5:1	Rev 1:14		
Zec 5:5	Rev 4:1		
Zec 5:9	Rev 4:2		

History

Not only are dreams and visions prevalent in every dispensation of the Bible, they have also been a consistent part of Church history. In order to give you a clearer view of the Church's experience with dreams and visions throughout the last 2000 years, I offer the following examples. (This section is provided for those who are interested in such historical studies. If you are not edified or helped by them, feel free to skim to the next section.)

1. Augustine — Rather than ignoring dreams as the contemporary Church has done, Augustine took the entire Twelfth Book in his *De Genesi ad Litteram to* explain his understanding of dreams and visions.

2. Polycarp — The book *Martyrdom of Polycarp* tells of Polycarp praying not long before his martyrdom, and being informed of what was shortly to happen through a symbolic vision. He saw the pillow under his head catch fire and realized that this image of destruction signified his own impending capture and death.

3. Justin Martyr — In his writings, Martyr said that dreams are sent by spirits. He believed that dreams are sent by both evil spirits and God.

4. Irenaeus — As Irenaeus refuted gnostic speculation in his writings, he indicated his clear view concerning dreams and the life of the Christian. In his principal work, *Against Heresies*, Irenaeus commented appreciatively and intelligently on the dream of Peter in the tenth chapter of Acts; he believed that the dream itself was a proof of the authenticity of Peter's experience. Again, he stressed the authenticity of Paul's dream at Troas. He also inferred from the dreams of Joseph in Matthew that Joseph's dreaming showed how close he was to the real God. In still another place, he explained that although God is Himself invisible to the eye directly, He gives us visions and dreams through which He conveys the likeness of His nature and glory.

5. Clement — In discussing the nature and meaning of sleep, Clement urged: "Let us not, then, who are sons of the true light, close the door against this light; but turning in on ourselves, illumining the eyes of the hidden man, and gazing on the truth itself, and receiving its streams, let us clearly and intelligibly reveal such dreams as are true.... Thus also such dreams as are true, in the view of him who reflects rightly, are the thoughts of a sober soul, undistracted for the time by the affections of the body, and counseling with itself in the best manner.... Wherefore always contemplating God, and by perpetual converse with Him inoculating the body with wakefulness, it raises man to equality with angelic grace, and from the practice of wakefulness it grasps the eternity of life (*Stromata*, or *Miscellanies*)."

6. Origen — In his great answer to the pagans, *Against Celsus*, Origen defended the visions of the Bible, saying: "...We, nevertheless, so far as we can, shall support our position, maintaining that, as it is a matter of belief that in a dream impressions have been brought before the minds of many, some relating to divine things, and others to future events of this life, and this either with clearness or in an enigmatic manner, a fact which is manifest to all who accept the doctrine of providence: so how is it absurd to say that the mind which could receive impressions in a dream should be impressed also in a waking vision, for the benefit either of him on whom the impressions are made, or of those who are to hear the account of them from him?" Having satisfied his parallel between dreams and visions, Origen then went on to discuss the nature of dreams.

In *Contra Celsus*, Origen further declared that many Christians had been converted from their pagan ways by this kind of direct breakthrough into their lives in waking visions and dreams of the night. He made it clear that many such instances of this sort of conversion were known.

7. Tertullian — Tertullian devoted eight chapters of his work *A Treatise on the Soul*, or *De Anima*, to his study of sleep and dreams. He believed that all dream, and evidenced it by the movement of sleeping infants. He believed that dreams occur from four sources: demons, God, natural dreams that the soul creates, and finally

"the ecstatic state and its peculiar conditions" or, in other words, the unconscious. Furthermore he states, "And thus we — who both acknowledge and reverence, even as we do the prophecies, modern visions as equally promised to us, and consider the other powers of the Holy Spirit as an agency of the Church for which also He was sent, administering all gifts in all, even as the Lord distributed to every one ..."

8. Thascius Cyprian, Bishop of Carthage in 250 A.D. — In a letter to Florentius Pupianus he said, "Although I know that to some men dreams seem ridiculous and visions foolish, yet assuredly it is to such as would rather believe in opposition to the priest, than believe the priest." In another letter he wrote that God guides the very councils of the Church by "many and manifest visions." He commended the reader, Celerinus, because his conversion to the Church had come through a vision of the night.

9. Lactantius, chosen by Constantine the Great to tutor his son. — In his *Divine Institutes*, he included a chapter, "The Use of Reason in Religion; and of Dreams, Auguries, Oracles, and Similar Portents," in which he cited examples to show that through dreams, a knowledge of the future is occasionally given to pagans as well as to Christians. His example of a logical fallacy is that of a man who has dreamed that he ought not believe in dreams.

10. Constantine — Lactantius writes of the heavenly vision that gave Constantine his great victory in 300 A.D. The story begins with Constantine being in desperate need and calling on God for help. "Accordingly he called on Him with earnest prayer and supplications that He would reveal to him Who He was, and stretch forth His right hand to help him in his present difficulties. And while he was thus praying with fervent entreaty, a most marvelous sign appeared to him from heaven, the account of which it might have been hard to believe had it been related by any other person. But since the victorious emperor himself long afterwards declared it to the writer of this history, when he was honored with his acquaintance and society, and confirmed his statement by an oath, who could hesitate to accredit the relation especially since the testimony of after-time has established its truth? He said that about noon, when the day was already beginning to decline, he saw with his own eyes the trophy of a cross of light in the heavens, above the sun, and bearing the inscription, CONQUER BY THIS. At this sight he himself was struck with amazement, and his whole army also, which followed him on this expedition, and witnessed the miracle.

He said, moreover, that he doubted within himself what the import of this apparition could be. And while he continued to ponder the reason on its meaning, night suddenly came on; then in his sleep the Christ of God appeared to him with the same sign which he had seen in the heavens, and commanded him to make a likeness of that sign which he had seen in the heavens, and to use it as a safeguard in all engagements with his enemies.

At dawn of day he arose, and communicated the marvel to his friends: and then, calling together the workers in gold and precious stones, he sat in the midst of them, and described to them the figure of the sign he had seen, bidding them represent it in gold and precious stones. And this representation I myself have had an opportunity of seeing (*The Life of Constantine I*, 28- 30)."

11. Socrates — One dream Socrates mentioned was that of Ignatius of Antioch. Ignatius had a vision of angels who sang hymns in alternate chants, and so introduced the mode of antiphonal singing (*Ecclesiastical History*, Vol. 35 and 36, by Theodoret).

12. Athanasius, Bishop of Alexandria from 328 to 373 — In his great masterpiece of Christian apology, *Against the Heathen*, he wrote: "Often when the body is quiet, and at rest and asleep, man moves inwardly, and beholds what is outside himself, traveling to other countries, walking about, meeting his acquaintances, and often by these means divining and forecasting the actions of the day. But to what can this be due save to the rational soul, in which man thinks of and perceives things beyond himself?...

For if even when united and coupled with the body it is not shut in or commensurate with the small dimensions of the body, but often, when the body lies in bed, not moving, but in death-like sleep, the soul keeps awake by virtue of its own

power, and transcends the natural power of the body, and as though traveling away from the body while remaining in it, imagines and beholds things above the earth, and often even holds converse with the saints and angels who are above earthly and bodily existence, and approaches them in the confidence of the purity of its intelligence; shall it not all the more, when separated from the body at the time appointed by God Who coupled them together, have its knowledge of immortality more clear? (II.31.5 and 33.3)"

13. Gregory of Nyssa — In his major philosophical work, *On the Making of Man*, Gregory deals directly with the meaning and place of sleep and dreams in man's life. He believed that when man is asleep the senses and the reason rest, and the less rational parts of the soul appear to take over. Reason is not, however, extinguished, but smolders like a fire "heaped with chaff" and then breaks forth with insights that modern dream research calls "secondary mentation." He went on to say that "while all men are guided by their own minds, there are some few who are deemed worthy of evident Divine communication; so, while the imagination of sleep naturally occurs in a like and equivalent manner for all, some, not all, share by means of their dreams in some more Divine manifestation. ..." His reasoning was that there is a natural foreknowledge that comes in an unknown way through the nonrational part of the soul — the "unconscious," according to modern depth psychology — and it is through this part of the soul that God communicates Himself directly.

Gregory then enumerated the other meanings that dreams can have, offering quite a complete outline of the subject. He suggested that dreams can provide mere reminiscences of daily occupations and events. Or, they can reflect the condition of the body, its hunger or thirst, or the emotional condition of the personality. Dreams can also be understood in medical practice as giving clues to the sickness of the body. Indeed, far from stating a superstitious belief, Gregory laid out quite well the principle upon which today's analytical study of dreams is based.

Gregory also told, in a sermon entitled "In Praise of the Forty Martyrs," of a dream that occurred while he was attending a celebration in honor of the soldiers who had been martyred. In the dream, the martyrs challenged Gregory for his Christian lethargy, and it had a profound effect upon his life.

It is clear that philosophically, practically and personally, Gregory of Nyssa believed the dream could be a revelation of depths beyond the human ego.

14. Basil the Great — In his commentary on Isaiah, Basil states, "The enigmas in dreams have a close affinity to those things which are signified in an allegoric or hidden sense in the Scriptures. Thus both Joseph and Daniel, through the gift of prophecy, used to interpret dreams, since the force of reason by itself is not powerful enough for getting at truth (S. Basilii Magni, *Commentarium in Isaiam Prophetam*, Prooemium 6f., J.-P. Migne, Patrologiae Graecae, Paris, 1880, Vol. 30, Col. 127-30)."

That Basil believed in continuing to consider dreams is indicated by the letter he wrote to a woman in which he interpreted the dream she had sent him. He suggested to her that her dream meant she was to spend more time in "spiritual contemplation and cultivating that mental vision by which God is wont to be seen."

15. Gregory of Nazianzen — In his second book of poems Gregory writes: "And God summoned me from boyhood in my nocturnal dreams, and I arrived at the very goals of wisdom (S. Gregorii Theologi, *Carminum*, Liber II, 994-950)." In another place he told that this nocturnal vision was the hidden spark that set his whole life aflame for God. In one of his poems, he spoke of the ability of demons to also speak through one's dreams. "Devote not your trust too much to the mockery of dreams, nor let yourself be terrified by everything; do not become inflated by joyful visions, For frequently a demon prepares these snares for you (*Carminum*, Liber I, 608-9, lines 209-12)."

16. St. John Chrysostom — In his commentary on Acts, volume one, he states, "To some the grace was imparted through dreams, to others it was openly poured forth. For indeed by dreams the prophets saw, and received revelations." According to Chrysostom, dreams are sent to those whose wills are compliant to God, for they do not

need visions or the more startling divine manifestations, and he mentioned Joseph, the father of Jesus, and Peter and Paul as examples of this truth (*Homilies on Matthew*, IV. 10f., 18; v. 5).

17. Synesius of Cyrene — Synesius wrote an entire book on dreams. He said, "One man learns ... while awake, another while asleep. But in the waking state man is the teacher, whereas it is God who makes the dreamer fruitful with His own courage, so that learning and attaining are one and the same. Now to make fruitful is even more than to teach" (Augustine Fitzgerald, *The Essays and Hymns of Synesius of Cyrene*, London, Oxford University Press, 1930, p. 332 [from *Concerning Dreams*]).

Synesius laid out a sound reason for discussing dreams and then enumerated the blessings to be gained from studying them. For the pure soul who receives impressions clearly, a proper study of dreams gives knowledge of the future with all that this implies. Important information is also provided about bodily malfunction and how it can be corrected. Far more important, this undertaking brings the soul to consider immaterial things and so, even though it was begun merely to provide knowledge of the future, it turns the soul to God and develops a love of Him. Synesius also told how dreams had helped him in his writings and in his other endeavors, and how they often gave hope to men who had been oppressed by the difficulties of life.

He made fun of people who relied on the popular dream books, insisting that only by constantly checking dreams with experience could they be understood. Their essential nature is personal, and they must be understood by the dreamer in terms of his own life. Some of them seem to be direct revelations of God, but there are also many dreams that are obscure and difficult to interpret. He suggested that anyone who is serious in studying them should keep a record so that he knows his sleeping life as well as his waking one. He even saw the connection between mythology and dreams, and explained his belief that the myth is based upon the dream; a true interest in mythology helps a man find the more vital meaning in his own dreams. Finally, Synesius showed the reason for his belief that dreams give hints about eternal life. As the sleeping state is to the waking one, so the life of the soul after death is to the dream life, and thus this state gives some idea of the kind of life that is led by the soul after death.

18. Ambrose — In Ambrose's famous letter to Theodosius calling for his repentance, he declared that God in a dream forbade him to celebrate communion before the Emperor unless he repented. These are his dramatic words: "I am writing with my own hand that which you alone may read.... I have been warned, not by man, nor through man, but plainly by Himself that this is forbidden me. For when I was anxious, in the very night in which I was preparing to set out, you appeared to me in a dream to have come into the Church, and I was not permitted to offer the sacrifice.... Our God gives warnings in many ways, by heavenly signs, by the precepts of the prophets, by the visions even of sinners He wills that we should understand, that we should entreat Him to take away all disturbances ... that the faith and peace of the Church ... may continue (St. Ambrose, Letter LI 14)."

Augustine tells how God revealed to St. Ambrose in a dream the hidden location of two martyred saints, who were then retrieved and given a proper consecration (St. Ambrose, Letter XXII; St. Augustine, *The Confessions*, IX [VII] 16; *The City of God*, XXII 8).

In St. Ambrose's more theological writings, Ambrose showed that an angel who speaks through a dream is functioning at the direction of the Holy Spirit, since angelic powers are subject to and moved by the Spirit.

19. Augustine — As has already been mentioned in number one of this series, Augustine wrote widely concerning the place and understanding of dreams in the Christian's life. His study of perception was as sophisticated as any in the ancient world. He saw reality as consisting of outer objects to which we react with our bodies, and the impressions of this sense experience, impressions that are "mental" in nature. We then have the inner perception of this sense experience, and finally the mental species in its remembered form. It is the action of the ego that unites these perceptions to the object. In one place, he calls the

faculty of imagination the bridge that mediates the object to consciousness, thus presenting almost the same thinking as that worked out by Synesius of Cyrene. Augustine saw man as possessing an outward eye that receives and mediates sense impressions, and an inward eye that observes and deals with these collected and stored "mental" realities that are called "memory."

In addition to the realities that come from outer perception and from inner perception of "memories," autonomous spiritual realities (angels and demons) can present themselves directly to the inner eye. These are of the same nature as the stored "mental" or psychic realities that are perceived inwardly. Augustine writes that men in sleep or trance can experience contents that come from memory "or some other hidden force through certain spiritual commixtures of a similarly spiritual substance (St. Augustine, *On the Trinity*, XI. 4.7)." These autonomous realities are nonphysical; yet they can either assume a corporeal appearance and be experienced through the outward eye, or they can be presented directly to the consciousness through the inner eye in dreams, visions and trances. Thus, through dreams, man is presented with a whole storehouse of unconscious memories and spontaneous contents; he is given access to a world that the fathers called "the realm of the spirit."

Just as angels have direct contact with man's psyche and present their messages before the inner eye, so also do demons. "They persuade [men], however, in marvelous and unseen ways, entering by means of that subtlety of their own bodies into the bodies of men who are unaware, and through certain imaginary visions mingling themselves with men's thoughts whether they are awake or asleep (*The Divination of Demons*, V. 9, N.Y., Fathers of the Church, Inc., 1955, Vol. 27, p. 430)."

In addition to presenting a theory of dreams and visions, Augustine also discussed many examples of providential dreams in the course of his writings. One of the most important of them was the famous dream of his mother Monica, in which she saw herself standing on a measuring device while a young man whose face shone with a smile approached her. She was crying, and when he asked why, she told of her sorrow that her son had turned away from Christ. He told her to look, and suddenly she saw Augustine standing on the same rule with her and she was comforted. Realizing the significance of the symbolism, she was able to go on praying for him with patience and hope; her dreams and visions are also mentioned in several other places in *The Confessions* (*The Confessions*, III. 19; V. 17; VI. 23; VIII. 30).

20. Jerome — In his early life, Jerome was torn between reading the classics and the Bible until he had this dream. "Suddenly I was caught up in the spirit and dragged before the judgment seat of the Judge; and here the light was so bright, and those who stood around were so radiant, that I cast myself upon the ground and did not dare to look up. Asked who and what I was I replied: 'I am a Christian.' But he who presided said: 'Thou liest, thou are a follower of Cicero and not of Christ. For "where thy treasure is, there will thy heart be also." ' Instantly I became dumb, and amid the strokes of the lash — for He had ordered me to be scourged — I was tortured more severely still by the fire of conscience, considering with myself that verse, 'In the grave who shall give thee thanks?' Yet for all that I began to cry and to bewail myself, saying: 'Have mercy upon me, O Lord: have mercy upon me.' Amid the sound of the scourges this cry still made itself heard. At last the bystanders, falling down before the knees of Him who presided, prayed that He would have pity on my youth, and that He would give me space to repent of my error. He might still, they urged, inflict torture on me, should I ever again read the works of the Gentiles ...

"Accordingly I made an oath and called upon His name, saying: 'Lord, if ever again I possess worldly books, or if ever again I read such, I have denied Thee.' Dismissed then, on taking this oath, I returned to the upper world, and to the surprise of all, I opened upon them eyes so drenched with tears that my distress served to convince even the incredulous. And that this was no sleep nor idle dreams, such as those by which we are often mocked, I call to witness the tribunal before which I lay, and the terrible judgment which I feared ... I profess that my shoulders were black

and blue, that I felt the bruises long after I awoke from my sleep, and that thenceforth I read the books of God with a zeal greater than I had previously given to the books of men (St. Jerome, Letter XXII, To Ekustochium, 30)."

Jerome's studies also gave him good reason to value dreams and visions. In commenting on Jeremiah 23:25ff., he shared Jeremiah's concern, indicating that dreaming is a kind of prophesying that God can use as one vehicle of revelation to a soul. It can be a valuable revelation from God if a man's life is turned toward Him. But dreams can become idolatrous when they are sought and interpreted for their own sake by one who is serving his own self-interest instead of God. The value of the dream depends upon the person who seeks it and the person who interprets it. Sometimes God sends dreams to the unrighteous, like those of Nebuchadnezzar and Pharaoh, so that the servants of God may manifest their wisdom. Thus it is the duty of those who have the word of the Lord to explain dreams (S. Eusebii Hieronymi, *Commentariorum in Jeremiam Prophetam*, IV. 23).

This word could not be sought, however, by pagan practices. In commenting on Isaiah 65:4, Jerome went along with the prophet and condemned people who "sit in the graves and the temples of idols where they are accustomed to stretch out on the skins of sacrificial animals in order to know the future by dream, abominations which are still practiced today in the temples of Aescylapius (*Commentariorum in Isaiam Prophetam*). Later, however, in the discussion of Galatians, he brought up specifically the dream in the sixteenth chapter of Acts in which Paul "was given the true light (lucam vero) (*Commentariorum in Epistolam ad Galatos*, 11)."

Jerome made no distinction at all between the vision and the dream. He clearly valued them both. Yet in the end, he fixed the ground firmly that would justify a growing fear of these experiences. In translating Leviticus 19:26 and Deuteronomy 18:10 with one word different from other passages, a direct mistranslation, Jerome turned the law: "You shall not practice augury or witchcraft [i.e. soothsaying]" into the prohibition: "You shall not practice augury nor observe dreams." Thus by the authority of the Vulgate, dreams were classed with soothsaying, and the practice of listening to them with other superstitious ideas.*

From here we enter the 1000 year period know as the Dark Ages, and little more is said until the writings of Thomas Aquinas.

21. Thomas Aquinas — Aquinas was greatly influenced by Aristotle and sought to reduce Christianity into Aristotle's worldview. This worldview left no room for direct spiritual encounter. Therefore dreams and visions were played down, along with experiences of angels and demons, the healings, tongue speaking and miracles. In the end, Aquinas' life contradicted what he had written. He did come into direct relationship with God through a triple dream experience and ceased to write and dictate. When he was urged to go on, he replied: "I can do no more; such things have been revealed to me that all I have written seems as straw, and I now await the end of my life (*Great Books of the Western World*, Vol. 19 [Thomas Aquinas], Chicago, Encyclopedia Britannica, Inc., 1952, p. vi)."

This was the turning point for the Church's view of dreams and their ability to carry revelation from Almighty God into the believer's life. Although the Church has flip-flopped back and forth somewhat in its view of the value of dreams, the pervading view today is much in line with the rationalism of our day, and very much out of line with the teachings of Scripture and the early Church fathers. One appears strange if he believes that God would actually communicate today to His children through the medium of dreams and visions.

22. Abraham Lincoln — Abraham Lincoln dreamed about his impending death just days before his assassination.

There are many more modern examples that could be quoted, but that is not our purpose at this time. There are entire books on the market today giving a Christian philosophical and theological base for interpreting dreams. There also are tes-timonial books concerning the variety of dreams and visions being experienced in the Church today.

As we have seen over and over again, dreams and visions are considered interchangeable, and so, even though much of this research deals primarily with dreams, it should be viewed in a wider scope to include visions as well.

It is time for the Church to return to a biblical understanding of dreams and visions and revelation.

New Testament Greek Words Describing Dream and Vision

In the Greek New Testament, there are many Greek words and phrases used to describe encountering God through dream and vision, and experiencing revelation. They are as follows:

Onar — a common word for "dream." Precisely, it is a vision seen in sleep, as opposed to waking. It is used in Matthew 1:20; 2:12,13,19,22 and 27:19.

Enupniom — a vision seen in sleep. It stresses the givenness, almost surprise quality, of what is received in sleep. It is used in Acts 2:17 and Jude 8.

Horama — translated "vision." It can refer to visions of the night or sleeping experiences, as well as to waking visions. It is used in Matthew 17:9; Acts 7:31; 9:10,12; 10:3,17,19; 11:5; 12:9; 16:9,10 and 18:9.

Opasis — can signify the eye as the organ of sight, an appearance of any kind, even a spectacle; but there are also two instances where it means a supernatural vision: Acts 2:17 and Revelation 9:17. The distinction between the perception of the physical and the nonphysical is lacking in the Greek. Both "seeings" are genuine perception.

Optasia — translated "vision." It has the sense of self-disclosure, of "letting oneself be seen." It is used in the following four passages: Luke 1:22; 24:23; Acts 26:19 and 2 Corinthians 12:1.

---

*   The word *annan* occurs ten times in the Old Testament. In most cases in the current versions, it is simply translated "soothsayer" or "soothsaying."

Ekstasis — the word from which the English word "ecstasy" is derived. It literally means "standing aside from oneself, being displaced or over against oneself," and ordinarily there is a sense of amazement, confusion and even of extreme terror. It may refer to either sleeping or waking experiences. Psychologically, both the dreams of sleep and the imagery that occurs on the border of wakefulness, hypnagogic or hypnopompic imagery, fit the condition that *ekstasis* describes. Although translated "trance," it is misleading to use the word "trance" as a direct translation. It is used in Mark 5:42; 16:8; Luke 5:26; Acts 3:10; 10:10; 11:5 and 22:17.

Ginomai en pneumati — translated "to become in Spirit" (Rev. 1:10). This signifies a state in which one could see visions and be informed or spoken to directly by the Spirit. Related phrases are found in Matthew 4:1; Mark 1:12; Luke 1:41 and 4:1.

Ephistemi, paristemi — simply referring to the fact that some reality stands by in the night or in the day. It is used in Luke 1:11; Acts 10:30; 16:9; 23:11 and 27:23.

Angelos or angel — literally meaning an actual physical envoy, a messenger, or a divine being sent by God, and *daimon, daimonion, diabolos* or demon, devil and satan, literally refer to nonphysical entities or powers from satan. Both angels and satan can be encountered in dreams and visionary experiences as shown in the following references: Acts 10:3; Jude 8; and many instances in the book of Revelation.

Blepo and *eido* — meaning "to see," "to perceive." These words are used to mean "see" in the normal outer sense, yet are also used to refer to seeing in the spiritual sense as evidenced in the following passages: Revelation 1:2,11; Mark 9:9 and Luke 9:36. Obviously, because of the dual use of these words to describe both inner and outer sight, the early Church considered visionary experiences just as easy to perceive and observe, and given as often and equally as valid, as the perceptions one has of the outer physical world.

Apokalupsis — translated "revelation," literally means disclosure, divine uncovering or revelation. It is used in Romans 16:25; 1 Corinthians 14:6,26; 2 Corinthians 12:1,7 and Galatians 2:2.

When considering the great variety of words used by New Testament Christians to describe their visionary experiences, we see that they have a vast number to select from, thus allowing them to very precisely delineate the exact type of visionary encounter they were having. Probably our poverty of vocabulary in finding one or two suitable words to clearly define our inner, visionary experiences demonstrates the poverty of direct spiritual encounter we all experience in the Western culture. May we restore to our vocabulary a host of suitable words to clearly define the variety of inner spiritual experiences we are having!

Defining Levels of Vision

1. Spontaneous Vision

We may receive a spontaneous inner picture in the same fashion as we receive spontaneous *rhema*. God may give a vision of the face of a friend or relative, and we just know we are to pray for them. The picture is light and gentle, and is seen within. It may be sharp or hazy, precise or unclear. As I poll Christian groups, I find that almost everyone feels they have sensed this type of vision.

2. Spontaneous Vision While in Prayer

These are identical to the previous level except that we receive them while seeking God in prayer. We have no part in setting them up. They just "appear," or pop into our minds. We may even find ourselves stretching or trying to change them in some way (although really we don't want to change them, because we want His visions, not ours). However, this in turn helps us to realize that it was His vision initially that lighted upon our minds (Dan. 7:1,13,14). About 70% of the Christians I poll sense they have experienced this type of vision.

3. Seeing a Vision Outside of Yourself

On this level, a person actually sees a vision outside himself, with his spiritual eyes. For example, Elisha prayed and said, " 'O Lord, I pray, open his eyes that he may see.' And the Lord opened the servant's eyes, and he saw; and behold, the mountain was full of horses and chariots of fire all around Elisha (2 Kings 6:17)." Only about 15% of the Christians I poll feel they have experienced this type of vision.

4. Vision While in a Trance

A vision can be seen while in a trance. Peter received a vision while in a trance in Acts 10:10-23. Trance-like visions are not very common in Scripture nor in the 20th century. About 5% of the Christian groups I poll have had trance-like visions.

5. The Visionary Encounter of Dreams

Paul received a vision in the night as he slept (Acts 16:9,10). Dreams are common in Scripture (about 50), and they are also common in the 20th century. About 85% of the Christians I poll feel they have had a dream that came from God.

Visions on each of these five levels are equally valid and spiritual, and all are to be thoroughly tested, weighed and considered.

Full Color, or Black and White Pictures?

The groups I poll are about evenly divided between those who see visions in full color and those who see in black and white. Some people seem to have much better internal antennas and clearer reception than others. My visions are nebulous, and black and white. Some people's are sharp, clear and full color; they roll off almost like a ticker tape. I am more left brain. I suspect that left brain people (analytical, logical) probably do not see as clearly as those God has gifted with more right brain leanings (intuitive and visionary). That is fine. When I need to see more clearly, I simply team up with one who is a seer, one who can see more clearly than I can. Jesus taught teaming up; He sent the disciples out in twos.

We are not in competition with each other. We give our giftedness to another to serve him or her.

Developing Your Ability to See in the Spirit

First, we must believe in the **value** of living in the world of dreams and visions. We must see it as the language of the heart, a primary means that God wants to use to communicate with us. Secondly, we must be willing to take the time to be with God, in quiet times, offering to Him the eyes of our heart that He might fill them with His dreams and visions. We want a flow of inner vision prompted and directed by the Holy Spirit. It is His vision we are seeking, not our own.

You will find that the more you present this channel to the Lord, the more it will be used. It will grow and grow until you reach the place to which God directed Dr. Cho, which was that "he must always be 'pregnant' in the form of dreams and visions." Our Lord Jesus set the example, for He did nothing Himself unless it was something He saw the Father doing (John 5:19,20).

The Bible says as we come to God, we must come in faith. We must also come to the world of dream and vision in faith. "Without faith, it is impossible to please God (Heb.11:6)." If we enter the world of dream and vision with doubt, we will find it taking us nowhere.

As we grow up, instead of rejecting the inner world as many of us were taught to do, we must learn to distinguish it from the outer world, yet live in it comfortably.

As we look at life, we see that we are more deeply moved upon and affected by images than by simple cognitive communication. For example, we prefer television over radio, a speaker who tells vivid stories over a didactic speaker, a testimonial book over a book of theology. Analytical thought does not have the same power as thinking in images. Images give us a way of thinking that brings us closer to actual experiences of the spiritual world than any concept or merely verbal idea. Dr. Cho found that the ability to become creative came into his life only as he learned to "incubate" the visions and dreams God gives to him.

As we look at the Bible, we find that God did not use systematic theology as His primary way of communicating Himself to us. Rather, He provided a series of powerful, true stories from

Genesis to Revelation, which, of course, involve image, pictures and parables. It was no accident that God chose to communicate Himself to us in this way. Rather, I am sure it was because He recognized it as the most effective means of presenting spiritual truths.

God sought to disclose Himself in the Old Testament through prophets (literally "seers"), and through the very beautiful picture of the Tabernacle (which in many ways still pictures our approach to Him as we understand the symbolism of it). Moreover in the New Testament, rather than just telling us how glorious and splendid and full of love He is, God sent His Son Jesus Christ to be the "radiance of His glory and the **exact representation** of His nature (Heb. 1:3, emphasis added)." Colossians 1:15 tells us that Jesus is the **image** of the invisible God. So, we see that when God most clearly and powerfully revealed Himself to us, He did not do so with words and rational concepts, but with the life of a person, His Son Jesus Christ, who was a living image of all God is. When the theology is beyond our understanding, we can look at the life of Jesus and, if we walk in Him, walk in God.

God uses images mightily in conveying Himself to us — not that we would ever trust in the image or bow down and worship it, but that it would lead us more fully to God. Jesus, Himself, taught with a great use of stories and parables rather than analytical concepts only, because He too grasped the power and value of the image in communicating spiritual realities.

Matthew 13:34 says, "**All** these things Jesus spoke to the multitudes **in parables** [as we shall see in a moment], and He was not talking to them **without a parable** (emphasis added)." Jesus turned everything in life into a parable. He converted issues into symbols of heavenly values and realities. All of life was a picturesque story to Him. Jesus lived, thought and spoke in the world of the vision (or parable), and that is an important key to the release of God's power through Him. Jesus turned the issue of getting a drink of water into a discussion of living water (John 4). He turned the sight of a field white for harvest into a spiritual reality that the people of the earth need to be spiritually harvested into the storehouse of

heaven. The commonplace pictures and images before Jesus were constantly used as stepping stones into pictures of spiritual realities.

Even though God has relied heavily on vision to convey spiritual realities and impart spiritual power, in the last 300 years, rationalism has gained gradual acceptance and has come to dominate Christianity. As a result, God's people have largely stopped receiving from God by way of the sanctified imagination. They have "hung up their receiver," believing that only analytical thinking is valid. They are so convinced of their position that anyone who actually believes in this world of spiritual experience given by the Holy Spirit (dreams, visions and images) appears strange to them.

Becoming Like Jesus

I desire earnestly to live as Jesus did, out of the Father's initiative, doing only what I see my Father doing (John 5:19,20; 8:38). However, before I can live that way, I need to learn how to become a seer. In a rationalistic culture where "seeing" is generally looked upon with scorn, it takes a monumental effort to become at ease with seeing vision as Jesus did.

Looking and Seeing

My experience, as well as the experience of many others, has convinced me that once we have grown accustomed to looking expectantly into the spirit world for a vision from the Lord, it readily appears. The simple act of **looking in faith** opens us up to begin seeing what is there.

I am convinced that the spirit world is there, whether I am seeing it or not. By becoming a seer, I am simply learning to see what is. When **learning** to see, I am learning to bring alive an atrophied sense (i.e., my visionary capacity) and then present it to God to be filled.

Once my visionary sense has been restored to life and is presented before Almighty God, I have the opportunity to live as did Jesus of Nazareth, out of the continuous flow of Divine vision.

The prophets of Israel could simply say "I looked," and as they quieted themselves before God "they saw" (Dan. 7:2,9,13). I have found that since I have reclaimed the use of my visionary ability, I too can simply quiet myself in the Lord's presence, look and then see the visions of Almighty God. I am a "seer" simply because I have become a "looker."

The Bible says we have not because we ask not. For years I never saw, because I never looked, nor did I ask to see. As I teach people to look, I witness their experience of becoming seers.

This sounds simple and it is for many, particularly those who are intuitive, spontaneous and visionary by nature, who have not cut off their natural spontaneous openness to vision because of the pressure of a culture that idolizes logical, analytical and cognitive functions.

Healing an Atrophied Visionary Capacity

However, for those like myself, who were born with the natural tendency toward the analytical and cognitive, and who have had these leanings reinforced by the rationalism of their culture, becoming a "seer" may not be so easy. Often the intuitive and visionary functions have literally atrophied and died through lack of use. Therefore, it is not as simple as just "looking" and "seeing."

When a muscle has atrophied, it must first be exercised and strengthened before the body can call it into use again. Even so, our atrophied, dormant capacity for visualization must be exercised and strengthened before the Holy Spirit can fill it and call it into use.

First, we must repent of the sin of scorning that which God has created, and secondly, we must ask God to breathe new life into it. Then we must stand and see if we can begin to walk. As we take our first wobbly steps, we are strengthened until we are free to walk with ease, allowing God to direct the paths for our feet. This is exactly what has happened with vision in my life and in the lives of many others.

Due to the scorn heaped upon it and its continuous disuse, my visionary capacity had atrophied and become useless. Therefore, when I began "looking to see" the vision God wanted to present to me, I saw nothing. I had so scorned my visionary capacity that it was unable to function when called upon to do so.

As pastors have often preached, our hearts are like a radio — we must tune them so we can hear God's voice. We must also tune them to see God's vision. However in this case, my heart's radio was not only out of tune, it was broken and in need of complete restoration by the Master. Therefore, I began the process of restoration by repenting of having scorned my visionary capacity. I asked God's forgiveness for not honoring and using that which He had created and bestowed upon me as a gift. I also repented of my participation in making an idol of logic and analytical thinking, a form of thinking that had swept over me as well as my culture. I covenanted to seek and honor His ability to flow through vision as much as I sought and honored His ability to flow through analytical thought.

Then I asked God to breathe upon my visionary capacity and restore it, to bring it back to life and teach me how to allow Him to flow through it.

Then I was ready to take my first few wobbly steps. As I sat in my study seeking God's face, I was drawn to a scene from the fourth chapter of John in which Jesus sat by the well and talked with a Samaritan woman. Sensing that God wanted to sit and talk with me, I pictured the scene with a slight adaptation. Instead of the woman talking with Jesus, I was the one talking with Jesus. As I peered intently into the picture, looking to see what might happen, the scene came alive through the Holy Spirit. Jesus moved and gestured, as someone does when he is talking. With His movement, there came into my heart His words and directives for my life.

This was the first time I had ever sought for vision in this way, and I was thrilled to see that Scripture so readily come alive and be taken over by the power of the Holy Spirit. I had in essence poised myself for the Divine flow by choosing a gospel story, meditating upon it and asking God to fill it. I found as I repeated this experiment in later days that God continued to move through these gospel scenes, causing them to come alive with His own life and become supernatural visions direct from the throne of grace.

Valid Questions

Now let us consider some rather common questions. First, "Don't I limit God by forcing Him to move in a gospel story that I present before Him to fill?" The answer is "Absolutely yes!" Of course, God has some variance as He comes alive in the gospel story. He can move it in one direction or another. However, if the gospel story is totally removed from what God wants to show me, I will find that nothing happens. The vision does not come alive. It remains dead. God is not able to move in it. I have had this happen, and in response I have simply relaxed and said, "God, how do You want to reveal Yourself in this situation?" With that, God implants the vision through which He can and does move.

The second question is, "Well then, why don't I just look for His vision in the beginning, rather than starting from a Bible story?" As I have said before, this works fine for the naturally intuitive and visionary person. However, the person with an atrophied visionary capacity will often need a learning tool to get him started. Once he is accustomed to vision, he will be able to discard the learning tool and simply "look" and "see."

The third question is, "Am I saying that my manufactured image is a Divine vision?" Of course not! My image is my image. God's supernatural vision is His vision. We never mix up the two. We never say that my priming of the pump is God's vision. It is simply my priming the pump. However, when the inner flow is experienced and the vision moves with a life of its own, flowing from the throne of grace, it is obviously no longer my own. At this point it has become God's. Mine is mine, and God's is God's.

The fourth question is, "Where in the Bible does it teach that we are to set the scene ourselves in order for God to begin flowing in vision?" Part of my response is, "Where does it say in the Bible that we are not to set a scene and ask God to fill it?" Since there is no clear verse for either position, we resort to pulling together several verses, which we then interpret in light of our chosen position. An alternative to this approach is to allow our brothers and sisters the Christian liberty to work out their own salvation in this area, since there is no absolutely clear biblical teaching on the issue. Perhaps the verses that most nearly can be interpreted as speaking against setting a scene are those verses that speak of avoiding vain imaginations and not setting up a graven image. A graven image is "an object of worship, carved usually from wood or stone (**Webster's Ninth New Collegiate Dictionary**)." Obviously, the scene we set in our minds is not carved or worshiped, but simply serves as a stepping stone to the living flow of Divine images. Webster defines vain as "having no real value: idle, worthless." I do not see a learning tool as something having no real value, as is true of a worthless idol. Learning tools are valuable and have a place. And the fact that the Bible speaks of vain imaginations tells us that there is also a "nonvain" use of imagination. I believe that the setting of a scene for God to fill is one of these "nonvain" uses of imagination.

On the Positive Side

On the positive side of this question of man's capacity to think visually, I would like to make two points. 1) All of the children and two-thirds of the adults I polled **normally** picture Bible scenes as they read them. As we pray for a spirit of revelation (Eph. 1:17), God causes the story to come alive and speaks to us out of it. This is essentially the same process we are describing. 2) One-fourth of the adults I polled normally picture the scenes of the songs they are singing; as God inhabits our praises, the visions come alive and move with a life generated from the throne of God. Both of these illustrate the very process I am describing.

Man's ability to think visually is currently being used unknowingly by many Christians, particularly those who are intuitive and visionary by nature. In reality, visual thinking is not a new thing. We are beginning to define and state clearly that which has been happening rather naturally among some. As a result of this clear definition and statement, all mankind can now be taught to become sensitive to a greater extent to the Divine flow within us.

A Temporary Learning Tool

It must be remembered that setting a scene is a temporary learning tool needed only by some. The naturally intuitive person will not need this learning tool. He will simply look to see, and the vision will be there. The analytically oriented person will put aside this learning tool shortly, as he, too, learns how to open himself naturally and normally to vision.

If we lived in a more biblical culture, perhaps we would not have so many obstacles to overcome before we could live normally and naturally in the Divine flow of vision. If our dreams and their spiritual meaning were a normal part of our conversation at breakfast with our families, as they were for Joseph and other Hebrews, we would find a natural skill built into our lives concerning visionary things. However, who in America takes their dreams seriously, discussing them regularly in a family gathering? Practically no one. If we did, we would be considered crazy. Is it any wonder that skill and openness to visions is almost totally lacking in our culture?

As a Church, we need to repent for allowing the rationalism of our time to distort our own perspective of a balanced lifestyle. Some fear that there may be seeds of Eastern thought in some of the teaching of the Church today. Did we ever stop to realize that Jesus was not a Westerner? God did not give us logic to idolize and put on a pedestal. He did not give us vision for us to squelch it with our scorn. No, it was others who encouraged these attitudes.

Church, let us come back to the balance of Jesus of Nazareth, who did nothing on His own initiative, but only that which He **saw and heard** the Father doing (John 5:19,20,30; 8:26,28,38). I have shared my struggles and experiences that have brought me closer to an ability to live this way. I challenge you to find the way that will **work for you**. The veil is torn, access is available, fellowship with the Holy Spirit is possible. Will you enter in? Will you seek the way? Will you enter within the veil and experience God in direct encounter, or will you be satisfied to experience Him second hand through the Book He has written?

Making Jesus Our Perfect Example

God is calling for those who will make Jesus their perfect example, who will aspire to live and walk as He did, who will do nothing on their own initiative, but will live as Jesus did, out of a constant flow of *rhema* and vision within them.

Will you search until you find the way to that lifestyle and experience? Will you continue on until you discover Him?

Will you find Him?

"You search the Scriptures, because you think that in them you have eternal life; and it is these that bear witness of Me; and you are unwilling to **come to Me, that you may have life**" (John 5:39-40).

Prayer: Lord, we come to You in repentance for allowing our culture to dictate to us, telling us that we are to scorn a part of our inner capacity that You have created and placed within us. We seek Your forgiveness and ask that You restore to our hearts a proper use of dream and vision. Restore our ability to hear and to see. Draw each of us into all that You have for us.

Summary Reflections on Dream and Vision

1. God does speak to us through dream and vision, as attested by hundreds of verses.

2. We do not presume to understand fully even the few disclosures of His transactions with the Father that the Lord has given us through the evangelists, yet it appears that **Jesus lived in a constant** flow of Divine images, as He "only did that which He **saw** the Father doing (John 5:19,20, emphasis added)."

3. Since Jesus is our perfect example, we are to learn to live the way He did, that is, constantly open to the Divine flow of vision.

4. The Bible tells us that God provides a ready and free flow of dreams and visions, as we experience the outpouring of the Holy Spirit. Therefore, the **normal Christian life is to experience vision readily** (Acts 2:17).

5. Samuel established schools of the prophets to train men to become seers (the original term for prophets). There is no indication that this process would not be continued. Today there are many Schools of the Prophets, once again training men and women to become seers.

6. The best way to train a person to become a seer is to train him to become a "looker." You will find scores of references from both Old and New Testament prophets saying, "I looked." Probably the major reason people are not seers today is because no one is instructing them to become lookers. We must once again learn to look to see.

7. We are commanded especially to fix our eyes upon Jesus (Heb. 12:1,2). The Greek for fixing our eyes is *aphorao* which literally means "to view with undivided attention by looking away from every other object; to regard fixedly and earnestly, to see distinctly (**The Analytical Greek Lexicon**, Zondervan)." According to the above definition, part of fixing our eyes upon Jesus is "to see Him distinctly." This is precisely what I am encouraging the Church to do as they pray, worship and walk through life.

8. May I suggest by way of a somewhat personal interpretation of Revelation 4:1,2 that we may be seeing John preparing himself to visually receive the bubbling flow of the Holy Spirit's vision. In chapter four, verse one, John said, "I looked," and we see him going through a door positioned in the heavens. **Immediately following his decision to answer the urging to go through this door, verse two records, "At once I came under the [Holy] Spirit's power, and lo ..."** (AMP). It is interesting that the Greek behind this specifically states at the beginning of verse two, rather than the beginning of verse one, that John came under the Holy Spirit's power. May I suggest that when John felt the call to meet God in the Spirit realm, he would visualize an open door in the heavens and, upon walking through it, would "come under the [Holy] Spirit's power," finding an active flow of Divine vision issuing forth. Admittedly this is a somewhat personal interpretation and you should feel free to set it aside if you are not comfortable with it. The interested student may want to search for other

places in Scripture where this process is indicated or taught. Please forward any research to me for future editions of this manual.

It is also interesting that one of the prophets' constant statements was, "I looked." The Bible clearly tells us that we have not because we ask not. Therefore, if we want vision, we most certainly will begin looking and asking for it, something that many of us have never been taught to do.

9. God uses images extensively in His communion with us, as evidenced by the following:

- God knows our needs. He knows that we are very aware of our own "story" and constant failing. He has provided in the Bible a sort of "story" recording His dealings with mankind. As we prayerfully ponder these Bible stories, we discover them merging with "our story" as God speaks to us from them. Although parts of the Bible contain systematic theology, God has made the Bible most largely narrative in scope.

- Jesus Himself is "the image, of the invisible God (Col. 1:15)." We see that when God most clearly communicated Himself to us, it was through the actions of a man's life and story (i.e. Jesus'), rather than simply the use of analytical, cognitive reasoning. Jesus said to Philip, "He who has seen Me has seen the Father; how do you say, 'Show us the Father'? (John 14:9)" The truths of the invisible God have been revealed to us through Jesus, His Son's, life story. In Jesus, we now have hundreds of snapshots (from the gospels) of God in motion.

- When God designed the Holy of Holies, the place where man would stand directly before the presence of God, God used an image to represent Himself to Moses and the other high priests. If God were opposed to the use of images to represent Himself to man, He could have had Moses stand alone in an empty room and speak to Him face to face and mouth to mouth without the use of images. However, God chose to use a symbol — the ark of the covenant and the mercy seat with cherubim on top.

- God's use of types throughout the Old Testament.

- Jesus' constant use of parables (picture stories) as He taught (Matt. 13:34).

10. I believe it is proper to enter into an image or picture to meet God in a direct spiritual encounter **because the structure of the entire Bible is such as to lead one into this experience.** As we have noted earlier, the Bible is primarily a book of powerful, life-changing stories, rather than a book of analytical theology. We are commanded to come unto the Lord as little children. When a child reads a story, he pictures the scene and action as he reads or listens. Most adults do so as well.

According to Ephesians 1:18,19, God wants to open the eyes of our hearts, granting us a spirit of wisdom and of revelation as we study. God desires to speak into our hearts as we study His Word.

Therefore I see the entire process of Bible study, as God has designed it, to involve entering into a Bible story, allowing God to speak to us out of the midst of the vision (created by the Word) which is set before our eyes, and living out that response.

11. As the vision within our hearts comes alive, we encounter God in the Divine flow that ensues.

- In Daniel 4:13-14, King Nebuchadnezzar encountered an angel in a vision **in his mind.** "I was looking in the **visions in my mind** as I lay on my bed, and behold, an angelic watcher, a holy one, descended from heaven. He shouted out and spoke as follows ... (emphasis added)."

- Daniel encountered the Ancient of Days and one like a Son of Man in a vision he had in his mind. "In the first year of Belshazzar king of Babylon Daniel saw a dream and **visions in his mind** as he lay on his bed; then he wrote the dream down and related the following summary of it.... I kept looking in the night visions, and behold, with the clouds of heaven one like a Son of Man was coming, and He came up to the Ancient of Days and was presented before Him.... As for me, Daniel, my spirit was distressed within me, and the visions in my mind kept alarming me (Dan. 7:1,13,15, emphasis added)."

- We see therefore that it is very biblical to encounter God, Christ and angels **in the visions of our minds** as these visions come alive with the flow of the Holy Spirit within us.

12. Our ability to see in the Spirit was designed to be presented to God and filled by God.

- We know that **everything** God created was good, and that "everything" obviously has to include our visionary capacity. As all that God has created is presented before Him to fill, God's kingdom is realized and His purposes established. As we present the eyes of our hearts to Him to fill, His vision fills our hearts. Our responsibility is to present all our capacities quietly before Him, allowing Him to move upon and through them. That includes our minds, our hearts, our hands, our mouths and our visionary capacity, along with everything else that we are.

- God generally will not force Himself upon the one who is not opening himself before Him. We generally will not speak in tongues until we offer Him our mouths. We generally will not receive words of wisdom and knowledge until we offer Him our minds. We generally will not receive visions until we offer Him the eyes of our hearts.

- Therefore, in cultivating our visionary capacity, we are presenting the eyes of our hearts before God, asking Him to fill them.

Allowing God to Restore Your Visionary Capacity

Some find that vision is almost completely, or even totally, impossible. There may be several reasons this is so. It is best to seek the Lord for revelation concerning what the block or hindrance is, and then ask for His revelation of the steps to take to heal the problem. The following are some common problems that I have run into, along with some solutions that have proven helpful.

Problem # 1 — Disdaining the Visual and Idolizing the Rational

Some have unwittingly been swept into the Westerner's idolization of logic and his disdain (or disregard) of the visionary. Westerners generally do not believe in the value and power of the visionary capacity within them. They do not hold it in esteem and honor, as one of the gifts that God has placed within man.

To heal this problem, one must: 1) repent for not fully honoring and using a gift and ability that God has placed within; 2) repent for idolizing logic and cognition; 3) state his commitment to honor and use his visual capacity as greatly as he honors and uses his analytical capacity; 4) ask God to breathe upon and restore his visual capacity; and 5) begin practicing and exercising it by learning to live in pictures as readily as he lives in thoughts. Then he is ready to begin presenting the eyes of his heart to God to fill, **by looking** for His vision as he walks through life.

Problem # 2 — Fear of Entering into Cultism

Some are unable to use their visual capacities effectively because they have been taught that it is cultish.

To heal this problem, one must: 1) realize that the ability to think and see using pictures was given to man by God, not by satan; 2) realize that even though satan seeks to fill man's visual abilities, so does God; 3) acknowledge that God does not want us to turn away from use of the visual capacity, but rather He want us to present it continuously to Him to fill; 4) renounce fear of receiving a satanic counterfeit, while confessing faith in God's ability to fill the visual capacity; 5) confess fear as sin and receive God's gift of faith; 6) realize that satan can attack the thought processes as easily as he can attack the visionary processes; therefore, both must be presented continuously before the Lord for Him to fill and to flow through.

Problem # 3 — Cutting Off the Visual Capacity In Order To Avoid the Sin of Lust

Some people have chosen to deal with the problem of lust by simply making a decision to cut off all use of the visual capacity. These people probably cannot visualize anything, including their living room couch.

To heal this problem, one has to: 1) realize that there are effective means of dealing with lust, other than cutting off one of the capacities that God has placed within; 2) learn to appropriate some of these other alternatives to effectively deal with the sin of lust; 3) repent for cutting off the visual capacity; 4) ask God to restore it and recreate it; 5) begin using it again; and 6) ask God to fill it with His Divine vision.

Problem # 4 — Cutting Off the Visual Capacity In Order To Avoid Some Unpleasant Visual Scene

Some people have cut off their sensitivity to the visual capacity because they have been trying to avoid seeing a scene of pain in their lives. This may be a scene of molestation or a recurring nightmare of snakes or some other terrorizing scene. They have decided that the most effective way of handling these terrorizing scenes is to cut off their visual capacities.

To heal this problem, one has to: 1) recognize and discover the precipitating reason for cutting off his visual sense; 2) offer the scene to God, asking Him to walk into it and heal it with His loving, all-powerful presence; 3) ask God to restore the use of his visual capacity; 4) begin again to use pictures and visions as he walks through life; and 5) present the eyes of his heart to God for Him to fill and flow through.

In summary, these are a few of the common blocks that keep people from living effectively in their God-given gift of dream, vision and imagination. May each one learn to fully use all the abilities that God has provided within man.

Suggestions for Becoming Open to Seeing in the Spirit

The following suggestions may help you begin to be open to God, allowing Him to fill the eyes of your heart with His dream and vision.

1. One must "be still" outwardly and inwardly so the Holy Spirit can issue forth with a flow of living images. Review the chapter on stillness. You will sense a bubbling flow within you as the vision comes alive with a "life of its own" (i.e. the Holy Spirit's life).

2. Enter a biblical story using vision. This is probably the most common way of all. Simply allow yourself to see what you are reading. And you can do more than just see the scenes yourself. After seeing the scenes, ask God to show you what He wants to show you, and a flow of inner images can take over that is directed by God.

3. Open the eyes of your heart during your quiet times, allowing God to show you things. I have found that **focusing intently** upon Jesus until He begins moving or speaking prompts the flow of the Spirit's images.

4. In intercession for others, see the person for whom you are praying, and then see Christ meeting that person. Relax and allow the vision to move under the direction of the Holy Spirit. Watch what He does, then pray that into existence.

5. Listen to your dreams, which are a natural expression of the inner world. Ask God to speak to you during the night (Ps. 127:2). When you awaken, **immediately** record your dreams and then ask God for an interpretation. He will give it. Read a good book on Christian dream interpretation. I believe the best is **Dreams — Wisdom Within** by Herman Riffel. Communion With God Ministries also markets a set of audio tapes, video tapes and a guide by Herman Riffel. These are a must for anyone who wants to begin working with their dreams. Without proper instruction and mentoring, a lot of error can come from faulty dream interpretation.

6. Praying in the Spirit opens up communication with the Holy Spirit and allows Him to arise, especially if you are presenting the eyes of your heart to God to fill.

7. Quiet prayer, simply affirming your love for Jesus and His toward you, opens you up to reflections and insights that are a form of vision in action.

8. When you come before the Lord in praise and worship, open the eyes of your heart to see what you are singing and allow the Holy Spirit to carry the vision where He wants.

Seeing in the Spirit, Not Worshiping an Image

God commanded the Israelites not to "make a graven image [literally "carved image"] or any likeness of what is in heaven above or on the earth beneath or in the water under the earth. You shall not worship them or serve them; for I, the Lord your God, am a jealous God (Ex. 20:4-5)." Therefore, we must carefully distinguish between seeing in the spirit and idolatry.

There is obviously no problem in receiving a vision from God as one prays and waits before Him. This has occurred throughout the Bible, one example being found in Revelation 4:2. Here John receives a heavenly vision of Christ, given by God, and as it unfolds, we find John actively involved, dialoguing with heavenly and angelic beings and participating in the dreams (Rev. 10:8-11).

However, when I set the first scene and look for a vision of Christ, do I find myself in violation of Deuteronomy 20:4, because I am making a likeness of a god that I am then bowing down and worshiping? No, definitely not.

God incarnated Himself in Jesus of Nazareth, "the image of the invisible God (Col. 1:15)." This God/Man then lived out a full life in our midst, showing us pictorially, over and over, the "radiant glory of God (Heb. 1:3)," revealing to us, image upon image, the kindness, gentleness, mercy and power of God. God is not only invisible, He is also visible in Jesus of Nazareth — the greatest of all images given to man — through the gospels as they record for us the powerful, life-changing stories of His life.

Now we have an image that is not a man-initiated image of the likeness of God, but a God-given image, perfectly portraying Himself to us in the multiplied stories **He has recorded for us**. Now, we can turn to the gospels, open to the story of His choice, read and see the invisible God in visible action. Often, the story itself will give us the precise answer to our need.

For example, in asking the Lord one day how I should counsel in the situation of an illegitimate pregnancy, the Lord immediately reminded me of the story of Jesus saying to the woman caught in adultery, "Go and sin no more." He did not condemn, reject or hate her; He received, protected and loved her, sending her on with His instruction. Thus was brought before my heart the story, complete with sound and vision — the story I could enter into and feel — the story and image of God's choice.

I did not bow down and worship that image of Jesus forgiving the adulterous woman. Rather, that picture instantly helped me to focus me on the eternal, invisible God Who revealed His love and mercy.

Carrying this one final step, I have found that when I want to commune with God in general, share love together, or share our lives together, I can focus my inner being on the invisible, intangible God and tune to Him by focusing on His Son, Jesus Christ, in one of the casual, relaxed scenes from the gospels. He becomes alive as His indwelling Holy Spirit quickens Him within me, and we commune together and experience any vision that He chooses to bring forth. We may walk together along the Sea of Galilee, sit on a mountainside, or experience any other scene He chooses to quicken to my heart. It is clearly commanded in Scripture that I "fix [my] eyes on Jesus, the author and perfecter of faith (Heb. 12:2)."

John "looked to see (Rev. 4:1)" what the Lord wanted to show Him. In verse two, the Holy Spirit took over and a heavenly vision unfolded before him. We, too, can look to see what God wants to unfold. I have looked at Jesus sitting on the edge of a well (John 4) and asked Him to speak to me the things He desires; and He has, through a gentle flow of spontaneous thoughts. I have noticed that as I look, the man sitting next to me on the edge of the well does not have a discernible face, but simply has the form of a man. Clearly visible features are unnecessary, even unimportant. For some reason, God does not allow the face to appear readily, and I have never tried to force it, because after all, we are seeking His vision, not ours. What is clear is His countenance of compassion, gentleness, peace, patience. (Incidentally, after using vision for a while in my life, Jesus' face did sometimes become clear. The first thing I noted were His eyes, filled with love and compassion.)

Thus, in no sense do I feel one is making a "graven image" or a "likeness." Rather, one is tuning in to God's image, Jesus Christ. Nor is one worshiping an image, because the image is readily alive with the moving of the Holy Spirit as He leads one into encounter with and the worship of the ever-living, invisible Almighty God.

One Inner Screen — Three Projectors

The diagram and chart on the following page can help you see and understand that the eyes of your heart can be filled by self or satan or God. May God guide you as you become open to His dream, His vision and His inner flow of Divine images.

Suggested Books on Using Vision When Encountering God

For a description of the practical way Dr. Cho lives, pregnant with dream and vision, read his book **The Fourth Dimension**.

For a good book describing the use of vision in the ministry of inner healing, read **You Can Be Emotionally Free** by Rita Bennett.

An example of the use of vision in inner healing in the New Testament is the twenty-first chapter of John where Jesus seeks to heal the deep hurt in Peter's heart caused by his threefold denial of his Lord. In order to minister deep, lasting healing, Jesus used imagery to deepen the reality of the forgiveness and love He was offering Peter. Both the hurt and the healing happen: 1) at twilight, 2) around a charcoal fire, and 3) involving a threefold confession. The Lord brings about an encounter that serves to remind Peter of his denial. Here the Lord shows something of what "drama" in His hands can do by way of healing memory and equipping for service. Simultaneously, **what had been** and **what was going to be** were present in Peter's mind and heart — a moment of intense, deep imagining and cleansing. It may well be compared with the Lord's use of "drama" in the parables; for all who are responsive, "my story is being told there." The Lord is **at work** in this activity. It is central to His ministry.

One Inner Screen — Three Projectors

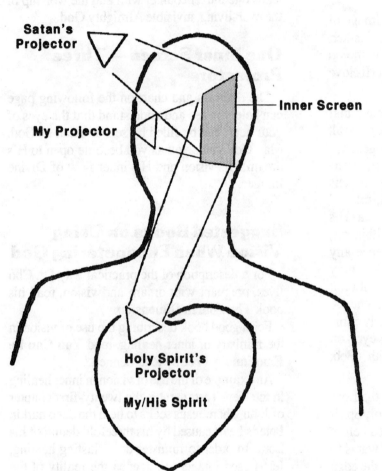

1. I am to instantly cut off all pictures put before my mind's eye by satan (Matt. 5:28; 2 Cor. 10:5).

2. I am to present the eyes of my heart to the Lord to fill. In this way I prepare myself to receive (Rev. 4:1).

3. The Spirit is to project on my inner screen the flow of vision which He desires (Rev. 4:2).

Testing Whether an Image Is From Self, Satan or God

SELF	SATAN	GOD

Find Its Origin (Test the Spirit — 1 John 4:1)

SELF	SATAN	GOD
Born in mind.	A painting of a picture. A flashing image. Was mind empty, idle? Does image seem obstructive?	A living flow of pictures coming from the innermost being. Was your inner being quietly focused on Jesus?

Examine Its Content (Test the Ideas — 1 John 4:5)

SELF	SATAN	GOD
A painting of things I have learned.	Negative, destructive pushy, fearful, accusative, violates nature of God, violates Word of God. Image is afraid to be tested. Ego appeal.	Instructive, upbuilding comforting. Vision accepts testing.

Seeing Its Fruit (Test the Fruit — Matt. 7:15)

SELF	SATAN	GOD
Variable	Fear, compulsion, bondage, anxiety confusion. Inflated ego.	Quickened faith, power, peace, good fruit, enlightenment, knowledge, humility.

Personal Application — Journaling Exercise

Ask the Lord the following questions. "Lord, how important is it to use the eyes of my heart? How have I been using them? How would you have me use them?"

Picture yourself and Jesus in a comfortable gospel story. See the scene around you. Then fix your eyes on Jesus. Smile! Enjoy His presence. Ask Him the questions written above. Tune to spontaneity and begin to write in the space below the flow of thoughts and pictures that come back to you. Do not test them while you are receiving them. Stay in faith. Know that you can test them later. Thank you, Lord, for what you say to us.

Prayer: "Lord, may the eyes of our hearts be constantly filled with Your vision."

Developing Dream and Vision — Class Worksheet*

Key Thought
Since dream and vision are used by God as primary avenues of spiritual contact, let us seek to become sensitized to their flow within us.

A. Why Develop Our Capacity for Seeing in the Spirit?

   1. _____

      a. _____

      b. _____

   2. _____

      a. _____

      b. _____

      c. _____

      d. _____

   3. _____

   4. _____

   5. _____

   6. _____

B. How to Develop Seeing in the Spirit

   1. _____

   2. _____

   3. _____

   4. _____

C. Principle of Negative Use

   _____

   _____

   _____

   _____

*   Use of this supplement is explained in the Teacher's Guide.

Chapter 6

New Testament Christianity and the New Age Movement

Many have noted that portions of what I teach here in **Communion With God** appear to have distinct counterparts among cult groups and the New Age movement. This concerns some people, so I have decided to include an entire chapter of my thoughts about the New Age movement and New Testament Christianity.

The New Age

The "New Age Movement" appears to be a loosely knit group of individuals who believe that we have entered a new age called the age of Aquarius. This age has allegedly replaced the age of Pisces, which represents the Christian era (pisces — fish — Christian symbol). The age of Aquarius (water bearer) is characterized by humanism (in a good sense), brotherhood and love. It is to be a golden age. It began, depending upon whom you ask, in 1904, 1936, 1962 or later. I personally reject such nonsense and believe we are living in the Church age in which we are to preach the Gospel of the Kingdom of our Lord and Savior Jesus Christ.

The New Age movement is causing much confusion among Christians as they seek to determine what the "New Age" is and how it is different from New Testament Christianity.

Because of a lack of understanding and definition of the New Age movement, Christians have even accused other Christians of being a part of it or having been influenced by it. Therefore it is time to write a chapter citing some of the differences and distinctions between new birth and New Age.

Before I began writing, I went to a local bookstore and purchased a 244-page reference manual entitled **The New Age Catalogue**. Broken into eight parts, it lists hundreds of books, authors, definitions, and magazine and video resources for those wanting to explore New Age teaching. I almost lost a trusted co-worker as she walked into my office and saw **The New Age Catalogue** sitting on my desk! She thought that if this was what I was into, it was time for her to step out. She was very relieved to discover I had only purchased the manual in order to have authoritative source material for this chapter!

The chart on the following page shows some of the basic distinctions between the New Age and New Testament Christianity.

By testing yourself or another using the nine basic distinctions listed, it should be quite easy to

New Testament Christianity	New Age
Who Is God?	
Yahweh, the personal Creator	The Evocative Other
The Standard for Truth	
The Bible	Evolving, eclectic
Who Is Jesus Christ?	
The Son of God	An enlightened teacher
What about Salvation?	
Purchased by the blood of Jesus	No such thing or, the process of integration
The Focus	
Christ centered	Man centered
The Power	
Through Christ	Through man
The Wisdom	
God's wisdom	Man's wisdom
The Next Age	
Brought about by God	Brought about by man
The Stance	
Man receiving from God	Man reaching to become god

determine whether a person is a "New Ager" or a New Testament Christianity. As you can see, there is a world of difference between the New Age and a New Testament Christian. There should be no need for confusion as to whether someone is one or the other. It should be obvious to all that just because a New Testament Christian is doing something that appears to be similar to the actions of a New Ager, those actions are no sign the Christian has been deceived by New Age methodology or teaching. Obviously satan is a counterfeiter. Therefore, things of the New Age are counterfeits of the truth of Christianity. As a result, there will be many similarities. Yet there will be many differences. The above list contains the foundational distinctions. Later I will give some more specific differences.

Why Is the New Age So Attractive to a Growing Number of People?

The New Age offers creativity and life to its followers. For example, David Spangler, who has been lecturing and writing on the New Age for 25 years, defines New Age as "the condition that emerges when I live life in a creative, empowering, compassionate manner."[1] That's an attractive prospect and goal for both Christians and non-Christians. He goes on to state, "I understand the New Age as a metaphor for being in the world in a manner that opens us to the presence of God — the presence of love and possibility — in the midst of our ordinariness."[2]

The ideals of the New Age are high and lofty and, if they can be achieved in even a small way by the power of man, they are tremendously enticing to a growing number of people. Therefore people flock to read and study the literature put out by the New Age.

Why Is the New Age So Deceptive?

One reason the New Age is so deceptive is that it espouses ideals and values that are very similar to Christianity. This, of course, should be expected, considering the fact that satan is the great counterfeiter. For instance, listen again to David

---

1   The **New Age Catalogue** by the Editors of Body Mind Spirit Magazine, Published by Doubleday 1988. Introduction
2   Ibid. Introduction

Spangler: "Inwardly, the New Age continues the historical effort of humanity to delve deeply into the mysteries of the nature of God, of ourselves, and of reality. In the midst of materialism, it is a rebirth of our sense of the sacred ... The New Age is essentially a symbol representing the human heart and intellect in partnership with God building a better world that can celebrate values of community, wholeness and sacredness. It is a symbol for the emergence of social behavior based on a worldview that stimulates creativity, discipline, abundance and wholeness; it is a symbol for a more mature and unobstructed expression of the sacredness and love at the heart of life."[1]

After reading definitions like the above, many Christians would respond with a feeling that Christianity itself holds to many of these ideals. However, the New Age believes man can reach for these goals and achieve them through his own effort, or if he does seek spiritual assistance, it is not restricted to Jesus Christ or God, but to any "good" spiritual energies that are floating around. Remember, the New Age movement is eclectic, and therefore is willing to draw from anyone's experiences or insight. They do not have a written standard against which to test all their experiences and teachings, as Christians do. For example, the following are some of the books and authors recommended in the **New Age Catalogue: Channeling — Investigations On Receiving Information From Paranormal Sources; The Sleeping Prophet, Develop Your Psychic Skills, and Crystal Healing** by Edgar Cayce.

What Should Be the Church's Response to the New Age?

Obviously we recognize it as a continuation of the deception that began in the Garden of Eden: "Man can become like God." It is the age-old lie that we can strive to reach divinity ourselves. Instead, Christians have discovered the freedom simply to rest in the Vine, experiencing the flow of the river of life that wells up within them by the Holy Spirit as they cease from their own labors and simply attune themselves to God.

We respect the New Ager's desire to become loving, creative and fulfilled, and we point them to the only true Source of such a lifestyle, Jesus Christ. New birth is mandatory as they acknowledge Jesus Christ, the Son of God, as their Lord and Savior and receive by faith His atoning work at Calvary.

We recognize that because New Agers are part of the great counterfeit, they may use words, phrases and techniques that have been borrowed from Christianity or Christian traditions. **Yet, we will not give over either these words or these experiences to the satanic counterfeit, as they are God's forever.** For example, New Agers have written on "the rainbow," which of course was part of God's covenant with Noah, and on "centering," which is a word and an experience that has been used for decades by the Quaker church. **The New Age Catalogue** even recommends the Christian book **Hinds Feet On High Places** by Hannah Hurnard (ibid. p. 89), published by Tyndale House Publishers, Inc. Being eclectic, we should expect them to draw from Christianity as well as anywhere else they desire to draw from. That does not concern us. We have a standard, the Word of God, and our acceptance of a truth is not based on whether or not a counterfeit group has yet picked it up. We look to see if it is taught in Scripture; and surely such things as centering or quieting our souls before the Lord, as is practiced by the Quaker Church, is clearly taught and demonstrated by King David in the Psalms as he states, "My soul waits in silence for God only (Ps. 62:1,5)."

Therefore we will expect the New Age to blur the line between truth and error through their eclectic nature, but we will walk calmly according to the eternal truths and experiences taught in God's Word. We shall not concern ourselves with how many cults are also drawing upon biblical concepts. We shall only concern ourselves with encountering fully and completely the God of Scriptures.

1   Ibid. Introduction

"One thing the New Age calls Christians to do is to enter fully into all of the dimensions of our relationship with Christ. The New Age has arisen to take the territory abandoned by the mainstream Christianity. Because Christianity (even most Charismatics) has neglected the intuitive and relational and has majored on the propositional and the analytical, a void has been left in the hearts of those who were seeking spiritual encounters. In the churches they met only doctrinal studies, so they sought for spiritual relationships within the occult and New Age teachings. The very best antidote for the New Age teachings is for Christians to enter into and live fully in the supernatural. This is certainly no time to draw back from supernatural living and retreat into a mere defense of orthodoxy. Because we have adopted this stance for the last half-century, we have opened the door for the New Age to fill the vacuum. There is a longing in the human heart for communication and a relationship with the Divine. Since the dawn of history, when God's people do not preach, proclaim and model the genuine article, men and women will wander into whatever appears to offer the fulfillment of their spiritual quest. We need to cast aside our hesitation and proceed strongly forward, the Word and the Spirit as our unfailing guide.

"The early Church made the tragic error (after about 150 A.D.) of majoring on defending orthodoxy in the face of the heresies of Gnosticism (which has recently arisen again as part of New Age teaching), Mystery Religions and State Paganism. While they were vigorously defending Christianity, formulating creeds (propositional statements of doctrine), and attempting to vanquish heresy by excommunicating heretics, somewhere along the line they forgot that Christianity is a relationship to be lived, not merely a theory to be proved. The rationalistic patterns of argument adopted from the Greek philosophers replaced the much more forceful arguments of a changed life and the miraculous interventions of Almighty God in the affairs of men. The Church largely lost the battle of ideas merely by conceding that the battle was confined to arguments over

ideas. The Bible is 90% narratives of God working in lives. Demonstrating God in our lives in all of His dimensions is our best defense. The best defense is still a good offense!"[1]

Additional Distinctions Between Christianity and the New Age

Since the New Age is seeking wholeness, life, love and creativity, it will obviously be reaching toward some of the same goals that Christianity reaches toward. Since the New Age is eclectic, it will be using some of the same approaches that Christianity uses, with some very subtle differences. Listed in the chart on the following page are some of these comparisons and some of the differences.

I believe that the New Age movement is a reaction to what God is doing in the Church of Jesus Christ. In 1900, the Holy Spirit began to move in new and powerful ways upon the Church. In just 90 years since then, we have seen over 400 million Charismatic and Pentecostal Christians worldwide who have been swept into these new (or restored) moves of the Holy Spirit. C. Peter Wagner estimates that 1.1 billion Christians will be sensitized to the Holy Spirit's flow by 2000 A.D. (**Target Earth**, p. 166). Gallop poll surveys have revealed that the individuals in this group that calls itself charismatic spend more time each week on the average in Bible study, prayer and church attendance than other Christians do. This is quite interesting. Regardless of your theological persuasion, the Bible says you can test things by their fruit. This surely is good fruit.

Therefore, I believe the New Age is satan's reaction to the mighty outpouring of the Holy Spirit that we are seeing in this century. I do not see it as something to fear or to flee from. Since when does light fear darkness? No, I stand against it in the power of the Holy Spirit and in the power of Almighty God! Often God has allowed tests to emerge within a culture so He can prove His supremacy over all else. Elijah and Baal are a classic example of this as Elijah proposed a test

1   From letter written by Rev. Maurice Fuller.

NEW TESTAMENT CHRISTIANITY	NEW AGE MOVEMENT
Intuitive Development	
The voice of God may flow through man's heart or spirit as intuitive thoughts, visions, burdens and impressions. Christians attempt to learn to discern God's voice, so they can hear and obey, thus experiencing abundant life.	Called intuition, New Agers recognize that as the voice of man's heart, it releases man's creativity, and thus they seek to cultivate it.
Contact With Spirit	
Christians seek fellowship with the Holy Spirit. They may also encounter angels sent from God.	New Agers seek fellowship with any beings in the spirit world.
Method of Quieting Oneself	
Christians often worship by fixing their eyes on Jesus, the author and perfecter of their faith.	New Agers use mantra.
Use of One's Visionary Abilities	
Visionary abilities are presented before God so He may grant Divine vision. They are recognized as a creative ability within man.	Visionary abilities are used by oneself to visualize one's goals. They are recognized as a creative ability within man.
Use of Writing in Spiritual Experiences	
Journaling is a way of recording what one senses God is speaking within him. Impressions sensed in the heart are registered in the mind and recorded by the hand. It is similar to the Psalms except that one's journal never becomes Scripture. Rather it is tested by Scripture.	Journaling is a way of recording what is flowing from the spirit world. One's hand hangs limp, and a force takes it over and guides it. The heart or mind of man is not involved nor is it submitted to Scripture. This is called "automatic writing."
The Planet Today	
Our world is being redeemed by the working of God through His Spirit, His angels and His working through His Church.	Our world is becoming better through man's efforts.
The Planet Ultimately	
New Heavens and a New Earth will come through God's direct intervention.	A new age will come through man's accomplishments.

to see who could call down fire from heaven. Whoever was successful was the one who served the true God.

You notice it is not the Pharisees or the false prophets who propose such tests or act with such courage and boldness. It is the prophets on the front line who prove God in the midst of their generation. I suspect that the books being written today by the Church about the New Age movement are not being written by the prophets. The ones I have read encourage a spirit of fear that we will be consumed, rather than a spirit of faith that we will conquer in this particular test. I believe the spirit of fear originates in satan, and the spirit of faith originates in God. Therefore I am very careful not to feed on anything permeated with the spirit of fear.

Let me suggest a prophetic stance in the midst of the dilemma in which we find ourselves. Since satan is obviously counterfeiting a truth of God, shouldn't we be asking what it is that God is doing in the area of vision and visualization? I propose the following five principles for people who are developing into visionaries. Each of these principles was discovered in Scriptures, and is rooted and grounded in Scripture.

Principles for Visionaries

1. Our goal is to be like Jesus who was a constant visionary.

> *The Son can do nothing of Himself, unless it is something He sees the Father doing... (John 5:19, emphasis added; also John 5:20; 8:38)"*

2. *We are to **look** for vision.*

> *Watch and pray ... (Matt. 26:41)*

> *Fixing our eyes on Jesus ... (Heb. 12:2)*

3. We are to look **in the vision** until the vision has stopped flowing.

> *Daniel said, "I was looking in my vision by night ... I kept looking until thrones were set up, and the Ancient of Days took His seat ... I kept looking in the night visions ..." (Dan. 7:2,9,13)*

> *... I was looking ... I was looking in the visions in my mind ... (Dan 4:10,13)*

4. We must realize that we can have encounters with Jesus, God and angels **in visions in our minds, and that these are actual spiritual encounters** (Dan. 4:4-5,10,13,14; 7:1,13-15; Matt. 1:20; 2:12,13,19,22).

5. The natural way to present the eyes of our hearts before God is to visually enter a Bible story in prayerful contemplation and allow God to move in it as He wills, or to fix our eyes upon Jesus, the author and perfecter of our faith (Heb. 12:1-2; Rev. 4:1-2).

Valid and Invalid Uses of Man's Visual Capacity

In a world where it is not enough just to identify the fact that man thinks visually as well as logically, it may be well to consider together some valid and invalid uses of man's visual capacity. The following are presented for your consideration.

Valid Uses

1. We often picture what we are saying.

(I.e., when the word "dog" is spoken, everyone automatically and instantaneously pictures a dog. It is the natural function of man's brain.)

2. A powerful orator will use picture words.

When Jonathan Edwards preached his great sermon "Sinners in the Hands of an Angry God," he pictured hell so graphically to his hearers that they literally clung to their seats so they would not fall into the great abyss. Today, powerful evangelists do the same type of thing as they preach.

3. Song writers often paint scenes to assist us in encountering God as we sing.

> *A wonderful Savior is Jesus my Lord,*
> *A wonderful Savior to me,*
> *He hideth my soul in the cleft of the rock,*
> *Where rivers of pleasure I see.*

> *He hideth my soul in the cleft of the rock*
> *That shadows a dry, thirsty land;*

He hideth my life in the depths of His love,
And covers me there with His hand,
And covers me there with His hand.

4. Picturing is sometimes used when memorizing information.

Probably everyone has used pictures occasionally to assist in memorizing a list of things. Jerry Lucas uses this approach extensively as he teaches people to memorize entire books from the Bible.

5. People visualize as they create something new.

Whether it is the homemaker redecorating her house or the architect designing a new building or the artist painting a picture or the child designing his latest invention, visualizing is obviously part of the entire creative process.

6. When writing out a prayer, we can use pictures to help us experience God.

*Thy lovingkindness, O Lord, **extends to the heavens**, Thy faithfulness **reaches to the skies**, Thy righteousness is like **majestic mountains**, Thy judgments are like **a great deep** (Ps. 36:5,6, emphasis added).*

Here, as in many other places, David is looking at creation and picturing God's greatness **as he prays**. It is apparent that David used visualization as he encountered God in prayer.

7. When reading Scripture, we see the scenes that the Bible so picturesquely sets.

God has chosen to use narrative as His basic writing style in communicating Himself to us. The Bible is 90 percent narrative, and 10 percent didactic. When it is read as a child reads, the narrative or story draws us into visualizing the scene which is being described. Since God's goal is for the Scriptures to come alive as we read, and that we find the vision moving with a life of its own, empowered by Almighty God.

8. In our imaginations, we are to keep the plans and purposes of ever before us.

Lord God of Abraham, Isaac, and of Israel, our fathers, keep this for ever in the imagination of the thoughts of the heart of thy people, and prepare their heart unto thee (1 Chron. 29:18 KJV).

Here David is praying that God will keep a clear vision of His purposes in the Israelites' imaginations.

9. God grants dreams and visions.

Hear now My words: If there is a prophet among you, I the Lord, shall make Myself known to him in a vision. I shall speak with him in a dream (Num. 12:6).

"And it shall be in the last days," God says, "that I will pour forth of My Spirit upon all mankind ... and your young men shall see visions, and your old men shall dream dreams" (Acts 2:17).

10. Divinely granted visions deepen one's faith, helping to release the creative miracle of God.

And He [God] took him [Abram] outside and said, "Now look toward the heavens, and count the stars, if you are able to count them." And He said to him, "So shall your descendants be." Then he believed in the Lord; and He reckoned it to him as righteousness (Gen. 15:5,6).

11. We are to fix our eyes on Jesus as we walk through life.

Fixing our eyes on Jesus, the author and perfecter of faith ... (Heb. 12:2)

It is appropriate to see Jesus (Immanuel — God with us), present with us as we walk through life.

12. We are to be seers, constantly seeing the Divine initiative. "Formerly in Israel, when a man went to inquire of God, he used to say, 'Come, and let us go to the seer'; for he who is called a prophet now was formerly called a seer. (1 Sam. 9:9)."

Jesus therefore answered and was saying to them, "Truly, truly, I say to you, the Son can do nothing of Himself, unless it is something He sees the Father doing; for whatever the Father does, these things the Son also does in like manner" (John 5:19, emphasis added).

Prompting Divine Flow
(Combining the natural and the supernatural

---

*The miraculous demonstration of God's power is released as **man acts in collaboration with God.***

Demonstrated on the Physical Level	Demonstrated on the Rational Level	Demonstrated on the Visual Level
1. **Situation** Peter walking on the water. (Read Matthew 14:22-23.)	1. **Situation** Luke writing his Gospel (Read Luke 1:1-4.)	1. **Situation** Habakkuk receiving visionary revelation. (Read Habakkuk 2:1,2.)
2. **Man's Part** Peter got up and walked, a very natural, physical function — something he could do on his own without miraculous intervention.	2. **Man's Part** Luke investigated everything carefully, writing it out in consecutive order — a natural, academic function, not needing miraculous intervention.	2. **Man's Part** Habakkuk quieted himself in the Lord's presence, to look, listen and write what he saw. Man can look with the eyes of the heart and be moved into direct spiritual encounter.
3. **God's Part** God added the supernatural element. Every time Peter's foot touched the water, God sustained it so it would not sink.	3. **God's Part** God added supernatural inspiration, by guiding Luke's thought process so the writing turned out to be Divinely inspired and perfect in content.	3. **God's Part** God added supernatural revelation by flowing through the visionary capacity, showing man visions of spiritual reality.
4. **How is a Miracle on the Physical Level Released?** Through a combination of the natural, physical abilities of man flowing together with the supernatural abilities of God.	4. **How is a Miracle on the Rational Level Released?** Through a combination of the natural, rational abilities of man flowing together with the supernatural abilities of God.	4. **How is a Miracle on the Visionary Level Released?** Through a combination of the natural spiritual visionary abilities of man, flowing together with the supernatural abilities of God.

May each of us present ourselves to God to fill and flow through.

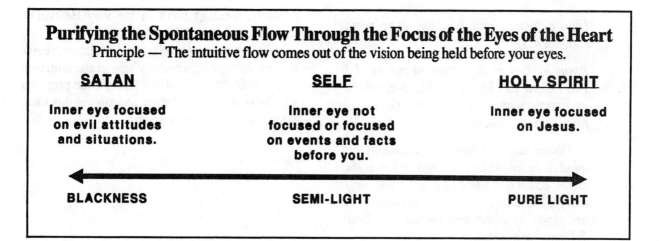

Purifying the Spontaneous Flow Through the Focus of the Eyes of the Heart
Principle — The intuitive flow comes out of the vision being held before your eyes.

SATAN	SELF	HOLY SPIRIT
Inner eye focused on evil attitudes and situations.	Inner eye not focused or focused on events and facts before you.	Inner eye focused on Jesus.
BLACKNESS	SEMI-LIGHT	PURE LIGHT

Improper Uses of Man's Visual Ability

1. One can follow the imagination of his own heart.

   But have walked after the imagination of their own heart, and after Balaam, which their fathers taught them (Jer. 9:14, KJV).

   In this case, man is using his capacities and God-given giftedness himself, rather than yielding it to God to use and fill.

2. Evil men will use their imaginations the same way they use every ability they have — for evil.

   But they hearkened not, nor inclined their ear, but walked in the counsels and in the imagination of their evil heart, and went backward, and not forward (Jer. 7:24 KJV).

3. Man can imagine evil against one another.

   How long will ye imagine mischief against a man? Ye shall be slain all of you ... (Ps. 62:3 KJV)

   Anyone can use his imagination to imagine evil, mischievous things and vain things.

4. Carving a graven image and worshiping it is strictly forbidden.

   The workman melteth a graven image, and the goldsmith spreadeth it over with gold, and casteth silver chains (Isa. 40:19 KJV).

   Thou shalt not make unto thee any graven image, or any likeness of any thing that is in heaven above, or that is in the earth beneath, or that is in the water under the earth (Ex. 20:4).

   And the residue thereof he maketh a god, even his graven image: he falleth down unto it, and worshippeth it, and prayeth unto it, and saith, "Deliver me; for thou art my god" (Isa. 44:17 KJV).

   "Graven image" literally means in the Hebrew "to carve, whether wood or stone."

   Fashioning an image of our own choosing and then bowing down and worshiping it is strictly forbidden.

5. Using our visual capacity in lust is strictly forbidden.

   I say to you, that every one who looks on a woman to lust for her has committed adultery with her already in his heart (Matt. 5:28).

The Place of Looking in the Vision in Your Mind and Meeting God

THESIS: As we look **"for** visions" and "in the visions" that appear in our hearts, we encounter God.

"I was looking" is found about 11 times in Daniel alone (NASB).

You ... were looking [in the dream] and behold ... (Dan. 2:31, Daniel to Nebuchadnezzar).

I saw a dream ... and the visions in my mind ... (Dan. 4:5).

I was looking in the visions in my mind I was looking as I lay on my bed, and behold an angelic watcher, a holy one, descended from heaven (Dan. 4:13).

... Daniel saw a dream and visions in his mind as he lay on his bed; then he wrote the dream down and related the following summary of it. Daniel said, "I was looking in my vision by night, and behold ..." (Dan. 7:1, emphasis added).

After this I kept looking in the night visions, and behold ... (Dan. 7:6, emphasis added).

I kept looking until thrones were set up, and the Ancient of Days took His seat ... (Dan 7:9, emphasis added).

Then I kept looking because of the sound of the boastful words which the horn was speaking: I kept looking until ... (Dan. 7:11, emphasis added).

I kept looking in the night visions, and behold, with the clouds of heaven One like a Son of Man was ended (Dan. 7:13,15-16,28, emphasis added).

A vision appeared to me ... and I looked in the vision, and it came about while I was looking that ... and I looked in the vision ... Then I lifted my gaze and looked, and behold ... While I was observing ... then I heard a holy one ... When I, Daniel, had seen the vision ... (Dan. 8:1-5,13 ,15, emphasis added).

And I heard the voice of a man between the banks of Ulai, and he called out and said, "Gabriel, give this man an understanding of the vision." So he came near to where I was standing, and when he came I was frightened and fell on my face; but he said to me ... (Dan. 8:16-17).

Samuel established schools of the prophets where men were trained in cultivating "prophetic vision," allowing God to fill their visionary capacity, meeting them in the way He wants, showing them the vision He wants.

I recommend that anyone who desires a greater understanding of the use of vision in encountering God within his spirit study through the prophets and the book of Revelation, examining this idea. Record what God shows you.

When the inner eye imagines evil and is focused on evil, destructive, fearful, accusative and negative contemplations, the spontaneous flow becomes satanic.

Because of the union of the Holy Spirit with our spirits, our spirits' flow now has intermittent injections of the Holy Spirit's ideas. Also, as I study the *logos*, the *logos* will begin flowing back through my spirit. However, my spirit may still flow on its own, with its own spontaneous thoughts.

When the eyes of the heart are focused on Jesus, the flow is Divine. Self's reactions and ideas are replaced by the pure flow coming from Christ.

The command to rule over our thoughts

We are destroying speculations and every lofty thing raised up against the knowledge of God, and we are taking every thought captive to the obedience of Christ (2 Cor. 10:5).

From My Journal

"The speaking of your spirit is to be the speaking of My Spirit, and it will be if you are centered and focused on me. As you look clearly and only to Me, the intuitive impressions you receive are from Me."

"Lord, when you say 'look to Me,' do you mean inner vision?"

"It is not absolutely necessary, although it is extremely helpful. Remember the pattern of My Son. He saw and heard.

"The looking with inner vision facilitates an easy, pure flow. However, the flow can come through inner dependence — simply 'relying on.' When looking to Me, you will find that intuition progresses beyond your subconscious knowledge to things that I reveal."

A Thoughtful Response to Some Valid Concerns

Q. Some ask, what is the difference between vision and visualization?

Visualization is when one manufactures the scene himself. Vision is when it flows spontaneously with a life of its own.

Q. Are we to seek visualizations or visions?

Visions, from the throne of grace.

Q. Is visualization ever right?

Yes, visualization is natural. All children do it and almost all adults also do it. Parents who are missing their children will picture their faces. Designers picture the new buildings they are planning. Homemakers picture how they could rearrange the furniture in their homes. Then they often go and do exactly what they have pictured.

Q. When is visualization wrong?

When I use it myself. I am supposed to do with my visual capacity exactly what I am supposed to do with every other part of my being — yield it to God to fill and to flow through supernaturally.

Q. How do you use the eyes of your heart as you approach God?

Generally, I do one of several things: One, I look to see whatever vision God would like to show me. Or, I may sing a love song to God, picturing the scene the words are describing, and ask God to move freely in the picture doing whatever He wants. He does. A third way I use the eyes of my heart is to devotionally enter a Bible story. As I meditate upon it, I realize that biblically speaking, meditation involves visualization. Therefore, I tend to picture the scene I am reading about, and I ask God to come alive in it and move in any way He desires. He does. I record in my journal what transpires.

Q. Why do I quote from various strains within Christianity and various people within Christianity, without warning readers of the error that may also be present in these streams or teachers?

First, it is not a commonly held assumption that to quote a person means total endorsement of all that person says or does. It should never be assumed that when I quote from a person or group, I am endorsing everything that person or group stands for. Actually, being as limited in scope as we all are, it is likely that none of us agrees totally with anyone or anything, except the words of Scripture. I even disagree with my own writings a few years after I have written them, and often go back and edit the manuscript. I suppose this will be a lifelong process.

Second, I encourage all participants of the **Communion With God** course to live under the active spiritual covering of their local pastors. Their pastors will be able to much more adequately instruct the parishioner as to the limitations of various teachers or streams of thought within Christianity than I will. I trust that each pastor will do that.

Third, I sense powerfully the desire of Jesus that we would all become one, so that the world would know ... (John 17). Part of my expression of this desire on Christ's heart is not to criticize my brother, but to hold up those things that I see to be good, knowing that light always overshadows darkness. We are commanded to test all things and "hold fast to that which is good" (not necessarily to stomp out evil). Light lifted up disseminates darkness.

Also, Jesus said that God rains upon both the just and the unjust, and that the children of this world are wiser than the children of the light. I may not like that verse but still it stands. I ask myself how could this be true, that the children of darkness could be wiser than the children of light, and one answer that comes to me is this: The Christian in our culture tends to devise theological boxes and stuff himself into them. Not much of a river is allowed to flow there (John 7:37-39). The heathen is more likely to be a hedonist, who will go with the flow and what feels good. He may have more likelihood of discovering the flowing river of God than the one stuck in a box.

Q. Some of your ideas are controversial and possibly incorrect.

That is very likely so. It is also the reason why I am so open to change and growth. I have a sign in my office that says "Don't bother to agree with me, I've already changed my mind!"

I will not be pushy about my ideas. I only present them. It is the work of the Holy Spirit to convince.

When I realize that one of my ideas is controversial, I will seek to present it in the most noncontroversial way possible. I will also state that it is a controversial idea and that no one needs to agree with it.

If you sense a desire to offer some correction, please know that I gladly welcome it and ask you to come alongside me (as the Holy Spirit does) to help me see and understand more clearly, rather than coming against me (as the accuser does), and seeking to destroy me.

Q. Doesn't visualization have to be expressly taught in the Scriptures before one should practice it?

Not necessarily. It seems to me that if Scripture allows for a practice or doctrine and provides underlying principles upon which it could be built, then the Church can build to the glory of God. If we choose not to take this position and require that the Scriptures needs to expressly teach a thing before the Church can practice it, then there will be many things that the Church must give up, including Sunday School, children's church, teen ministries, health care in such areas as dental work and corrective lenses, Christian radio programs, Christian TV programs, and on and on. Who is prepared to tell the Church to give up all of these things?

Nor would I say that the Bible has to use an express word before we as the Church can use it. For instance, we use such words as "rapture" and "trinity," even though they are not found in Scripture.

Q. What is your personal standing on the great creeds of the faith?

I hold to the statement of faith of the National Association of Evangelicals as well as the Apostles Creed. I am a member in good standing of a large Assembly of God church in Buffalo, New York. I have worked as a pastor among conservative Christian churches for 18 years. I graduated from Roberts Wesleyan College, a Free Methodist institution. I walk in a submissive relationship to four other mature, well-recognized pastors of conservative Christian churches with over 80 years of pastoral experience among them.

Q. What is "Christian Mysticism"?

Christian Mysticism can be traced back through essentially all of Church history. Mysticism is "the belief of immediate personal awareness of our union with God." There have been two basic strains of mystics within the Church. One is the "mystics of stripping away or of silence." They speak of the world of Divine reality as darkness, a desert, an unknowing — empty from a human point, but full with Divine presence and love. The way to that Divine reality is a stripping away of the consciousness of objects and ideas (i.e. Eckhart, John of the Cross, Cloud of Unknowing). The second type of mystic is the "mystic of clarification or spiritual vision." They speak of a world of spiritual reality that is characterized by light — a light as indescribable and enigmatic as the dark, but experienced like the full blaze of a life-giving sun, in comparison to which the material and impermanent light of this world is pale and shadowy. The way to this is an increased inner focusing and awareness (e.g., Augustine, the Victorines, Greek Orthodox mystics, Bonaventure). It seems to me that coming to Christ the Light and allowing Him to heal and transform one's being is much more effective than trying to strip away at yourself. Can self really overcome self? Or is it Christ, the Light of the world, who overcomes self? If self overcomes self, is that not a dead work and simply Phariseeism?

The desired result of mystical (spiritual) encounter with God is that one's life and person may be conformed to the humility and servant likeness of Christ. Many mystics have been critics and reformers of the Church, drawing strength for this vocation from their inner life. (See **Abingdon Dictionary of Living Religions** by Keith Crim pp. 511-514.)

Q. Since it appears to be mostly "kooks" who claim to hear from God, wouldn't it be better if we stayed away from this area?

The problem is not actually hearing from God, it is claiming to hear from God when you really do not. The best safeguard against people who claim to hear from God is to actually hear from God yourself. The best defense against impostors is having the real thing. Possibly these "kooks" are only "kooks" because we have not shepherded them into maturity and skill in the areas of hearing God's voice and seeing His vision. Maybe their presence and claims are our fault because we have left them high and dry and shepherdless, having to forge ahead on their own with no pastoral covering.

If we were to shun hearing from God because there are impostors, then to be consistent we would have to shun learning the Scriptures because some have grossly misinterpreted them. How foolish.

Q. Would you offer a critique of Dave Hunt's book **The Seduction of Christianity**?

My heart was deeply grieved as I encountered the accusation flowing through David Hunt's book **The Seduction of Christianity**. The book, published by Harvest House, attacked many of the most significant spiritual leaders in the Church today: Dr. Paul Yonggi Cho, Dr. Robert Schuller, Dr. Kenneth Hagin, Rev. Earl Paulk, Rev. Robert Tilton, Charles Capps, Frederick Price, Kenneth Copeland, Norman Grubb, Bill Volkman, Agnes Sanford, Ralph Wilkerson, John and Paula Sandford, Richard Foster, Morton Kelsey, C.S. Lovett, Rita Bennett, Dennis and Matt Lynn, Ruth Carter Stapleton, John Wimber, Francis MacNutt, James Dobson and others.

What man could possible have the audacity to touch such a vast array of God's anointed and call them down one after the other, describing how each one has been "seduced" by the cult philosophies of our time? What do all of these men and women have in common that would throw them into one group for criticism and censure?

One thing held in common by these men and women is that they believe in having a positive mental attitude. They also believe they can see in the spirit the visions of Almighty God and speak them forth in a creative way. Thirdly, they believe that Christians become expressions of God to the world in which they live. And finally, these people hold a worldview that light is advancing rather than darkness. These beliefs do not strike me as being cultish. As a matter of fact, I have found nearly a thousand Scripture verses that substantiate these beliefs, which I have presented in a book, **Seduction? A Biblical Response.**

Dave Hunt reasons that since some cults hold the above mentioned beliefs, any Christian who also believes these things must have been seduced by the teachings of these cults. It strikes me as totally backward to first discern what cults believe and then compare the beliefs of Church leaders to these beliefs. A much more sound practice would be to examine the *positive* teaching of the Bible on these subjects and then hold up the beliefs of these men to the teaching of Scripture — something Dave Hunt never quite gets around to doing.

Since the book has such great power to confuse and persuade, let me suggest the following strengths and weaknesses of the book.

Strengths:

1. Dave Hunt is obviously *a scholar concerning the beliefs of modern day cults.* He has done much research and is to be commended for his research ability.

2. This book will cause all Christians to be *more aware of the possibility of deception* in the age in which we live. It will therefore inspire all Christians to take a deeper look at the biblical foundation for their beliefs.

3. This book will help *Christians clarify and deepen the messages* in the areas which he attacks. Thus, the end product will have value.

Weaknesses:

1. Because Dave Hunt has spent so much time studying cults, *he focuses on the beliefs of cults, rather that on Scripture.* He compares the teaching of outstanding Christian leaders, such as Paul Yonggi Cho, Robert Schuller, Kenneth Hagin and Earl Paulk against what cults believe, rather than against what the Bible teaches. This is a *backward approach* when testing for error and a fundamental flaw in his book.

2. Mr. Hunt is not a "*Berean*," in that a Berean "examines the Scriptures daily, to see whether these things are *SO.*" Whenever Dave Hunt does go to Scripture, he seeks to prove that these things are NOT SO, rather than to examine the truth in them. For example, when coming against the belief in a positive mental attitude, David Hunt never once examines Philippians 4:8 or any of the hundreds of verses that speak of the scriptural command to have a positive mental attitude. This, then, becomes *another fundamental flaw* of the book, in that he is seeking to prove error rather than seeking to prove truth, as did the Bereans.

3. David Hunt accuses leader after leader in the Church of today and *appears more as "the accuser of the brethren" than the comforter.* Accusation is the center of satan's work (Rev. 10:10- 12), and the Church needs to be careful not to become his mouthpiece. Accusation permeates this book. We have been entrusted with the ministry of reconciliation, not with the ministry of destruction, and I sense that this book will bring much destruction to the body of Christ at large.

4. If one has read many of the authors that Dave Hunt quotes, he will find that over and over Mr. Hunt slants and alters the intent of what the author was saying. Some material is taken directly from various authors; however, unless you have read these men extensively, you will not recognize the slant that makes their teachings appear evil, when in actuality they are not. Therefore, I would suggest that no one take the statements at face value, but instead carefully read a fair amount of material by the Church leader being slighted so the reader can form his own unbiased opinion.

5. Dave Hunt fails to see that *the presence of a counterfeit proves that there is also a real, and that this real thing has value.* The book needs a much stronger thrust in describing the real things that are originals from which the counterfeit came. Let us not just concentrate on what we are against. Instead, let us emphasize what we are for.

A Final Note

I have prepared a study manual entitled **Seduction?? A Biblical Response**, which is built around four concordance studies, including approximately 1000 verses of Scripture. In it, I respond to four of Dave Hunt's basic seduction charges by allowing the reader to examine several hundred verses and establish his own understanding of what the Bible teaches in these four areas. They are: 1. How God Uses Vision and Image; 2. Becoming Expressions of God; 3. A Positive Mental Attitude and the Word of God; and 4. Worldview: Advancing Light or Advancing Darkness? This study manual can be ordered from Communion With God Ministries, 1431 Bullis Rd., Elma, NY 14059 ($7.95).

I did write to David Hunt when his book first came out and told him that I would like to build a friendship relationship with him and discuss the concepts he was writing about. Two years later he wrote back to me and said he did not see much point in a relationship with me since he felt the differences between us were too great. Oh, well! You can't win them all! However, a year after that, he was willing to debate me on the John Ankerberg show on the topic of visualization. I declined, telling them that I believe the biblical injunction: If you have a problem with a brother, go to the brother and work it out. Then if you can't come to terms, get two or three others to come and help you. Only then, if you still have not worked it out, bring the matter before the Church. I said that until Dave Hunt and I had taken the first two steps, I was not willing to take the third step and debate him on national television. I also insisted that we would spend the time building a positive theology of how God desires to use visualization, instead of tearing down others. I was refused on both counts. Therefore the debate never materialized. I am sure it was for the best.

Probing Deeper

The following two articles have been written by a theologian friend of mine, Rev. Maurice Fuller. Maurice Fuller is pastor of Queen's Park Full Gospel Church in Calgary, Alberta, Canada. He is Academic Dean of Calgary School of the Bible and a member of the Board of Regents of the Association of Church-Centered Bible Schools.

"There have been a number of people who have embraced and been blessed by the concepts in **Communion With God**, but who have had struggles (or have talked with those who have had struggles) with the concept of "visualization" or "seeing in the Spirit." What seems to be the cause of the problem is not the possibility of having a dream (while sleeping) or a vision (while awake) or any kind of visual experience in the Spirit when it is sovereignly initiated by God. But the idea of our initiating the vision, "using vision" (as we are urged to do in **Communion With God**), or "priming the pump" (as Mark Virkler expresses it) does go counter to what many of us were taught. Nor has it helped us when Dave Hunt suggests in **Seduction of Christianity** that the concept (of

visualization) is never so much as mentioned (in the Bible) much less explained or taught,'[1] and that '... all idols are fronts for demons. This is what makes visualization of Jesus or God not just a minor error but extremely dangerous.'[2]

"Unquestionably, there is a kind of visualization that is occultic and demonic, and much also that is just plain nonsense. But is there a **genuine** seeing in the Spirit? There is definitely a philosophical as well as a physiological difference between 'seeing' and 'looking for.' The first is almost involuntary, while the second is definitely an act of our will.

"First, there is the fact that it **does** happen. Many of us have pictured Jesus in our minds and, as the picture took on life, have seen Jesus do a variety of things. These experiences have been of immeasurable blessing to us. Jesus has become more real to us and we have experienced a greater closeness and intimacy with Him. Many times others have been ministered to as we have, in the Spirit, seen Jesus go to them, lay His hands on them, etc. (even though these people have had no knowledge of what we were seeing in the Spirit). The effect of looking for Jesus and seeing Him move and work in various ways, in the context of quietness and stillness in the presence of God, by true, dedicated believers in submission to God and to the leadership of a local church, has been overwhelmingly positive and beneficial.

"Second, to answer the question, is it **right** to 'look for' Jesus in vision, we must ask another question. Is it right to listen to **hear** from God? Is it right to pray for wisdom and then, as an act of our will, listen for His voice in answer to our prayer? Few Christians would have a problem with this. This is what prayer is all about. This is what communion with God is all about — centering down and, as a deliberate act, listening for His voice, or writing down what comes into our spirits from Him. What is often not understood is that the acts of hearing and seeing are actually very closely related. Complete understanding is often dependent on **both** hearing and seeing. We do not doubt that it is right to seek a work or *rhema* from God. We not accept only a *rhema* that comes

1   Hunt, David. **The Seduction of Christianity**, Harvest House, 1985, p. 114.
2   Hunt, p. 167.

spontaneously or sovereignly initiated by God, but also that *rhema* which we have asked for, waited for and actively listened for with the ears of our spirits.

"What is the connection between hearing and seeing, between word and vision? In Scripture they are intimately connected. Faith, in Romans 10:17, comes from a *rhema* from God. We have probably thought of a *rhema* only as a word, heard with our spiritual ears. But a *rhema* can also be seen. Numbers 14:11 asks, 'How long will they not believe Me, with all the **signs** which I have performed among them? (NKJ, emphasis added)' Here, believing (acting on our faith) is not dependent only upon God's words that they have heard, but also upon God's signs that they had seen. Both are *rhema*. Deuteronomy 29:2-4 also connects the two, 'You have seen all that the Lord did before our eyes ... the great trials which your eyes have seen, the signs, these great wonders. Yet the Lord has not given you a heart to perceive [understand] and eyes to see and ears to hear, to this very day (NKJ).'" What their eyes saw and their ears heard should have produced perception or understanding — which is what faith is. The fact that it didn't indicated some flaw in their character. Psalms 74:9 further links word with sight, hearing with seeing: 'We do not see our signs; there is no longer any prophet; nor is there any among us who knows how long (NKJ).'

"The ideas of seeing and hearing are inseparably linked in John 6:45,46: 'It is written in the prophets, "And they shall all be taught by God." Therefore everyone who has **heard** and learned from the Father comes to Me. Not that anyone has **seen** the Father, except He who is from God; He has seen the Father (NKJ, emphasis added).' Jesus further stated in John 14:9: '... He who has seen Me has seen the Father ... (NKJ).'

"Seeing the Lord is never simply for the sake of having a visual experience. It is always accompanied by a word from Him. What is seen is also itself a visual word, an illustrated word, a verbal picture. Wilhelm Michaelis says, 'Often seeing and hearing together constitute the totality of sensual (of the senses) and spiritual perception.'[1]

"In our seeking for a word or *rhema* from God, what we receive may be in the form of a vision, a word in our spirit, a word through journaling or some other form of communication. We keep not only the ears of our spirit open but also the **eyes** of our spirit. In the same way that we **listen for** a word, we also **look for** a vision. Both of them constitute Divine communication (*rhema*) to us. Both are scriptural and both are valid. God has given us the spiritual capacity for both of them and will respond to us as we actively seek Him in both of these ways."

Looking For Vision

"In the first article of this series we talked about the philosophical rationale for looking for vision. Looking for vision was understood as being distinct from receiving vision that is sovereignly initiated by God. We suggested that listening for *rhema* is, to most believers, as acceptable as hearing *rhema* that is sovereignly initiated by God. Most of us believe it is quite legitimate to actively seek an answer from God to some questions we may have. We even accept that it is proper to initiate the process though journaling.

"Is it legitimate to actively seek vision and even to initiate the process?

"On what premise is it also legitimate to actively seek vision and even to initiate the process? In the realm of the physical, we have the same ability to look to see as we have to listen to hear. In our powers of recall or memory (a function of the human spirit), we can recall both words and pictures. In fact, it is quite impossible to remember apart from pictures. We initiate this process and, as with initiating vision, the results sometimes surprise us. We are astonished many times at what our self-initiated process of recall has brought back to our remembrance. Having these God-given abilities, then, can we utilize them equally to touch God, who indwells us and has become one spirit with us?

"Logically, it would certainly seem that we could. To some, however, this activity is very risky. But the same dangers lie in the path of listening for God to speak as do in the process of

1   **Theological Dictionary of the New Testament.** Vol. V., p. 341.

looking for Him to reveal Himself in vision. The possibility of contacting alien forces exists in one as well as the other. In fact, as the Jehovah's Witnesses are evidence, people can go off into error merely by reading the Scriptures. But the same protection (a committed life and the Holy Spirit) is also present in all of these processes.

"But what saith the Scriptures? Are there biblical examples of people looking for vision? I believe there are. Let us consider Psalms 27:4: 'One thing I have desired of the Lord, that will I seek: that I may dwell in the house of the Lord all the days of my life, to behold the beauty of the Lord, and to inquire in His temple.'

"Three things David desires and seeks after: to dwell, to behold and to inquire. Since the first and the last desires present fewer problems, let us look at them first. 'Dwell' is the Hebrew *yashav*, with the meaning of 'to abide, dwell, remain.' It sometimes means 'to sit.' The idea seems to be of unhurried dwelling or remaining in the house of the Lord, the place where God was uniquely present. Indeed, David desired that his entire life might be spent in this intimate spiritual intercourse.

" 'Inquire' is the Hebrew *baqar* which means 'to meditate or reflect upon, to investigate.' Keil and Delitzsch define the word in this passage as 'contemplative meditation that loses itself in God who is there manifest.'

"But what does 'behold the beauty of the Lord' mean? Let us first note that 'seek' *baqash*, in the first part of the verse, indicates a seeking with the intention that the object of the seeking be found. When it is used for seeking God (as it is here), it can mean 'to seek after a word or a revelation from God.' It is well also to note that this seeking is not merely a seeking for some novel experience. The word or revelation will contain commands or instructions that are to be obeyed.

" 'Behold' is in Hebrew *chazah*, a word used both for the natural vision of the eyes and for supernatural visions. It is safe to say that here it does not mean natural vision, but a supernatural vision of the Lord. It is rarely used, in fact, for natural vision, but seems in the Old Testament to have the predominant meaning of 'a spiritual seeing, a vision from God.' So here we have

David seeking for a supernatural vision of the loveliness and beauty of God. Keil and Delitzsch describe the experience as 'His revelation, full of grace, which is there visible to the eye of the spirit.' Seeking vision is for the purpose of fully realizing His will for us.

"Again, the vision that is seen is not merely for the purpose of a novel and entertaining or ecstatic experience. The vision seen with the eyes of the spirit has precisely the same function as a word heard with the ears of the spirit. It is a *rhema* from God that, according to Romans 10:17, brings faith to our heart. It is always instructive or hortatory. To seek for vision in a flippant manner is an invitation to deception. To have all of the senses of our spirit open, seeking for an auditory or visionary *rhema* with a humble submission to His authority and a commitment to obey Him, is an invitation for God to reveal Himself to us in an infinite variety of ways. It is for the purpose of fully realizing His will for us."

Theological Word Book of the Old Testament, (Chicago: Moody Press, 1980) Vol. I, p. 105.
Keil and Delitzsch, (Grand Rapids: Eerdmans, 1985), Vol. V, p. 357.
Keil and Delitzsch, p. 357.
Theological Dictionary of the Old Testament, (Grand Rapids: Eerdmans, 1974), Vol. II, p. 238.
Keil and Delitzsch, p. 357.

Personal Application

Use the following page for journaling. Picture Jesus with you in a comfortable setting. Possibly go for a walk along the Sea of Galilee or sit with Him on the mountainside as He teaches the people. As you enjoy being with Him, relax, still yourself and fix your gaze upon Him. You may see Him as a Being with long flowing robes and a loving gentle countenance. You may see a twinkle in His eyes and laughter on His lips, because He enjoys so much spending this time with you. Enjoy being with Him. Ask Him what He wants to tell you. If you have a more specific question than that, ask Him that question now.

Write it in the space below. Then tune to spontaneity, fix your eyes on Jesus and begin writing in simple childlike faith out of the flow that comes bubbling up from your heart. Record what He wants to say to you. Don't test it now. Test it later. Just simply write in childlike faith.

Please journal now, before going on. Begin this journaling exercise by writing out the question you want to ask the Lord.

Chapter 7

The Pharisees' Struggle With the Holy Spirit

Self-Evaluation: Discerning a Pharisaical Tendency

How would you handle the following situations? Circle the best answer.

Situation # 1

A recognized Christian leader is discovered associating with individuals of **known** disrepute. It is best to:

a. love him and accept his actions.

b. pray for his return to solid Christian relationships.

c. go and rebuke him privately.

d. rebuke him openly.

Situation # 2

A teacher urges his followers not to share their deeper insights with certain people because they are not spiritually attuned enough to receive them. This is an example of:

a. spiritual arrogance.

b. isolationism.

c. wisdom.

Situation # 3

A young teacher boldly leads his followers into breaking one of the Ten Commandments, as it has been interpreted and understood for centuries in your church. He says that human need takes precedent over their interpretation of the commandment. It is best to:

a. renounce him as a heretic.

b. ask him to explain why he is doing this and seek to enlarge your perspective to include his views.

c. try to get his followers away from him.

Situation # 4

A new "religious teacher" comes to your city and begins drawing people away from the established churches and teachings with his own charisma and new interpretations of Scripture. His views are different than the Church believes. The "gullible" flock to him because he supposedly does great miracles and feats of healing. It would be best to:

a. keep your distance from him so you don't get caught up with him.

b. urge all to keep their distance from him.

c. seek to undermine his authority by showing that he has deviated from the beliefs held by the established Christian Church over the last several hundred years.

d. go and listen to him, and try to understand his new beliefs and power. Then go to Scripture and try to prove him right.

e. seek to show that his views are very similar to cultist groups.

f. try to deepen your own convictions by seeking additional biblical support for the position which you and the Church have held for years.

Answers

Situation # 1 The correct answer is "a." Compare Matthew 9:9-17 — Jesus associating with tax collectors. Principle: We are not to judge others' actions without first discerning their heart motives (Matt. 7:1; 9:12; Rom. 14:10-13).

Situation # 2 The correct answer is "c." Compare Matthew 7:6 — casting pearls before swine. Principle: All people are not equally ready at a particular point in time to receive a particular insight. Wisdom must be used.

Situation # 3 The correct answer is "b." Compare Matthew 12:1-8. Jesus broke the fourth commandment, "on it [the seventh day] you shall not do any work (Ex. 20:10)," by picking and eating grain. His response was that "the Sabbath was made for man, and not man for the Sabbath (Mark 2:27)." Principle: Man was not made to serve rules, rules are made to serve man (Mark 2:27).

Situation # 4 The correct answer is "d." Compare Matthew 5:21-48 — Jesus's reinterpretation of beliefs with the simple statement, "But I say unto you." Principle: When confronted with a new truth, we are to examine Scripture to seek to prove the idea right (Acts 17:11).

Would I have crucified Jesus? Would you have crucified Jesus? It is hard to say. But when I look at these four modernized stories from the gospels, I am afraid I might have. That is why I think it might be wise for all of us to study the principles of phariseeism that follow. Then we can become aware of and remove any tendencies of phariseeism from our hearts.

The Pharisees' Struggle With the Prophetic Word

I believe it might be the legalism and phariseeism within us all that causes us to react to the prophetic word in our midst.

I believe God is doing a new thing in His Church. I believe He is restoring elements of Christianity that have been lost for centuries. And I believe a number of books on the market today may be the pharisaical reaction to the new movings of God in our day.

Religious people have never responded well to innovation or change. They generally stone the prophets whom God places in their midst. Stephen said in Acts 7:51,52, "You men who are stiff-necked and uncircumcised in heart and ears are always resisting the Holy Spirit; you are doing just as your fathers did. Which one of the prophets did your fathers not persecute? And they killed those who had previously announced the coming of the Righteous One, whose betrayers and murderers you have now become." To prove His point, they stoned him on the spot.

In light of Stephen's sermon and murderous death, it might be wise not to directly confront the pharisees of our day, since they carry the spirit of murder around with them and enjoy killing all those who disagree with them.

I believe the problem today is not just the possibility of New Age error creeping into the Church. I suspect that equally pervasive is the problem of the established, fundamentalist, legalistic pharisees in our midst and within us all, who are at war with the innovative, unpredictable movings of the Holy Spirit. It seems to me that the issue that is coming to the forefront is not so much whether certain people have been seduced by the New Age, but whether the phariseeism within us all is holding back what God wants to do in His Church. With that in mind, let us examine legalism, phariseeism, spirit flow, and how each of us can avoid stoning the prophets.

The pharisees of our generation still struggle with the prophetic word and seek to kill those who are carrying it. It is interesting that even though the Pharisees were the biggest problem Jesus had to face when He walked this earth, we have essentially no books exposing the problem today.

The only book I have found is **The Pharisees' Guide to Total Holiness** by William Coleman. It strikes me as strange that we have no proliferation of books on the number one problem that Jesus faced. Could it be that we might have a blind spot?

Overcoming the Phariseeism in Us All

How would I know if I have any tendencies toward phariseeism in me? I had never studied phariseeism or read a book on it or heard a sermon on it. Many of us would be hard put to list 40 principles of phariseeism, and we would find it even harder to state that we have applied these principles to our lives and purified our hearts of all phariseeism. The following list is simply a few of the tendencies of phariseeism that are mentioned in the New Testament. Please score yourself to see how you do. Be honest as you answer these questions. Answer them from your "gut response" rather than after theological deliberation. Let the answers reflect who you really are.

Symptoms of Phariseeism

Circle "yes" if you generally do or believe the following statement.

Circle "no" if you generally do not believe or do the following statement.

1. I come alongside people who hold different positions than I do (John 16:7). yes no

2. I come against people who disagree with me (Rev. 12:10). yes no

3. When someone disagrees with me, I seek to discover the truth in what they are saying (Acts 17:11). yes no

4. When someone disagrees with me, I seek to prove that they are wrong (Acts 17:11). yes no

5. I find it easy to accuse and put people down (Rev. 12:11). yes no

6. I look for ways to build people up and encourage them (1 Cor. 14:3). yes no

7. When I go to the Scriptures, I try to find verses that prove a person is right (Acts 17:11). yes no

8. When I go to Scriptures, I try to find verses that prove a person is wrong (Acts 17:11). yes no

9. I use the Scriptures to encourage people and build their hope in who Christ is in them (Rom. 15:4, Phil. 4:13). yes no

10. I enjoy debates where I can try to trap my opponent (Matt. 22:15-40). yes no

11. I try to phrase questions in such a way that I might have grounds to accuse a person, based on his answer (Matt. 22:15-40). yes no

12. I try to show people the ease of living out of Divine grace (Matt. 23:4). yes no

13. I help those who are burdened down (Matt. 23:4). yes no

14. I like people to notice my religious deeds (Matt. 23:5). yes no

15. I like to be honored by men (Matt. 23:6). yes no

16. I like to be called by my full title (Matt. 23:7). yes no

17. I instruct people in the many commandments that will help them become more holy (Matt. 23:13; Gal. 4:3). yes no

18. I am precise and demanding when it comes to obeying the rules I have established (Matt. 23:23). yes no

19. I emphasize love and mercy more than I emphasize justice and rightness (Micah 6:8). yes no

20. I tend to overlook the little things while keeping my eyes fixed on the more important (Matt. 23:24). yes no

21. I tend to get caught up in the little things and overlook the big issues (Matt. 23:24).   yes no

22. I devote more time and care to inner attitudes than I do to outer appearance (Matt 23:25).   yes no

23. I take more time and care on outer appearance than I do on caring for the condition of my heart (Matt. 23:25).   yes no

24. I think the harder I try to be good and right, the better I will become (Rom. 7).   yes no

25. I have discovered that when I stop striving and instead yield myself to the in-working power of Christ, He works more easily within me (Rom. 8).   yes no

26. I focus on containing the outside, yet my heart rages with evil within (Col. 2:20-23).   yes no

27. I see hypocrisy within myself (Matt. 23:29-31).   yes no

28. I tend to feel that life is found in the study of the Scriptures (John 5:39,40).   yes no

29. I feel that life is found in the experience of Christ (John 5:39,40).   yes no

30. I can see prophets in my community (John 6:42).   yes no

31. I seldom judge by outer actions alone. I try to look into the heart and perceive the heart motive behind the action (John 7:24).   yes no

32. I tend to judge by outer actions and appearances (John 7:24).   yes no

33. I try to destroy people (either verbally or actually) rather than love them (John 8:37,40,44).   yes no

34. I live out of the voice and vision of God within me (John 5:19,20,30).   yes no

35. I live focused on the principles within Scripture (John 5:39,40; Heb. 12:2).   yes no

36. I trust the theology I have built (Gen. 2:16,17; John 24:21-32).   yes no

37. I trust the flow within me (John 7:37-39).   yes no

38. I tend to say that those who I disagree with have demonic influences in their lives (John 8:48; 10:20).   yes no

39. I find it difficult to be taught by those I view to be beneath me (John 9:34).   yes no

40. I tend to think that those of the persuasion of my particular church or group are the most right and most likely to make it to heaven (John 10:16).   yes no

Non-pharisaical answers. Grade yourself. For every answer you have incorrect, place a "P" next to it. Then total the "P's" to find any tendencies of phariseeism within you. Look up the supporting verses, pray over them and ask the Holy Spirit to heal any such tendencies within you.

1. yes	2. no	3. yes
4. no	5. no	6. yes
7. yes	8. no	9. yes
10. no	11. no	12. yes
13. yes	14. no	15. no
16. no	17. no	18. no
19. yes	20. yes	21. no
22. yes	23. no	24. no
25. yes	26. no	27. yes
28. no	29. yes	30. yes
31. yes	32. no	33. no
34. yes	35. no	36. no
37. yes	38. no	39. no
40. no		

The Pharisee's Struggle With Grace

A great English preacher at the turn of the century said, "If you have preached on grace and have not yet been accused of lasciviousness, you have not yet preached on grace." Grace is so contrary to law that there is a constant battle between the two. Having grown up under law, it is almost impossible to free my heart from it. The law says, "Do." Grace says, "Believe what Christ will do." The Law says, "Strive;" grace says, "Cease striving and enter Christ's rest." Preachers of law focus on 1) you and 2) the rules you are to be keeping. Preachers of grace focus on 1) Christ and 2) the flow of His life within you. Preachers of law preach from Mount Sinai. Preachers of grace preach from Mount Calvary. Preachers of law bring guilt and condemnation into the lives of their hearers. Preachers of grace bring freedom, release and peace into the hearts of their hearers.

Preachers of the law come against preachers of grace. Paul said, "Having begun by the Spirit, are you now being perfected by the flesh? (Gal.3:3)" I preached law for ten years before I learned grace. I discovered grace when I discovered God's voice within my heart. When I journaled, I found that God was not beating me. He was loving me. Even though I was berating myself, God was not chastising me. After a year of journaling, I decided to stop flogging myself since God wasn't beating me. Boy, did I feel better after making that decision! Then I decided I would stop beating the sheep with the Word of God. You know, there really is something sick and sadistic about a person who regularly punishes himself and others. No wonder the world laughs in derision at "the Church."

I know of nothing other than an ongoing encounter with the voice of God that can truly release a person from legalism so he can live in the Spirit of Almighty God.

Much of the battle in the Church today is between preachers of law and preachers of grace. Two helpful books that chart the differences between law and grace are **Abiding in Christ** by Andrew Murray, and **Abide in Christ** by Mark and Patti Virkler.

My Testimony of How God Moved Me From Boxes to Rivers

I grew up loving boxes. What do I mean by that? I mean that I enjoyed establishing theological systems and principles that I put together into a systematic grid of truth. Then I tried to stuff my life into it. Sounds inviting, doesn't it?

For instance, I established my theology concerning how much to witness, how much to pray, how much to disciple others, how to handle fear, anger, discouragement and guilt, how to properly crucify my flesh, how to rejoice without ceasing, etc., etc. Then I sought to live out of all these principles that I had established.

I discovered, however, that while I focused on one set of rules/principles, I forgot another, and as a result, I always felt guilty, condemned and depressed. I hadn't learned yet to fix my eyes on the Author of the rules. Instead, I was fixing my

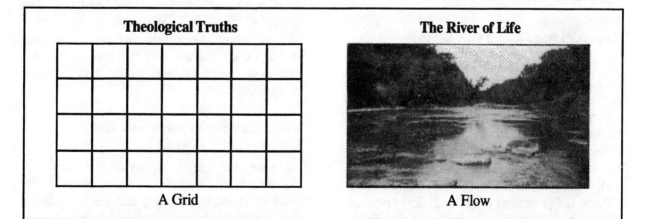

Theological Truths

A Grid

The River of Life

A Flow

eyes on the rules. I hadn't yet come to realize that the end of the Law is always death, and that if I tried to live out of laws, I would always be experiencing a death process working within me. For me, this death took the form of guilt, accusation, condemnation and depression. Not exactly the abundant life that Jesus spoke about.

For several reasons my boxes never seemed to work. First, the expectations of the laws that I had discovered within the Bible always left me feeling guilty, knowing I could never measure up. Second, my boxes always seemed to need adjusting. They never seemed any bigger than I was. (That should have been a clue that they were mine and not God's!) When I first became a Christian, my box describing who was a Christian was quite small. It included my church and me. Eventually, I enlarged it a bit and let some other Baptists in. Then I enlarged it some more and let some Methodists in. Then I accepted the Pentecostals and Charismatics into my box. (I had to revamp the entire box to do that!) Eventually, I even discovered Catholics who were genuinely saved.

By then I had altered my box so many times and so drastically that I wasn't even sure about the value of building theological boxes. They seemed so small, so inadequate and so imperfect. They didn't seem like a very effective approach to living life. Plus, they always created so much division. Rather than maintaining the unity of the Body of Christ, I was always segregating it, based on my limited theological understanding. I began to wonder if this truly was the way we were to live, or if God had a better plan.

Discovering Life in the Spirit

But then something new began to enter my life. I began to learn the ways of the Spirit of God. I learned to hear His voice and see His vision. I learned to open my heart to the intuitive flow of the Spirit of God within me. I learned to live out of the stream that was welling up within me. Jesus had spoken of these streams, but I had never really understood what the experience was. " 'From his innermost being shall flow rivers of living water.' But this He spoke of the Spirit,

whom those who believed in Him were to receive ... (John 7:38,39)"

When I learned to recognize the voice of God as the bubbling flow of spontaneous ideas that welled up from my heart as I fixed my eyes upon Jesus, I discovered a new way of living, that of living out of the Spirit of God rather than simply the laws of God — not that they are in any way opposed to each other. It is just that the Holy Spirit has such great finesse in handling the laws of God that my shallow boxes were mere mockeries of His vast truth.

When struggling with a situation, I found that if I used my own theological boxes to deal with it, I would end up with narrow, judgmental decisions. However, if I went to Jesus in prayer and tuned to the flow of the river within, He would bring other principles to my attention that I had more or less forgotten. He would ask me to apply these over and above the principles that I had been trying to apply earlier. It's not that some principles are right and some are wrong. It's that some are more weighty than others. Some are the true heart of the matter, and some are simply the periphery. Jesus told the Pharisees of His day that they strained at a gnat and swallowed a camel. "Woe to you, scribes and Pharisees, hypocrites! For you tithe mint and dill and cummin, and have neglected the weightier provisions of the law: justice and mercy and faithfulness; but these are the things you should have done without neglecting the others (Matt. 23:23)."

I found that I generally forfeited the principles of mercy and faithfulness when dealing with others. I was harsh and severe in my judgment of them, and rather than being faithful and loyal to them, I came against them, more as the accuser of the brethren. Therefore, I assumed a satanic stance, rather than a Holy Spirit stance, that is, I tended to "come against" rather than "coming alongside."

The Accuser's Stance or the Comforter's Stance?

It took me years to come to grips with the realization that satan was the accuser of the brethren (Rev. 12:10), and that the Holy Spirit was the One who came alongside and helped

(John 14:16). Even when we are terribly wrong, God does not take an accusative or adversarial stance against us. For example, when the world had just committed its most hideous crime (i.e., crucifying the Son of God), rather than accusing and condemning, Jesus said, "Father, forgive them; for they know not what they do (Luke 23:34)."

As I began to examine my own life, I realized that I often took accusative and adversarial stands against people with whom I didn't agree. I felt it was what God wanted me to do. However, finally it dawned upon me that the accuser's stance is satan's stance (the word "devil" literally means "accuser") and the comforter's stance is the Holy Spirit's stance. Since this revelation, I have made a commitment *never* to take an accuser's stance against anyone. No longer will I be the expression of satan. If someone is struggling, hurt, down or in error, I have one, and only one, posture. That is, to come alongside him and comfort him, to be faithful to him and thus preserve the dignity of all men and the unity of the Body of Christ.

As I began to live out of the river that flows from within, I became less judgmental and less narrow-minded. I developed "largeness of heart," a trait that Solomon had (1 Kings 4:29). However, I became increasingly concerned about my more embracing attitude (i.e., my tendency to freely embrace so many). It seemed a bit liberal to me. I wasn't too sure about it at first. However, I was coming to realize that my narrow, theological boxes could be more easily equated with phariseeism than I cared to admit. I knew that it was time to make a change. (I had never studied the principles of phariseeism and applied them to my life, but I was becoming uncomfortable, thinking that maybe a number of them perhaps fit very well.)

Discovering Certainty in the Spirit

As I prayed about my growing tendency toward embracement and my growing disregard for boxes, I asked God several questions. The first one was, "Lord, can I trust the intuitive flow?" You see, I was losing my nicely defined fences. I was no longer so sure where the boundaries were.

I was concerned about falling into cultism. After all, if you get into flow and you don't have clear edges, what keeps you ...? The Lord answered me this way: "Mark, you can trust the intuitive flow of My Spirit more than you can trust the boxes you build with your mind." What He said made all the sense in the world. I began to wonder, "Where does it say in the Bible that we test for truth **using our minds**? Isn't the test so often made in our hearts, through discernment?" As a matter of fact, Jesus Himself recommends that we go with the intuitive flow over and above the analysis of the mind when He says, "When they arrest you and deliver you up, do not be anxious beforehand about what you are to say, **but say whatever is given you in that hour; for it is not you who speak, but it is the Holy Spirit** (Mark 13:11, emphasis added)."

Therefore, I began to set aside my love for boxes and for theological grids of truth. I came to cherish instead the intuitive, healing flow from my heart, from the One so much wiser and more embracing than I. I dismantled the idolization of my mind and established my heart as the throne which God has chosen as the center of life and the central avenue through which to communicate with mankind. I began to experience the fact that those who are led by the Spirit are not under the law (Gal. 5:18).

My second question for the Lord was, "Well, then, God, what about laws and rules and boxes? Should I scorn them as having no value? What is a proper attitude toward the Law, toward laws?" The Lord gave me several answers. First, the Law keeps us in custody (i.e., keeps us from killing ourselves), before we come to the point of being led by the Spirit (Gal. 3:23). Second, it is a tutor that leads us to Christ (Gal. 3:24). A tutor is one who teaches us a lesson. The law teaches us that we can never fully keep the law. Therefore, we must abandon ourselves to grace. Wow! What a release! Third, even though we study the laws of God, we never fix our eyes upon them. Instead, we fix our eyes on Jesus, the Author and Finisher of our faith (Heb. 12:2). So when I look at a situation, I do not approach it with laws on my mind. I approach it as Christ would, with love first and foremost.

Loving Mercy, Not Justice

The Lord showed me that I loved justice, judgment and precision, more than I loved mercy and love. I approached people first with judgment, and only secondarily with love and mercy. He showed me that He was the opposite of that. He approached people with love and mercy first, and only secondarily with justice. He reminded me of the Micah 6:8 balance: "He has shown you, O man, what is good; and what does the Lord require of you, but to **do justly**, and to **love mercy**, and to walk humbly with your God? (NKJ, emphasis added)" He said to me, "Mark, you love justice and only do mercy. I love mercy and only do justice. You are the inverse of Me." With that I was cut to the quick and began to change, seeing the imbalance within me.

Finally, the Lord began to show me the proper place and purpose of laws and rules within my life. He said, "The Sabbath was made for man, not man for the Sabbath (Mark 2:27)." I tended to get that all mixed up. I used to start with the rule and think that my purpose was to obey it. Jesus says, "No." We start with man and his fulfillment, and rules are meant to serve man. They are there to assist in releasing the maximum amount of life possible. Jesus Himself came to give us life, abundant life. Therefore, I am learning to begin with the goal of "life" and see what application of which rules releases the most life within and through me. If I don't begin and end with the goal of life, I generally begin and end with the goal of obeying the rule. And man was not created so that he could keep a bunch of rules. He was created to experience abundant life.

How to Avoid Stoning the Prophets

Have you thrown a stone at a prophet lately? Would you know it if you had? Do you know who the prophets of the 20th century are? Do you know what the prophetic messages are that God is giving to the Church in this generation?

You say, "I don't even think there are prophets restoring truth in this generation. I don't see any!" Neither did the people during the time of Jesus' earthly ministry see any prophets in the land. The Church has a history of being blind to the prophets in her midst. Not only has she been blind to them, but she has rejected them and stoned them.

Jesus said that "Elijah already came, and **they did not recognize him**, but did to him whatever they wished. So also the Son of Man is going to suffer at their hands (Matt. 17:12)." Jesus' brothers could not see him as a prophet, much less as the Son of God. They even mocked Him (John 7:2-9).

This is a serious indictment against us all, because each of us is part of the Church, and each of us has a built-in blindness to the prophets in our midst, as well as a tendency to stone them. Therefore, rather than point critical fingers at those who, in other times, stoned the prophets whom God had sent them, let us carefully examine this tendency in our own lives and seek to rid ourselves of it completely, so as not to be found guilty of the same sin.

Who are the prophets of our age? What are their messages? I do not purport to know them all or to be able to give you a complete list of them here; however, I would like to give you a sampling of some of those who have touched my life. If you do not agree with my appraisal of all those who follow, please do not stone me! Rather, simply say, "That point doesn't register with me right now, so I think I will put it on the back shelf for awhile and bring it back down for examination at a later date." This kind of response will produce a lot less bloodshed and allow me to arrive safely at my next birthday, which both my family and I would deeply appreciate.

The further back into history that we look, the easier it is to identify the prophets. The closer we come to the day in which we live, the more difficult it becomes for the Church to clearly recognize its prophets. Although some individuals may discern these prophets very quickly, the Church, as a Body, reaches that point more slowly.

Probably all would agree that Martin Luther, John Calvin, Charles Wesley and Charles Finney were prophets of their day, restoring truth to the Church. At the beginning of the twentieth century, God began to restore the truth of the Baptism of the Holy Spirit and the availability of the gift of speaking in tongues. This restoration was not easily received, and some Pentecostals found their homes and churches burned by other Christians who were convinced these people had moved into error. However, by 1982, the **World Christian Encyclopedia** reported that there were 100 million Pentecostals/Charismatics worldwide. C. P. Wagner reports that there will be an estimated 1.1 billion Pentecostals/Charismatics and other Spirit sensitized Christians by the year 2000 (**Target Earth**, page 166, published by University of the Nations and Global Mapping International, 1989). Such numbers have brought a large portion of the Church to accept the validity and authenticity of this experience. Yet, do all accept the validity of this prophetic word to the Church? No, certain groups of "Bible believing" Christians still hold out, unable to receive the prophetic word in their midst.

In the 1940's, the message of the place of physical healing in the life of the Christian was presented to the Church by Oral Roberts and others, and Christians began to find that they have power through the Holy Spirit over sickness and disease.

In the 1950's, Kenneth Hagin appeared on the scene, teaching the place of faith, and the power released in confessing the Word of God over a situation.

In the 1960's, Derek Prince began teaching the Church the place of deliverance as part of an overall prayer ministry.

In the 1970's, Derek Prince taught the place and role of a shepherd, and the need for the Christian to have a covering in his life. Bill Gothard defined this as an accountability relationship and encouraged every Christian to establish accountability relationships in his or her life.

Dr. Paul Yonggi Cho restored to the Church worldwide the truth of home cell groups and demonstrated the effectiveness of this truth by building a church of over one-half million members, a phenomenon never before realized in the history of Christianity.

Time seems to be condensed in the 1980's as we see God restoring an array of truths to the Church. Inner healing, as part of the overall prayer/counseling ministry of the Church, is being discovered and applied with great healing benefits to those who receive this ministry. Self-esteem and the dignity of man have been called the New Reformation by Robert Schuller, an ingredient he says we missed in the reformation of the 1500's. Union consciousness (1 Cor. 6:17), the realization that through the new birth man has been joined to Almighty God, is a truth God is restoring to the Body of Christ from several sectors: Norman Grubb, and those who are involved in the faith movement.

The truth that not only does God desire to commune with His people, but He has enabled us to do so, is one of the truths being restored during this decade. This has been evidenced through the growing realization that it is possible to teach the Church to hear God's voice clearly and to see easily into the spirit world.

Dance, as a part of praise and worship, is continuing to be restored in a variety of expressions throughout the Body. Not only do we see untrained spontaneous dance, but there is now emerging skilled and artistic dance as spiritual expressions of praise and worship. The use of banners and pageantry as a means of manifesting praise and worship is also returning.

A theology of dominion as a result of the death and resurrection of the second Adam is being brought to the Church from numerous quarters today, including such men as Earl Paulk, David Chilton and others.

The above list obviously is not complete. It serves only as a sampling of suggested prophetic truths that God is restoring to the Church in our generation. How did you respond? Did your heart say "yes" to some and "no" to others? Did you feel like casting a few stones as I went down the list? If so, I want to remind you that stone-casting is our typical response to the prophets in our midst. Stephen, in reciting the Israelites' history, summed it up by asking, "Which one of the prophets did your fathers not persecute? And they killed those who had previously announced the coming of the Righteous One, whose betrayers and murderers you have now become (Acts 7:52)." To demonstrate the degree of their openness to hearing this kind of statement, we find that they "covered their ears, and rushed upon him with one impulse.... and began stoning him ... (Acts 7:57,58)," thus proving the point of his entire delivery, which is that **we have a tremendous tendency to stone the prophets in our midst.**

Why do we respond this way? If we can identify the reasons for this response, we can more effectively keep it from occurring in our lives.

Reason # 1 — Often the prophetic word is veiled, being revealed only to those with spiritual understanding.

For example, Malachi said, "Behold, I am going to send you **Elijah the prophet** before the coming of the great and terrible day of the Lord. And he will restore ... (Mal. 4:5,6)." The Jews took this literally and looked for Elijah to return. However, Luke very clearly says that John the Baptist fulfilled this prophecy, because he came **"in the spirit and power of Elijah ...** (Luke 1:17, emphasis added)" Jesus said that "all the prophets and the Law prophesied until John. And if you care to accept it, he himself is Elijah, who was to come. He who has ears to hear, let him hear (Matt. 11:13-15)."

Second, as we speak forth a new idea or concept, we will not do it the first time with the finesse and clarity that will develop as we say it over and over, allowing time for it to be sharpened and clarified by the response of the Body of Christ. Therefore, when you hear a new word being spoken, approach it with the understanding that it may be nebulous and as yet not well-defined. Rather than coming against it, which is the work of satan, the accuser, come alongside it, which is the work of the Comforter. Seek to ground it biblically and clarify it. Sometimes, after trying to ground a new message in Scripture, you will find that it is impossible to find any biblical support for it at all and will then have to reject it as a false word.

Reason # 2 — In the zeal of our new discovery, we try to cram a prophetic truth down the throats of unready and unwilling victims.

How many of you, when you were first saved, rushed out and tried to get a close friend saved when he was not ready for this? You most likely caused a substantial reaction! How many of you did the same thing when you were baptized in the Holy Spirit? Those who have a prophetic message need to be aware of this tendency and learn to back off and wait a bit for the timing of the Lord, rather than sharing it with everyone they meet. Some are not ready for this message. On the other hand, if we are hearing a prophetic message, we need to pray for God to enlarge our hearts, so that we can be open to mull it over prayerfully under the illumination of Scripture.

Reason # 3 — Those who hear the prophets do not always make the message theirs before passing it on, and thus they dilute or distort it.

Kenneth Hagin spent 50 years meditating on the Word under the illumination of the Holy Spirit and found that it had become so fleshed out in his life, and his faith had so deepened, that as he spoke it forth, the power of the Word would be released into the situation at hand. One of his adherents shared with me with great pain that she had confessed the Word of healing over her baby until it died of a problem that could easily have been handled by the doctors. Because she had not had the life experience of Kenneth Hagin and the inner intuitive and visionary nature of Kenneth Hagin, she was not able to see the same power released that Kenneth Hagin has, and tragedy resulted. This type of occurrence does not make Kenneth Hagin's prophetic word wrong; however, it does demonstrate the great need for intense clarity and understanding and wisdom as we pass along a prophetic word.

Reason # 4 — There is a tendency toward eccentricity as the prophet continually shares only his new revelation.

Some people cast demons out of doorknobs and off the sidewalk. This makes us tend to reject the deliverance ministry. However, one extreme is as bad as the other. We must not throw out a prophetic truth because the prophet or one of his adherents becomes out-of-balance. One-third of Jesus' prayers for supernatural intervention were deliverance prayers (25 out of 80). If He is the perfect balance and goal of my life, then presumably one-third of my prayers for supernatural intervention should also be deliverance prayers.

Some people have carried the message of shepherding to the point of extreme dictatorship. Does that mean I should reject completely the place of accountability relationships and submission?

Some people believe that if you really have faith for divine healing you should never go to a doctor. Does that mean I should reject prayer for divine healing when I am sick?

No, in each of the above cases I need simply to recognize the tendency toward eccentricity as a truth is being restored and smile, letting the pendulum take its necessary swing, being as careful as possible to find a balance. Admittedly, this balance may not always be possible until we have worked with the particular truth for a period of time.

Reason # 5 — There may be pride on the part of the speaker.

As the sharer of the new revelation speaks, he may do so with a condescending attitude, implying, "I have something you don't have"; "I'm better than you"; or "Here, let me educate you." This will generally provoke such a reaction in our flesh that we will have a hard time getting past it.

If you are the sharer, be careful of this kind of spiritual pride. If you are the hearer and detect an arrogant spirit, ask God for the grace to stand above it so that your heart can hear and respond to the prophetic word that is being delivered, even though the messenger is manifesting some imperfections.

Reason # 6 — There may be pride on the part of the hearer.

We may struggle with our own pride as someone shares a new insight with us. "How can anyone know something I don't know?" "I've been a Christian longer than he has." or "Can anything good come out of Nazareth?" Beware of this pride and ask God for the grace to crucify it whenever you sense it emerging.

Reason # 7 — Sometimes the hearer examines Scripture to prove that the word of the prophet is not so.

There is enough tension in Scripture that we can generally find verses that appear to speak to the opposite of almost any truth we believe. For instance, if you believe you have to love your brother to get to heaven, I can quote the words of Jesus when he said, "If anyone comes to Me, and does not hate his own father and mother and wife and children and brothers and sisters, yes, and even his own life, he cannot be My disciple (Luke 14:26)."

If, on the other hand, you believe that you must hate your brother in order to get to heaven, I can quote John's command that "The one who says he is in the light and yet hates his brother is in the darkness until now (1 John 2:9)." So I say again, there is enough tension in Scripture to make almost any truth appear wrong, **if we have a mind to do so.** However, we are to be more noble-minded that this. "Now these were more noble-minded than those in Thessalonica, for they received the word with great eagerness, examining the Scriptures daily, to see **whether these things were so** (Acts 17:11, emphasis added)."

The Bereans sought to prove the truth of a new message, rather than the error of it. This is as the difference between night and day, between God and satan, between taking the accuser's stance and the Comforter's stance, between coming against and coming alongside to help. Make a determination always to come alongside and help, rather than to come against and accuse. Let our hearts and minds be used by God and not by satan.

Reason # 8 — The hearer may fix his vision on a few extreme examples of the prophet's message, instead of fully seeking out the core of the message.

I am amazed at how much this is being done, even by national leaders who are frequently seen on television. They write articles telling of a few extreme examples of a prophet's message, then couple these with a verse that is on the opposite end of the tension point in Scripture, thus "proving" their point: "The prophet is deceived!" What a sad day for the Church, as the sheep become convinced of such reasoning, although in actuality they themselves are being deceived while they proudly believe they have been spared from deception. Who really is being deceived? You decide.

How foolish to gaze on the extreme! Instead, we are to reach in and discern the core of the message and seek to clarify and confirm it with Scripture. We know the extreme will always be there. Satan will make sure of that, in hopes of getting us to reject the message. However, as children of the light, we do have spiritual discernment. We must look for the heart of the message. We must examine Scripture daily to see if these things are so. We must come alongside as helpers, giving greater clarity to the message. We must become the expressions of the Comforter, rather than the accuser. **We are children of the Light.**

If after reading this chapter, you discern that you have cast a few stones that you ought not to have cast, ask His forgiveness and ask that by His grace you may be sensitized to discern satan's attempts to draw you into stoning the prophets of our generation.

A New Reformation in Christendom

The last Reformation in Christianity occurred in the 1500's at a time when the Western world was just discovering the scientific method and rationalism. Although the Reformation healed much within Christianity, it may have left some gaping holes as it sought to be palatable to the world in which it lived. It did not lay much stress on dreams and visions and the voice of God guiding the believer by day and by night. The stress was not on spirit encounter, but on the fact that every believer had the right to approach God for himself, even though it may have been more from a theological bent than one of ongoing spirit encounter.

At the beginning of the twentieth century, God began emphasizing the work and moving of the Holy Spirit, and before the century is over 1.1 billion believers will have found a new walk of intimacy with the Spirit of God. I believe this century will be seen by historians as a century of Reformation as the Church discovers the role of the Holy Spirit in their lives corporately and individually. I believe we are in the midst of a New Reformation within Christianity. That is why we are suffering so many birth pangs. During the last Reformation, we martyred and killed those who led the way, only to recognize their vast contribution and pioneering spirit after their life's blood had been spilt. Today these martyrs are our heroes.

May we not take the lives of those who stand out in front and lead us. May we be willing to doubt our own infallibility just a bit and honor the voice of God in the midst of His Church. We truly are living in the most remarkable age of Christendom. We are seeing 78,000 new believers being added to the Church every day and 1600 new churches being started in different places of the world each week.[1] No other time in Church history has seen such awesome movings of God.

Let us be open to what God is doing. Let the murderous spirit of religion be cast back to the pit of hell where it came from! Let our hearts overflow with humility and meekness as we watch what God is doing. It is truly a "new age"! The theology we have has essentially been passed down for three hundred years. We need to again search the Scriptures in light of God's movement in today's world and allow Him to reinterpret things that have stood for centuries. Who will have the courage to do so? The Kingdom of God suffers violence, and violent men take it by force. Will you wrestle with your theology and allow it to be transformed by the wonder of what God is doing in this present day?

A Prophecy for the Body of Christ — Received Through Journaling

A spirit of criticism has been released in My Church. My Church has begun to bite and devour one another. Have I not warned you in

My Word to beware that ye not bite and devour one another lest ye be consumed?

Behold, have I not given you the ministry of reconciliation? Have I not called you to be peacemakers?

Blessed are the peacemakers. Blessed are those who build bridges. Blessed are those who pour forth the healing oil of My Holy Spirit. Blessed are they, I say.

Blessed are ye to have them among you. Blessed are you when they speak forth their words of healing. Blessed is My Kingdom because of their fragrance.

Behold, this day I command you to fulfill the responsibility of being peacemakers — each and every one of you. None is exempt. None may disobey. All must speak forth My words of love, My words of peace, My words of comfort. You may not attack one another. You must not attack one another.

Behold, I have spoken. Behold, you are to hear and obey. It is I, the Lord, who has commanded ye this day. Behold, it is not to be taken lightly. You are to hear and obey My word.

—Received 12/27/87 - 3:45 AM through Mark Virkler

I Thought I Knew: The Kingdom That Almost Was

Let me close this chapter with a story/parable.

As a native of the land of Israel, I was taught about the great coming deliverer. He would come as the mighty and strong arm of the Lord, freeing His people from the yoke of oppression. He would restore the kingdom of David, establishing righteousness in the land. The Father would grant unto Him an eternal kingdom, one that would not pass away. He would rule the earth in righteousness and glory. His glory would cover the earth. He would be the great Messiah! He would be called Immanuel, "God with us!"

Therefore, it was with great exuberance that my brother came running to me one day saying, "We have found the Messiah, the One of whom the Scriptures speak!" I raced with him to this One

whom he had discovered and followed after Him for a great many days.

I watched Him heal the sick, proclaim release to the captives, and teach, saying, "The Kingdom of God is at hand." For more than three years He proclaimed this great message. **We believed!** The great Deliverer was in our midst. No longer would we be subject to cruel oppressors, such as Rome. We waited excitedly for Him to establish His throne. All the Scriptures would be fulfilled. All I had been taught would soon be realized.

But then tragedy struck. The King was betrayed by one of His own followers. Sold for 30 pieces of silver, the price of a slave, He was whisked through a mock trial and crucified on the same day. All of my hopes turned to ashes. Life became empty. The King **did not rule.** He never even got the chance to set up His kingdom before His tragic death. All my beliefs were dashed to pieces. All my hopes were gone.

What about all the teachings of the Word? They were **not fulfilled.** My faith was shaken. I returned to my home and my job in listless despair. Maybe all of life was a cruel hoax. The teachings I had learned from my youth were wrong. Maybe even the Scriptures were a fraud. I was filled with hopelessness and confusion.

And then the cry came: **He had risen and ascended** to the Father. We were to wait in Jerusalem for the promise of the Father, His Spirit, to baptize us in power. He **had set up** His kingdom, and now we were going to help Him establish it.

As I waited, I went back to the Word. I reexamined the book of Isaiah. I discovered verses I had never understood before — about a suffering Servant who would come as a Lamb before His slaughterers.

Maybe the Word was true after all! Maybe it was only the interpretations that I had been taught that were not true. It amazed me how different the Word looked now, in light of the events around me.

Maybe the simple teaching of the Word is not enough. Maybe we need to search the Word **in the light of our experiences in life.** Maybe the Word will always speak in somewhat new and different ways to me as life progresses around me. Maybe

I will never have full understanding in this life, but only that which is revealed to me in the context of my own life. Maybe full understanding will have to wait for eternity.

Lord, speak to me. I'm a bit unsure. How do I fit together the testimony of your Word and the testimony of life? In what way should they be blended? How exactly do I discover truth?

Personal Application

Record below what the Lord speaks to you concerning the above questions. Tune to spontaneity, fix your eyes upon Jesus, and begin to write in simple childlike faith. Begin by writing down a simple question you want to ask the Lord.

Chapter 8

Journaling — A Means of Discerning God's Voice

Journaling is a biblical method that can be used to help one grow in discernment of the voice of God in his heart. It has been a most helpful tool for me. It has been the tool that has taught me to discern God's voice. Journaling, as I use the term, is simply keeping a notebook of one's prayers and what one senses to be God's answers. We have 150 psalms that were written this way, as well as the books of the prophets and the book of Revelation. Clearly, it is a common biblical experience.

Some have asked if it is not true that the journaling commands and examples we find in Scripture are different from the journaling we are doing, in that in Scripture, all the journaling became Scripture. Not so! In First Chronicles 28:12-19, we have an example of journaling that did not become Scripture, exemplifying the exact procedure we are recommending. In verse 19, David says, "The Lord made me understand in writing by His hands upon me, all the details of this pattern." That was the pattern for the temple, which is not recorded in its entirety in Scripture.

God is speaking to His children much of the time. However, we often do not differentiate His voice from our own thoughts, and therefore, we are timid about stepping out in faith. If we can learn to clearly discern His voice speaking within

us, we will be much more confident in our walk in the Spirit. Journaling is a way of sorting out God's thoughts.

One of the greatest benefits of using a journal during your communion with the Lord is that it allows you to receive freely the spontaneous flow of ideas that come to your mind, **in faith** believing that they are from Jesus, without short-circuiting them by subjecting them to rational and sensory doubt while you are receiving them. You can write in faith believing they are from the Lord, knowing that you will be able to test them later.

I found that before I began keeping a journal, I would ask God for an answer to a question, and as soon as an idea came into my mind, I would immediately question whether the idea was from God or from self. In doing so, I was short-circuiting the intuitive flow of the Spirit by subjecting it to rational doubt. I have found that the flow of God is arrested by doubt. He that comes to God must come in faith (Heb. 11:16). I would receive one idea from God and doubt that it was from Him, and therefore receive no more. Now, by writing it down, I can receive whole pages in faith, knowing I will have ample time to test it later.

Keeping a journal greatly facilitates the flow of *rhema* into your heart. Also, maintaining a journal keeps your mind occupied (therefore, out of the way) and on track as you are receiving God's words. Another advantage of writing revelation down is given in Habakkuk 2:2,3. Habakkuk was told that he should write down what he received, because there would be a period of time before it came about. Therefore, your journal becomes an accurate reminder of revelation God has given you that has not yet come to pass.

After keeping a journal for ten years, I cannot fully express how it has deepened my relationship with Christ. It has been one of the most helpful tools I have discovered for growth in the spirit.

The Difference Between Journaling and Automatic Writing

Obviously automatic writing is satan's counterpart to journaling. Those who have experienced automatic writing before becoming a Christian tell me that in automatic writing a spirit comes and controls the person's **hand**, whereas in journaling there is a spontaneous flow of ideas birthed by God in their **hearts** and then recorded in their journals by a hand freely under the person's own control. Therefore in journaling, the entire being is involved, the heart, the mind and the mind's guiding of the hand in writing, whereas in automatic writing only a limp hand is involved. The rest of the individual is bypassed by the evil spirit that controls the hand.

The Difference Between Journaling and Adding to Scripture

One of the most common objections to journaling is that it seems to come perilously close to writing new Scripture and, thus, adding to the word of God. Some take this objection and use it against hearing from God in any fashion apart from reading the Scriptures. This is an honest objection and since adding to Scripture is forbidden, we must not dismiss the matter lightly.

To help us understand the distinct difference between the Scriptures and what God speaks to us in journaling, let us examine the instances of God speaking to individuals in Scripture and compare them with written prophecy.

An example of oral prophecy is found in First Samuel 12:1-15. Nathan prophesied against David for his sin of adultery. It was a message from the Lord, but it was for that specific situation only.

Examples of more general prophecy can be found in the books of Isaiah and Jeremiah. These prophecies contained words not only for the prophet's own time, but also for the remote future. They are timeless, relevant and valid for every generation.

So we see the essential difference between prophetic utterance and journaling today, and written Scripture. The first has local and temporal significance; the second is timeless. It refers to all ages and all people. It is only if an attempt were made to make prophetic utterance or journaling timeless and universal that we would be adding to Scripture. This we must not do. Journaling most often is for us, personally, and for no one else. It is for where we are right now. Further, journaling will give us a greater appreciation for the Scriptures because we will have a more intimate relationship with the Spirit who inspired the biblical writers. We can see similarities between the way the Word came to them and how His personal word comes to us.

Practical Suggestions For Journaling

1. Since you are coming to meet with your Creator and Sustainer, and commune with Him, your time of journaling should be when you are in your prime condition and not overcome by fatigue or the cares of the world. I find early morning best for me. Some find the middle of the night best for them. Find your best time with God and use it.

2. A simple spiral-bound notebook is sufficient. If typing comes easy for you, you may want to type rather than write. One man communes with God in his car using a tape recorder. He simply speaks forth the words he feels are coming from God. So, even a tape recorder may be a good means for some.

3. Keep your journal secluded and use codes when necessary. As you bare your soul to God

and He counsels you, some of your material will be of a private nature and should be kept secluded. Grammar and spelling are not critical when journaling.

4. Date all entries.

5. Include in your journal your communion with God, your dreams and their interpretations, visions and images the Lord gives you, and personal feelings and events that mattered to you (i.e., angers, fears, hurts, anxieties, disappointments, joys, thanksgivings).

6. As you begin journaling, you will find that the Holy Spirit grants you healing, love and affirmation as He speaks edification, exhortation and comfort to your heart (1 Cor. 14:3). He will lead you into a fuller love relationship with Jesus and provide the encouragement and self-acceptance the Divine Lover wants to give to you. Then, as times goes on, allow your journaling to expand into a flow of the gifts of the Holy Spirit (i.e., prophecy, word of wisdom, word of knowledge, discerning of spirits, etc.). If you seek to use your journal to cultivate the gift before you have sharpened your journaling ability through use, you may find that your mistakes will set you back so severely that it will be hard to press on with use of a journal. After your journal is firmly established and sharpened through much use, you will find the gifts of the Holy Spirit beginning to flow naturally through it. Allow them to come in their time.

7. Have a good knowledge of the Bible so that God can draw upon that knowledge as you journal. Not only is *rhema* tested against the *logos*, **but it is also built upon the *logos*.** God told Joshua to meditate, confess and act upon the Law of God day and night so that God could give him success (Josh. 1:8). If I fill my heart and mind and life with God's principles, and then pause in dependence upon Him in a given situation, my spirit will bring forth, through a flow of spontaneous thoughts, a perfect construction of exactly the right biblical principles. Thus I am able to speak a more pure, life-giving word from God. *Rhema* is built upon the *logos*, in that God, by His Spirit, is selecting, through illumination, the specific principles that apply and then is constructing them in precise order. My mind cannot pick out

and construct with nearly the precision that my spirit can. Thus, *rhema* is grounded in *logos* and is illumined by *logos*.

8. Those wanting to add more structure to their journaling may use the first few pages to list people and items God is burdening you to pray for regularly. You may also want to list the seven areas of prayer listed on a summary page at the back of this manual.

9. When you begin to journal, **write down** the question you have, rather than just thinking it. This simple act will assist greatly in facilitating the Lord's response.

10. As you are learning the art of journaling, you may want to journal daily until it is established in your life. Then you should be free to be spontaneous about your journaling. I generally journal several times a week.

11. Skip a line in your journal when you move from God speaking, to you speaking, and vice versa. This will help you keep the transitions clearer when you reread it.

12. Reread your last journal entry before you begin your next day's entry. It helps you check whether or not you have been obedient to the previously spoken *rhema* word.

13. I review my entire journal when the notebook is full and write a brief summary of the key themes God has spoken about to me. I put this summary in the front of my next journal.

14. I have found that every time I have asked the Lord for a date, the dates have always been wrong. Therefore I have stopped asking. I suspect the desire for dates is more of a witchcraft thing and the answer I get back is coming from satan. When God speaks, He simply says "soon," which means anytime in the next 1000 years. He says, "Trust me." Therefore, I recommend that you don't ask for specific dates in your journal.

Safeguards for Your Journey Inward

1. Cultivate a humble, teachable spirit. Never allow the attitude, "God told me, and that's all there is to it." All revelation is to be tested. In learning any new skill, mistakes are inevitable.

Accept them as part of the learning process and go on.

2. Have a good knowledge of the Bible so that you can test your *rhema* against the *logos*.

3. God gives one revelation for the area in which God has given him responsibility and authority. A wife and homemaker will receive revelation for within the home. A husband will receive revelation for shepherding the home and functioning in his business. A pastor will receive revelation for the church over which God has made him responsible. Along with God-given authority comes God-given revelation to wisely exercise that authority. Therefore, look for revelation in the areas over which God has given you authority and responsibility. Stay away from an ego trip in which you begin seeking revelation for areas in which God has not placed you.

4. Be fully committed to a local body and under a spiritual counselor. Walk together with others who are on the inward way. Realize that until your journaling is submitted and confirmed, it should be regarded as "what you **think** God is saying."

5. Ascertain whether your journaling experiences lead to greater wholeness and ability to love and share God. If your experiences become destructive to you, you are contacting the wrong spirits and you should seek out your spiritual counselor immediately.

A Brief Introduction to Christian Dream Interpretation

This powerful and exciting subject is almost entirely untaught in Christendom today. Since I mentioned above that I record dreams and their interpretation, I felt I should share at least a bit more about this topic at this time. My mentor in this area has been Rev. Herman Riffel, a mature man, who I consider to be the foremost authority alive today on Christian dream interpretation. We have a cassette series of 22 half-hour sessions of teaching by Herman on Christian dream interpretation, which is available for purchase,

along with a study guide. They can be ordered through Communion With God Ministries. Herman Riffel is also available to come to your church to conduct seminars on Christian dream interpretation. He may be contacted at 2015 Stone Ridge Lane, Villanova, PA 19085 (215-527-5389). It is a life-changing seminar.

The following are two articles that Herman has written for me during the last year. I include them to give you a taste of Herman's ministry and a brief introduction to the concept of Christian dream interpretation.

By Day and By Night

"It was a beautiful day for mountain climbing. The sky was blue, and the sun had taken off the morning chill. My wife and three children and I had hiked beyond the tree line, well above the hills and forests below.

"To the right of the trail, the mountains rose up sharply; to the left, the path dropped off toward the ravine.

"I was leading the way, my family right behind me: wife, Lillie, a strong resourceful woman; Elaine, intelligent and charming; David, with his quick head for mathematics and love of detail; Edward, blue-eyed and blond, our real nature lover.

"The trail at the start was about three feet wide and covered with pebbles. It began to narrow as it wound its way up and around the mountainside. Finally, the trail was so narrow that we stopped, and I made a sickening discovery. We had come too far; I had led my family into a situation of great peril.

"Suddenly I felt the stones give way under my feet, and with a shock, I realized that all of us were going to slide and tumble down to the chasm below!

"Then I awoke![1]

"I knew God had spoken to me in a dream. I listened and realized that He had shown me a picture of my inner thoughts at the time. It was very much like Ezekiel's vision (chapter 8), only

---

1   Taken from **Dreams: Wisdom Within** by Herman Riffel, Destiny Image, 1990. Can be obtained from author.

my situation was momentary, quickly confessed and cleared.

"That was twenty-five years ago, but it was the beginning of the realization that 'by night and by day' God speaks to us. He speaks not only during the day, but in the night as well. As the Jewish Sabbath began in the evening, so God begins His conversation at night. He speaks to us in our dreams, or night visions, as Daniel called them, in the most elementary language of mankind, but unfortunately lost to most of our Western culture.

"We know that God speaks to us during the day, but I learned that even that is unfamiliar to many Christians. After being a pastor for twenty-five years, my wife, Lillie, and I were invited to share our experience with over one thousand missionaries in many countries. When we spoke to them of how God had led us, they would frequently ask, 'How do you know the voice of God from all the other voices that we hear — the voice of public opinion, the voice of our own desires, the old voice of authority or of prejudice, and the voice of temptation?' I had already been working on this subject for years, and after much discussion with the missionaries, I began to write the book **The Voice of God** and later wrote **Learning to Hear God's Voice.** [1]

"There is no greater privilege than to hear from the God who controls all the universe. Scientists spend fortunes in money and years of time trying to get a word from outer space. Yet God created us so that we can communicate directly with Him. Adam and Eve never needed a lesson on learning to hear God's voice. Yet the recognition of that voice was lost. By the time Samuel came 'the word of the Lord was rare; there were not many visions (1 Sam. 3:1).' So it is in our nation today. We need to raise up a band of those who can reliably hear the voice of God and act on it.

"It is amazing that we can learn to hear God's voice and receive instruction from Him. He speaks to us continually, whether it is by dreams at night, or by word or vision during the day. However because of our rational training in the Western world, we must learn to listen to God with our hearts, as well as to listen to the world

with our minds. If we are to learn to hear God reliably so that we can speak, even to the nations as the prophets did, then we must exercise discipline and receive training. We cannot afford to be slipshod about such an important subject."

Why Are There No Josephs or Daniels Today? - There Are Astrologers!

"Before we criticize President and Nancy Reagan for their interest in astrology, we had better take a hard look at the Church. Why are there no Joseph's and Daniel's today? There was a Joseph who stood before Pharaoh of the mighty Egyptian empire, and interpreted his dream and saved the nation of Israel. We also remember and respect Daniel, who stood before a succession of emperors of the Babylonian and Medo-Persian empires. Why are there no such great interpreters of dreams today?

"The evident reason is that we have not only neglected the language of dreams, but we have practically turned it over to the enemy. Men and women, including presidents and kings, have known that there is truth beyond the scientific realm, but in a time of great crisis, as it was when the president was shot, and the real way to the unknown is missing, they will seek after whatever is available.

"There is a great blind spot that the Western Church has had concerning dreams. Even those who have believed in the supernatural seem to be afraid of this area. Yet the Bible is full of examples of God's use of dreams to guide, encourage, warn, enlighten and instruct His people.

"The cause of this blind spot is centuries old. It is found in a philosophy that has sadly affected the Western world, including the Western Church. It is the Aristotelian philosophy that says that valid knowledge can only come from the five senses and reason, entirely discounting the spiritual realm. This is the philosophy our Western world has followed to the point that it has exhausted itself, finally learning to scientifically destroy itself. In its emptiness, it knows that there must be something beyond, but since the

1   **Learning to Hear God's Voice** by Herman Riffel, Chosen Books, Fleming Revell Inc., 1986.

Church generally has failed to demonstrate the power of the supernatural, the world has turned to occult sources. It has dabbled in seances and drugs to find the 'out of this world' experiences.

"Finally, the Church, in its helplessness, reluctantly came to the recognition that God still speaks today. So we have come to accept the validity of prophecy, of words of wisdom and knowledge, and even tongues.

"However, the blind spot the Church has not yet faced is the vast area of the dream and vision. For twenty-five years I have been studying this subject, since a dream spoke to me decisively. But my persuasion comes not simply from my experience, but rather from what the Scriptures have to say about God's consistent communication with man through dreams and visions. The amount of positive material related to dreams and visions in the Bible is staggering.

"When I added all the positive statements about dreams and visions in the Bible, the great events surrounding them, and the prophecies that issue out of them, the sum total of that material was almost equal in size to the New Testament. Yet when the subject of dreams and visions is mentioned in the Western Church, the very few seemingly negative verses on that subject are quoted against the validity of the dream. I shall refer to those Scriptures later.

"Look for a moment at a partial list of God's great saints of the Bible who were guided, warned, instructed, or illumined by dreams and visions. The list includes Abraham, Jacob, Joseph, Gideon, Solomon, Job, Elisha, Daniel, Ezekiel, Zacharias, Mary, Joseph, Jesus, Peter, John and Paul. Besides these, we find God speaking to believer and unbeliever alike through dreams and visions.

"See the great events that hinged on dreams and visions. God put Abraham into a deep sleep to receive the covenant affecting both Jew and Christian ever since his day. Joseph was able to save his nation and sit at the right hand of the great Pharaoh of Egypt because he had learned to interpret dreams correctly. Solomon, through a dream, received the promise of wisdom to rule Israel at its high point of history. Daniel was elevated to become the president of the vast Babylonian empire, because he understood the language of dreams. Ezekiel saw visions from heaven and prophesied of his people's future.

"God is still looking for those whom He can use to interpret His voice to those who cannot understand it."

I trust the above two articles will whet your appetite with the realization that God can and does speak to us through the dream. However, before you begin to work with dreams seriously, I ask that you purchase some of Herman Riffel's materials on the topic so you enter the area with knowledge. Otherwise, you can reduce it to spoken nonsense. Now let us turn to an example of journaling.

An Example of a Prophetic Word Flowing Through Your Journal

After you have acquired skill in journaling by doing it regularly for six months to a year, you may find the gifts of the Holy Spirit beginning to flow through your heart and pen. One of these gifts is prophecy. I have found that I can ask the Lord for a prophetic word for our Sunday service, and He will give it to me before the service begins — possibly even several days before. I write it down and share with the pastor in charge of the service that I have a word from the Lord. He then asks me to come and share it at an appropriate time. One such prophecy which I shared at Full Gospel Tabernacle on December 5, 1987, follows.

"My children, fear not your weaknesses. Be not discouraged by them. Are they mightier than I? Are they greater than the living God?

"NO! They are not! No! They are simply to be consumed by MY power.

"Even as you are consumed in MY Presence, so are your weaknesses consumed by MY Power. MY Power and MY Presence are one. Therefore when you are consumed in your weakness, you are not consumed in MY Presence. Conversely, when you are consumed in MY Presence, MY

Power has consumed you, and your weaknesses are no more.

"So come My children unto Me, and you shall be healed."

Mistakes in Your Journaling!!!

There will be times, especially when you are just beginning, that you will find errors in your journaling. How do you handle this? I didn't handle it very well during my first year. Usually I would become angry, fearful, discouraged — tempted to throw my journal down and quit. I did that at least a half-dozen times during my first year. I was of the opinion that since it was supposed to be God's words, it had to be right; and if it wasn't right, then it wasn't God, and the whole exercise in journaling was a farce.

As I reflect on my initial responses, I realize how immature they were. Who does anything perfectly the first time? Who ever began riding a bike without first falling more than once? Who ever learned to play tennis without first missing the ball? The fact is, there is always a practice time before we perfect any skill. And even when we have become skillful, we still make mistakes from time to time. We must carry this same attitude and realization into our spiritual growth as well. If we do, the pressure of having to be perfect in our journaling is removed. We will allow ourselves the freedom to fail at times, without giving up the whole enterprise. We simply laugh and say, "Whoops, that was a mistake!" and go on. I encourage each of you to adopt this attitude.

Some of the Most Common Reasons for Mistakes in Journaling

1. Improper Focus — Sometimes you may discover yourself inadvertently praying with an idol in your heart. That is, you are focusing more intently on the "thing" you are praying for than you are on Jesus Christ. Thus the answer comes back through the "thing" rather than purely from Jesus' heart. The solution — fix your eyes on Jesus as you pray. Watch Him address the thing you are praying about.

2. Improper Interpretation — Sometimes I think God has said a certain thing. I go out and act on it, but it doesn't come to pass as He said it would. I have often found that as I go back and read the actual words that are in my journal, they are different than I had thought them to be. I had immediately jumped to a conclusion, interpreting the words in a certain way. However, when I looked again at the actual words, I found that these actual words were fulfilled. It was my interpretation that was wrong. The solution — be careful not to interpret what God says. Ask Him to interpret it. He will.

3. Not Acting as God Instructs — I have found that if I do not act on the words of God in the way and according to the timing which He gives me, the release of God's perfect will into the situation can be hindered. The solution — do what God says, when He says it, the way He says to do it.

4. Not a Large Enough Conduit to Release God's Power — God chooses to have His power flow through human channels, allowing His will to be released. These channels most often are individual Christians. If God has spoken that His will is to do a supernatural feat through me, and my channel is clogged or constricted through improper spiritual care and exercise, my constricted channel can thwart God's miracle, and my journaling may appear to be wrong. However, my journal probably did reveal God's perfect will, but it was not accomplished because my channel was too small to allow a sufficient amount of the Holy Spirit's energy to touch the point of need.

5. Not Having the Right Word in Your Vocabulary to Fit the Feeling Within Your Spirit — As God gives impressions within our hearts, our spirits search for an adequate vocabulary to attach to these impressions so they become understandable. If I do not pause to get exactly the right word, or if I do not have the right word in my vocabulary, I may hastily assign a wrong word to the inner sensation and find I have botched up my journaling. The solution — wait for the "right" word to be formed within your heart, the word that fully and completely conveys the feeling of your spirit.

6. Blocking the Divine Flow by Having Your Sights Fixed on a Limited Number of Options — Sometimes when I ask a question, I am looking for a "yes" or a "no," and have thus closed my heart to other creative possibilities. Often God has creative approaches to situations that I never hear because I am locked into a narrow framework. In this case, I may find myself journaling the answer I most want to hear, since I have blocked the Divine flow. The solution — be careful to be open to limitless possibilities.

7. Some of God's Commands in Your Journal Are Never Meant to Be Fulfilled. They Are Simply Positioning Moves. — "Now it came about after these things, that God tested Abraham, and said to him, 'Abraham!' And he said, 'Here I am.' And He said, 'Take now your son, your only son, whom you love, Isaac, and go to the land of Moriah; and offer him there as a burnt offering on one of the mountains of which I will tell you' (Gen. 22:1,2)." Later, the angel of the Lord countered this command, saying to Abraham, "Do not stretch out your hand against the lad, and do nothing to him; for now I know that you fear God ... (Gen. 22:12)."

I believe this happens many times in our lives. God speaks a certain thing, moving us in a certain direction for a period of time, and then after getting us to a certain point or action, He totally reverses His command. I believe this is done in order to position our attitudes in holiness before Him, and to more effectively position us and others for future purposes that He has planned.

Therefore, we must be open to this eventuality and hold on to all words loosely. It is Christ Himself, and Christ only, to whom we hold tightly.

8. God Will Not Violate Man's Free Will. — God desires that all men come unto repentance; however, some do not. Therefore, God's perfect will is not always realized in each person's life. When we are journaling and a word is given that involves another person, we need to realize that that person can choose a direction contrary to God's perfect will, and that our journaling, even though it may be reflecting God's perfect will, may not be fulfilled.

9. Be Extremely Cautious if Your Journal Speaks of the Death of Someone of Whom You Would Like to Be Freed. — If you believe you are being told that your spouse is going to die and you are going to marry another, this should be dismissed, or at least set on the back shelf and left alone. Every close relationship contains a certain amount of stress. There may be a conscious or unconscious desire to be freed from the relationship. This unconscious desire can emerge in your journal and appear to be the voice of God. If it is truly of God, it will happen. If not, it will simply be forgotten. Do not incubate such a vision or speak it or act upon it. It is very often from the deceiver. This is one of the ways satan comes to us as an angel of light. He will use Scripture to prove his point; however, his message betrays him. He is speaking of death. Leave it alone. Instead, focus your journaling on ways of enhancing your relationship with that person and give increased attention to cultivating your relationship with the Lord.

10. Beware of Your Own Strong Desires as You Journal — If you feel strongly about a certain thing, it is very easy for your own desires to come through your journaling. Prominent examples would include: romance, sexuality, power, greed, lust, fame. These things can flow so easily and effortlessly into your journal that you are almost certain it is Christ, yet it is only a reflection of your own desires. Therefore, crucify your own desires daily and walk near the cross of self-sacrificing love. Make sure your journaling comes only from that vantage point. Submit any questionable journaling in these areas to those over you.

Sometimes when you submit your journaling to your spiritual friend, you find that he disagrees with your journaling. In this case, make sure that he has not just answered "off the cuff," or just given you "his best opinion" concerning the issue. You are not asking for his best opinion. You are asking him to pray about it and get back to you, telling you what God is saying to him concerning the issue. The solution — ask him to pray about it and tell you what God tells him.

These cover a few of the most common reasons we discover errors in our journaling. Accept your errors with grace and laughter, and go on, knowing that practice makes perfect (Heb. 5:14).

Samples of Journaling

Often individuals have me read entries from their journals to help them in confirming that it truly is the voice of God speaking to them. Several of these individuals have allowed me the privilege of passing their journal entries along to you so you may be blessed by hearing the kinds of things which the Lord is speaking into their lives. Celebrate the goodness and greatness of God as you read.

"You feel the immediate victory and slaughter of the evil one is the goal. I feel the process is the goal. You see I can instantly slaughter the evil one. Yet I have not. I am letting him perform his greatest efforts against My body and then I shall utilize **both his and My efforts together** to demonstrate My victory. Thus I shall rule over all — both the forces of good and the forces of evil. And My triumph shall be unquestionable.

"Therefore fear not the process nor the intertwined defeats. I shall in My time thoroughly and totally defeat the enemy and shall be Lord over all.

"Has not the process always been integral to my plans? Consider Joseph's many years of slavery before being exalted to Pharaoh's right hand. Consider Moses' 40 years on the backside of a desert before being exalted by My right hand. Is not the process integral to the victory? Consider My Son's death and torment before being exalted to My right hand.

"Fear not the process. Fear not for the victory, for it shall surely come SAITH THE LORD.

"CELEBRATE the process. CELEBRATE the struggle. CELEBRATE the defeats, for all shall be swallowed up in My victory and I shall be Lord over all. I shall rule over the light as well as the darkness. My glory shall shine forth as never before and all mankind shall see it."
From Mark Virkler's journal
December 27, 1987

"Why does Dad always get so mad all the time?"

"Benji, I'm bringing you through many tests right now. And I'm teaching you and him many things. You are now going into spiritual adulthood, and you must learn many things. Your dad and mom will get stricter on you for a short time, and during this time I will teach you many things. Some of your friends will dislike you because you are getting wiser and more spiritual. I love you and your parents love you, and I will be interceding for you at the right hand of the Father during this time."

"Lord, will you help me have a better attitude towards my elders and my school work?"

"Yes! All you have to do is ask for my help!!"

"Please help me have a better attitude."

"OK. But first I want you to yield yourself to Me and allow Me to take control."

"OK. I want You to take all control over me and I yield myself to You."

"Benji, you will have a better attitude all the time. You are very very special to Me. Thank you for yielding to Me!"

"I love You very much!"

"I love you, too, Benji."
Benji, a 10-year-old boy at a "Communion With God Seminar" in Springfield, October 30, 1989

I'd like to share with you an incident that happened at Y.W.A.M. Holsted, October 19th.

"Lord, please speak to me about this Discipleship Training School as I walk through these delightful grounds. Lord, I feel Your presence, Your closeness in the beauty of this place."

"What do you see lying on the ground?"

"Lord, I see many fallen chestnuts. Some are completely exposed, their hard, prickly shells have long since broken open and they are bright and shiny."

"What else do you see?"

"Lord, some have only a crack in their shells, others are partly exposed and some are still unripe and are on the trees."

"My child, this is a picture of the different stages of My children within this school. Some have allowed Me to break open their hard shells that they had placed around themselves for protection. They are open and exposed, and My Holy Spirit will continue to do a deep work in their lives. Others are partly open and, as the power of My Holy Spirit is released, their bondages will break asunder. Others are in different stages of openness, and some are not ready at this present time. Remember the chrysalis? It is not My purpose to wrench away hard shells before the maturing process is completed. If you help the butterfly to break the shell it will be damaged and it will die. My timing is always perfect. So allow Me to initiate and My people to respond at their own pace."

Jean Turner

A testimony from a "Communion with God Seminar" in England

Saturday, October 3, 1987

Remember, Journaling is Only a Tool

We do not worship the tool or get stuck on the tool, as fantastic as journaling is. No, we come to the Creator and Sustainer of our souls, the Lord God Almighty. Can He speak outside of our journals? Obviously, yes! I have discovered that after journaling for awhile, I am much more aware of the inner sensation of the flow of the Spirit of Almighty God. Now even without my journal at my side, I find myself hearing that intuitive voice within speaking to me. Do I continue to journal? Yes, because it is such a powerful tool. Does God speak outside my journal? Yes, through many ways. One way is the continuous flow of His Spirit within me. Another is the counsel of friends.

Another is the Bible. Another is circumstances of life. Another is dreams. When all these line up, I feel most confident that I am truly flowing in God. I do not live out of any one of the above, but rather out of all of the above.

Do I sometimes miss God? I imagine so. It's so hard to tell. There are really so few mentors in this area to show us the way. I accept the fact that we are children just beginning to learn to walk in the realm of the Holy Spirit. I expect that in such a stage of growth there would be numerous mistakes. However, I just keep on pressing on. Lord, keep me from faltering.

Books of Collections of People's Journaling

Talking With Jesus by Evelyn Klumpenhower

A daily devotional set up for 365 days of the year. Very inspiring.

Devotional of Hebrews by Rev. Peter Lord

Peter Lord is the Pastor of a 6000-member Baptist church in Titusville, Florida. He starts each entry with a verse from Hebrews and follows it with the journaling the Lord gave Him concerning that verse. Very powerful. The first book I know of that consists of a man's journaling. A landmark book.

Hearing God by Rev. Peter Lord

An excellent complement to **Communion With God**. Peter Lord is on my board of advisors and shares similar insights from his life's experience of over 30 years in the ministry.

Each of these excellent books may be ordered through Communion With God Ministries.

Worksheet for Classroom Use[1]

A. Key Thought
Journaling, writing out your prayers and God's answers, offers new freedom in hearing God's voice.

B. Three books of the Bible that clearly illustrate a form of journaling:
1. _____
2. _____
3. _____

C. Ways in which journaling is extremely helpful in one's prayer life:
1. _____
2. _____
3. _____
4. _____
5. _____

D. Four values found in hearing His voice more clearly:
1. _____
2. _____
3. _____
4. _____

Prayer: "God, may You teach us to clearly discern the flow of Your voice and vision within our hearts."

---

[1]   The use of this supplement is explained in the Teacher's Guide.

Personal Application

Begin keeping a journal on a daily basis for a while, allowing this new avenue of prayer to take root within your heart. On the blank page that follows, write a journal entry now before going on. Ask the Lord to speak to you. If you have a specific question, write it below. If you do not have a specific question, write out the following: "Lord, what would you like to say to me?" **The simple act of writing down an initial question in your journal is critically important in prompting Divine flow. Do not overlook this step.**

Chapter 9

Habakkuk: Combining Stillness, Vision, *Rhema*, and Journaling

One day as I was praying, I took a pencil and paper and wrote down a question for Jesus to answer. As I finished writing, I focused the eyes of my heart on Jesus, picturing myself sitting next to Him on the edge of a stone well (i.e., John 4). I peered at Him intently, waiting for Him to answer. All of a sudden, into my heart came an idea which was not my own, but was an excellent response to the problem. I wrote it down and turned my gaze again upon Jesus. Again, an excellent thought came to my heart, and I wrote it down. After a bit, I found I had written two paragraphs, and as I looked at the content, I was amazed at how perceptive and wise it was. I said, "I bet this is from the Lord!!!"

I repeated this experiment in the following days during my devotional time. When spontaneous thoughts would come, I would react to them with my own analytical thoughts and questions, and He would then respond to my questions. I found I was dialoguing with the Lord! An experience I had always dreamed of and never experienced was finally happening. I was learning to converse with God! My search for a full relationship with the King of Kings was finally being rewarded. As I experimented with this over the next few months, I became increasingly convinced it was

the Divine wisdom and love of Almighty God that was flowing through my pen. During those first days and weeks, I took much of my journaling to a spiritual mentor over me, who was able to hear the voice of God, and asked him to confirm whether or not it really was God. He told me it was! This confirmation from another continued to spur me on. Each person who begins journaling should have a spiritual mentor with whom he shares his journaling. **This is a critically important step!**

Then one day, God showed me how absolutely biblical my experience was. He showed me how perfectly it paralleled Habakkuk's experience. Habakkuk was a prophet who heard the voice of God. In Habakkuk 2:1-3, he tells us how he heard God speak. I was "blown over" by the revelation. Let us examine it together because I believe in it we have a summary of the previous chapters of this book, as well as a pattern for hearing God's voice that can be used by many.

> *I will **stand** on my **guard post***
> *And station myself on the rampart;*
> *And I will keep **watch** to see what He will*
> *speak to me,*
> *And how I may reply when I am reproved.*

Then the Lord answered me and said,
"Record the vision
and inscribe it on tablets ..."
(Hab. 2:1, 2, emphasis added).

Habakkuk is seeking a spiritual experience. He wants to hear the *rhema* of God directly in his heart so that he can understand the mess he sees around him. **First,** he goes to a quiet place where he can be alone and become still. He stations himself there waiting for God to speak. **Second,** he quiets himself within by "watching to see" what God will say. The Hebrew word *sapha,* translated "keep watch," literally means "to watch closely, to be alert, to look expectantly, to wait for an answer from God." I believe he had some way of looking specifically toward God. In chapter one, verse one, it says that this is the "burden which Habakkuk the prophet *saw* (emphasis added)." So in some sense, God's *rhema* was couched in vision. As we have seen, focusing the eyes of our hearts upon God causes us to become inwardly still, raises our level of faith and expectancy, and makes us **fully** open to receive from God.

Third, when God begins to speak, the first thing He says is "Record the vision." Habakkuk wrote down what he was sensing in his heart.

These three elements — becoming still, using vision, and journaling — are the elements used by the prophet Habakkuk to hear the voice of God. And those with whom I have shared this approach have discovered that they, too, are able to discern His voice. I believe this is a God-ordained pattern that can assist one on his approach to God and help lift him to the level of the spirit. Until I combined **all three** of these elements in my devotional life, I was not able to discern God's voice and commune with Him. I often had become frustrated and uncertain about what God really wanted. These elements truly have transformed my devotional life. In my earlier Christian life, I had quit singing the song "Sweet Hour of Prayer" because I never had sweet hours of prayer. Now, I can sing the song again because I find that I can enjoy dialoguing with God by the hour and leave fully charged with His life and love.

Some Personal Lessons in Hearing the Lord's Voice

1. God does not require more of you than you are ready to give. He will provide an alternate, easier path if you request it.

2. Christ often speaks back using Scripture. *Rhema* is grounded in *logos.*

3. When His inner voice lines up with inner thoughts you already have, rejoice. Don't doubt that it is His voice and assume that they are just **your own** thoughts. What is happening is that you were already picking up God's spontaneous thoughts before you began your prayer time. Your prayer time simply has confirmed what you already had been sensing from God.

4. When the Lord's words do not come to pass as you expected, go back and ask Him why. He will tell you. If the issue generates into a confusing mess that you can't understand, that's fine. Just put it on the back burner and maybe some day you will receive understanding about it. If not, you will understand it in eternity. I have several confusing messes on my back burner. One stayed there for eight years until God finally granted me understanding of it through another person in the Body of Christ, who explained to me what the Lord had meant.

5. Initially, I looked upon my experiences as experiments. I was unsure and only acted on one-half to two-thirds of them. My confidence grew as I saw the positive results.

6. I found I could react to His ideas with my own meditated thoughts and questions, and that Christ would react to my thoughts with His forthcoming words. I still recognized a distinction between His spontaneous thoughts and my meditated thoughts.

Things to Consider

• When Oral Roberts was asked, "How do I go about learning to hear God speak to me?" he replied, "Wanting it badly enough to work on it."

• You will not learn much about the inner world until you take time to be quiet and look within.

• Relating to the inner world is complex and takes as much time and effort as relating to the external world.

My Experience of Inwardly Quieting Down and Allowing Jesus to Speak

1. I still myself in the Lord's presence, most often through worship, singing in the Spirit, or devotionally entering into a Scripture passage. My outer being is quieted, my inner being is quieted. I am in neutral, poised before my Lord.

3. The Lord speaks His thoughts through His Spirit into my heart (1 Cor. 2:9,10).

4. His Spirit is in union with my spirit (1 Cor. 6:17).

5. Spontaneous thoughts and impressions flow from the Holy Spirit to my spirit, going directly to my mind, where they are registered.

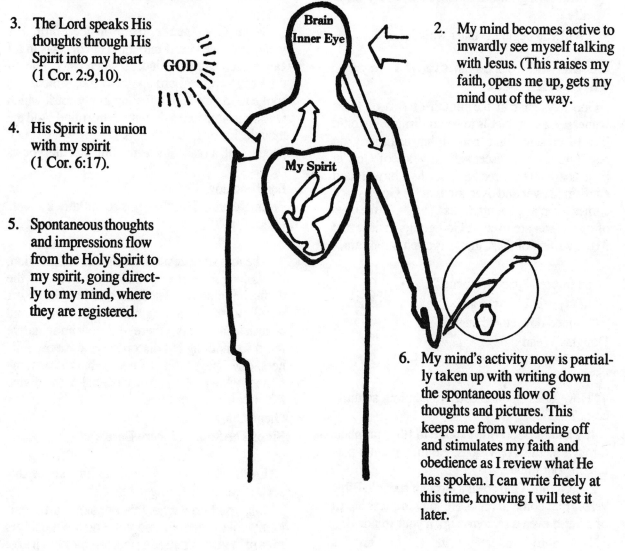

2. My mind becomes active to inwardly see myself talking with Jesus. (This raises my faith, opens me up, gets my mind out of the way.)

6. My mind's activity now is partially taken up with writing down the spontaneous flow of thoughts and pictures. This keeps me from wandering off and stimulates my faith and obedience as I review what He has spoken. I can write freely at this time, knowing I will test it later.

7. When desiring God to speak, I no longer look and listen outwardly into the cosmos, but inwardly into my spirit.

8. While momentarily pausing for a new thought or the right word to come forth in the sentence I am writing, my mind tends to easily get involved in meditating on that thought. Instead, I send it back to focus on Jesus. **One's own thoughts** can easily rush ahead of the Spirit, resulting in impurity. As I wait for a moment, focused on Him, He places the "right" word or thought into my heart.

- Learning to walk in the inner world is similar to learning to walk physically. There will be stumbling, falling and getting back up again.
- Westerners are underdeveloped in their understanding and differentiation of the inner life.
- Will you begin the inner walk?

Confirmed by The Mouth of Two or Three Witnesses

God says that at the mouth of two or three witnesses, every fact is to be confirmed. I would like to present some confirming testimony on how others have discerned the voice of God in their hearts. The three basic truths I have found confirmed over and over, are that: 1) God's voice comes often as a spontaneous thought, 2) the eyes of our hearts are used as God grants vision, and 3) the writing of these things is often important.

"an impression came to me."

"In my mind, I saw a girl sitting at the table ... "

"I jotted down the thoughts."

Douglas Wead

From **Hear His Voice**, (pp. 84, 94, 79)

"How does spontaneous revelation actually come?

1. Pictures. God often spoke to [the] prophets through pictures or visions. He may plant a picture in your mind...

2. Scripture. God speaks through specific Bible verses that come to mind. He may impress a part of a verse even a reference upon your mind.

3. A word. God may bring to your mind a specific word or piece of advice that did not come as the result of a detailed thought process. It was more spontaneous and given as if dropped into your mind. The thoughts that come from the Lord in this way are usually unpremeditated and spontaneous in character and come more in a flash without a logical sequence; whereas, when we are consciously thinking, or even daydreaming, we usually connect one thought with another."

Larry Tomczak

From "Spiritual Gifts and You"

Charisma, October 1981 (p. 57)

"The way my guidance comes ... is intuitive. Gut feelings. Instincts."

Francis MacNutt

From **Hearing His Voice** by John Patrick Grace (p. 57)

"When God speaks to me in the Spirit, His voice translates itself into thought concepts that I can conceive in my mind. So when I say, 'I heard the Lord,' or 'the Lord spoke to me,' I mean He spoke to me through a feeling in my spirit which was translated into a thought in my mind. And the thought immediately brings with it what young people call 'a rush.' It's something that hits you as right."

Ben Kinchlow

From **Hearing His Voice** by John Patrick Grace (pp. 78,79)

"The lost art of Jesus is His use of imagination. 'Jesus looked at reality through the lens of the divine imagination. The imagination is the power we all possess of seeing harmonies, unities, and beauties in things where the non-imaginative mind see nothing but discords, separations, ugliness. The imagination of man is but the window or door which, when thrown open, lets the divine life stream into our lives.' "

Glenn Clark

From **The Soul's Sincere Desire**

"Lord, what do you want to say about this session we are listening to today?"

"Bill, you know what this session can mean to my children, because you know what it has meant in your life these past ten months (note: Mark conducted a "Communion With God" seminar in this same church ten months earlier). I have anointed Mark to deliver this message to My people. All who will open their hearts to this truth will have a river of life flow through them, and I will be able to use them to encourage, to build up, to heal, and to perform in my body all that I speak of in My word. My children have never really known how to do this before. I will use this to bring my bride to a fullness it has never known, if they will heed what is being taught here today."

Bill Woosley
A confirming journal entry
Received and read before a group taking a
"Communion With God" seminar with me in
Springfield, Missouri
November 28, 1989

"Learning to hear God through journaling has been the most exciting and revolutionizing thing to happen in my life. It has brought extreme change to my life and that of my family. It has caused me to have constant and lasting joy in my life. It has given me wisdom and guidance in every area of my life. As a woman, I journal about everything from what I wear each day to what His will is for my life. Hearing each day what my Father wants me to eat, has helped me to lose 60 pounds. Journaling has given me such confidence in myself. For many years satan has torn at my self-confidence in **every** area of my life. But now, I ask Jesus what He thinks of me. His thoughts of me are so beautiful, loving and caring. He tells me I am unique and special and He planned me just the way I am even before the world began. 'Wow!' now that's special!

"I find that if I arise very early in the morning before the rest of my family, I can be quiet and alone with my Lord. Before the noise of my daily life begins, I can hear Him so easily. It starts my days out just right!

"There have been many times in my life that I have not followed God's will for my life, simply because I didn't know what it was. I was so busy 'feeling in the dark' for His will: going through 'open doors' and resisting the 'closed doors.' But now that I can hear God, I can know what His will is each and every area of my life. Praise the Lord! I have not made any monstrous mistakes in my life since I learned to journal.

"But you know, I've found out the neatest thing! Jesus told me that even while I was so busy trying to find His will for my life, He had His hand on me even then. He tells me now that He planned the parents I would have, the husband and even the three boys I would have. Even while I was struggling, He gently guided me through my life.

"But I cannot praise my Father enough for making it possible for me to actually learn to hear Him through journaling. My life will **never** be the same!"
Paulette Wolsey
A confirming testimony

Conclusion

These testimonies confirm that God does use the tools of spontaneous thought, spiritual vision and writing things down as means of establishing communion with us.

From My Journal

I will close this section with a poem from my journal that describes my experience of learning these truths. This was the first poem I had written in thirteen years, so I can truly say it was of the Lord. I do not write poetry.

Coming Apart Unto Him

Lord, You spoke in Your Word what You'd
    have me do.
To come apart and wait upon You.
That You would renew the strength of my life
And let me soar into heavenly heights.
Lord, it's so hard to come apart to You.
There are always so many things to do.
In the natural it seems like a fruitless waste
To fritter away my time into space.
But You're opening my eyes, allowing me to see
The value of coming apart unto Thee
That out of my stillness You finally get through
To speak to me plainly things concerning You.
Spirit to spirit impressions flow,
It's Your voice to me, so the story goes.
I look and I listen attentively,
Recording the thoughts You give to me.
I'm enticed by Your speaking into my heart,
Giving clarity and faith through what You
    impart,
In a moment saying more than I can in a month.
Clearly, powerfully, and it's more than a hunch.
Lord, I'm learning to come apart unto You.
To open my spirit and let You speak through.
That waiting on You is not vain,
It's the most precious experience I can gain.
Lord, You are filling all of my dreams.

You've filled my life with reality from Your
    scheme.
You fill my religion with Your grace,
Lifting me high above time and space.
As Jesus, may I come apart from life,
Waiting on You to regain new life,
Speaking it forth to the world around,
Sharing with them the life I've found.
Lord, teach me to look only at You
Not the wind and the waves, and all the to-do.
To stand firm and fast in what You speak
As I pray and fast, Your face to seek.
Lord, teach me Your voice more pointedly,
Keep me apart and waiting on Thee.
Allow Thy fullness my eyes to see,
Lord, I come apart to wait upon Thee.

Personal Journaling Application

Choose a gospel story that is comfortable to you. You may want to reread it so it is fresh in your mind. Picture the story. Enter it, becoming one of the characters. Allow yourself to be present with Jesus. Fix your gaze upon Him. Ask Him the question that is on your heart. It may be as simple as "Lord, what do you want to speak to me?" Or it may be a more specific question. Tune to spontaneity and begin writing out of the flow that bubbles up within you. Don't test it as you receive it. Test it after the flow is finished.

Begin by writing the question below that you want to ask the Lord. Then enter the vision.

Chapter 10

Moving From Soul to Spirit

Because of the overemphasis on the mind and sense knowledge in Western civilization today, it is very easy to attempt to live the Christian life out of one's soul (mind, will and emotions) rather than one's spirit (deep, consuming, underlying attitudes, motivations and character). The Christian life, including prayer, is to flow from your spirit, not your soul.

Discerning the Spirit

(Underlying Attitudes, Motivations and Character Traits

1. You are discerning the spirit when you sense the underlying attitudes, motivations or character of a person. For example:

1 Kings 21:1-5 ... a sullen spirit

Prov. 11:13 ... a faithful spirit

1 Pet. 3:1-4 ... a quiet spirit

2. Being tuned to the Spirit involves being tuned to the spontaneous thoughts, feelings and visions that come to you rather than only the meditations of your mind.

Restoring Your Spirit

(Eating, Drinking, Breathing)

God jealously desires the spirit, which He has made to dwell in us (James 4:5). As Jesus was growing up, He grew "strong in spirit." We also need to grow strong in spirit. Our spirits were made to be filled with God. We restore our spirits by filling them with the Lord, digesting only His words, drinking much from His spirit, and breathing His *rhema.*

The Spirit's Food — Digesting the *Logos*

The Spirit's food is the Bible. Joshua was told that if he would meditate on it, practice it and speak only the Word, his way would be successful (Josh. 1:8). Satan is constantly trying to keep Christians from doing that. He is constantly throwing his thoughts into our minds (John 13:2) and trying to remove God's thoughts from our minds (Luke 8:12). We are told that the mind is a battlefield and that we are to destroy speculations and take every thought captive to Jesus Christ (2 Cor. 10:5).

From a quick scan of Scripture, we can see that satan's thoughts are those that are negative and destructive, while God's thoughts are positive and upbuilding. Satan will attack us with guilt, inferiority, failure, defeat, condemnation, fear, worry, anxiety, doubt, uncertainty, bondage, narrow-mindedness, prejudices, uncontrollable thoughts, impure pictures, wanderings, weakened concentration, confused ideas, memory failure, etc.

It is important to discern when your mind is under satan's control and call upon the Lord for release — turning your mind back to Him. It is also important that you watch carefully the thoughts you ingest, that they in no way contaminate or weaken your spirit.

Satan can only attack your thought life when an opening is provided for him. A mind unrenewed by God's Word, cherishing sin, misunderstanding God's truth, accepting suggestions, lying blank or passive, affords an opportunity for satan to attack. A Christian, waiting quietly before the Lord for His thoughts, does not have a blank or passive mind. His heart is still and his mind is quiet, but it is actively focused on his Lord and Savior, Jesus Christ.

The Spirit's Water — Drinking the Spirit (Praying in the Spirit)

It was Jesus who likened the indwelling Spirit to a flow of living water (John 7:38-39). Paul said that when you speak in the Spirit, you are speaking to God. Your spirit is speaking mysteries, and you are building yourself up (1 Cor. 14:2,4).

I believe praying in the Spirit is to be a part of our prayer life (1 Cor. 14:15); it serves an important role in energizing our spirit by opening us to the Divine flow.

The Spirit's Breath — The *Rhema* of the Spirit

It is the *rhema* spoken by the Spirit that produces life (John 6:63). The thoughts of my mind (when not illumined by the Holy Spirit) are of the flesh and result in bondage and death. God speaks to me through my spirit (Prov. 20:27), teaching, guiding and comforting me (John 16:13).

One must tune one's senses to the impressions of his spirit, above the meditative thoughts of his mind. In this way he tunes to spontaneous flow rather than analytical thought.

Summary

To pray and live out of a restored spirit:
1. Digest the Word - Food
2. Pray in the Spirit - Drink
3. Stay Tuned to His Spirit - Breath

These three keys, although somewhat difficult to discover (it took me five years), are quite simple and easy to accept — but extremely difficult to practice. It will take a great amount of adjusting and persistence for a Westerner to put these truths into his everyday living. Most Westerners accept, without hesitation, the thoughts of satan throughout the day, not even suspecting they are coming from him, but assuming they are simply their own. A real move away from rationalism must take place in our hearts until we perceive the spiritual warfare surrounding spontaneous thoughts (2 Cor. 10:4,5). By destroying the speculations in our minds, we are destroying satanic fortresses. This will not be done through our own efforts, but only through calling upon the Divine power of the indwelling Christ. The goal and objective is to be transformed by totally renewing our defiled minds with the Word of the Lord (Rom. 12:1). Only then will we experience His will (Rom. 12:2).

Most Westerners will also find it difficult to pray **much** in the Spirit. Once again, we are so caught up in rationalism that to even believe in the value of praying in the Spirit (a super-rational experience) is difficult, much less to practice it in one's daily prayer life. We must move toward the spiritual until we reach the balance of praying regularly with the Spirit and praying regularly with the mind (1 Cor. 14:15).

Finally, most Westerners will find it extremely difficult to stay tuned to their spirits, having been trained all of their lives to live out of the reasonings of the mind (i.e. to eat from the forbidden tree of knowledge of good and evil). To retrain oneself to now begin living out of the spontaneous, intuitive impressions of the Spirit (i.e. to eat from the tree of life) is a formidable task, and will only be done through persistence, and much effort and calling upon the grace of the Lord Jesus

Christ. In a way, I am hesitant to give forth the truths of heart communion in such a simple, straightforward fashion. First, one tends not to appreciate what he has not personally struggled to achieve; and second, these truths appear so simple that they may only be half-tried or untried, and then either let go or subjected to severe, premature judgment. However, I must trust in the Lord's grace to accomplish His work in our hearts. He is able, and He is faithful. We can only bow our knee before Him, acknowledging our weakness and inability to impart changes in another's life and His supreme ability to change us as He wills.

From My Journal

I have found nothing as effective as the application of these three keys (digesting the Word, praying in tongues, staying tuned to His Spirit) to cause me to overcome my great personal war against accusation, condemnation, depression, doubt and insecurity within my own heart. An example from my journal of the way He has helped me deal with it follows:

"Lord, I have so many questions. Will you please answer them?"

"Lay aside all thoughts but those that come from Me. This will overcome the uncertainty and accusation in your heart. Act immediately in faith on those things that I speak to you ..."

He then went on to instruct me on several specific actions that resolved my questions. Once again, His *Rhema* was the life that set me free from my personal bondage. Praise His glorious Name!

Personal Application

Prayer: "Lord, is there a word you want to speak into my heart that will set me free in some area of my life? If so, I am open for You to speak."

Fix your eyes on Jesus, tune to spontaneity and begin to write what flows within you.

Chapter 11

Tuning Your Heart to Hear God Speak

"But just as it is written, things which eye has not seen and ear has not heard, and which have not entered the heart of man, all that God has prepared for those who love Him. For to us God revealed them through the Spirit; for the Spirit searches all things, even the depths of God" (1 Cor. 2:9,10).

Tuning Your Heart's Radio to Receive God's Signals

Our mind and physical senses cannot receive the fullness of God's revelation to us. It must come to our hearts intuitively through the operation of the Holy Spirit, living **within** us (1 Cor. 2:9-16).

I have heard it used in sermon illustrations that our hearts are like a radio, which we need to tune to hear the signals that are coming from God. I would agree with that. However, no one could ever offer me a tuning knob that would allow me to tune my heart more perfectly to the voice of God. Therefore that sermon illustration always left me frustrated.

In this chapter we are going to look at ways God has said we can tune ourselves to pick up His voice. Most of the aspects of tuning deal with preparing the condition of your heart, since it is into the heart that God speaks. We will look at three biblical examples of approaching God to hear Him speak: the first is the tabernacle experience; the second is Habakkuk; and, the third is the instructions given in Hebrews 10:22.

Learning to Operate the Radio (The Tabernacle Experience)

On the mountain, God gave Moses the design for the tabernacle, which Hebrews 8:5 tells us is a copy, a shadow and a pattern of the heavenlies. It not only established the way for the Israelites to approach Him and hear His voice, but it also establishes the way that we approach God and hear His voice. The tabernacle depicts the spirit, soul and body of man. The outer court corresponds to man's body, where we receive sense knowledge. It was illuminated by natural light. The Holy Place corresponds to man's soul. It was illuminated by oil in a lampstand, which corresponds to the Spirit revealing truth to our minds. The Holy of Holies represents man's spirit, where the Shekinah Glory lightens our innermost being, giving us direct revelation within our hearts. Therefore, God speaks to us on three levels. The Gospel of Luke was written as a "Holy Place experience," as God illumined Luke's mind with truth (Luke 1:14). Revelation was written out of a "Holy of Holies experience" as John received direct vision and *rhema* from God. The following sketch of the tabernacle may help you see these truths.

Each of the six pieces of furniture represents an experience in our approach to God.

1. The Brazen Altar — The Cross (Ex. 27:1-8)

This signifies our initial commitment to make Jesus Lord of our lives and present ourselves as a living sacrifice to Him (Rom. 12:1,2). This is an absolute prerequisite to approaching God.

2. The Brazen Laver — God's Word (Ex. 30:17-21)

This signifies our washing ourselves by applying the *logos* to our lives. The applied *logos* has a cleansing effect on our lives.

3. The Table of Shewbread — The Will (Ex. 25:17-21)

As flour is ground fine for the making of the bread, so our will is ground fine as we totally commit our way unto the Lord.

4. The Seven-branched Lampstand — Illumined Mind (Ex. 25:31-39)

God illumines truth to our mind as we study His Word.

5. The Altar of Incense — Emotions (Ex. 30:1-10)

Through the offering up of a continuous sacrifice of praise, our emotions are brought under the control of the Holy Spirit.

6. The Ark — Direct Revelation of the Spirit into our Hearts (Ex. 25:10-22)

Out of worship and stillness, we enter heart-to-heart communion with God. God's Shekinah Glory fills our hearts.

For a more complete study of the above truths, I recommend the tape series "The Way into the Holiest" by Derek Prince, and the study booklets that go along with it. This series may be ordered from Derek Prince, P.O. Box 306, Dept. 6, Ft. Lauderdale, FL 33302.

The Rough-Tuning Dial to Receive Direct *Rhema* (Habakkuk's Pattern in Hab. 2:1-3)

Rhema is spontaneous thoughts, ideas and impressions that come to your heart from God. We open ourselves to *rhema* by:

- Quieting the outer noise by going to a quiet place.
- Quieting the inner noise by looking to Jesus (using vision).
- Keeping your mind from wandering by use of a journal.

For a more complete study, review the chapter in this manual on Habakkuk.

Fine-Tuning Dial to Receive Direct *Rhema* (Heb. 10:22)

... we have confidence to enter the holy place by the blood of Jesus, by a new and living way which He inaugurated for us through the veil, that is, His flesh, and since we have

The Tabernacle Experience — God's Design for Approaching Him

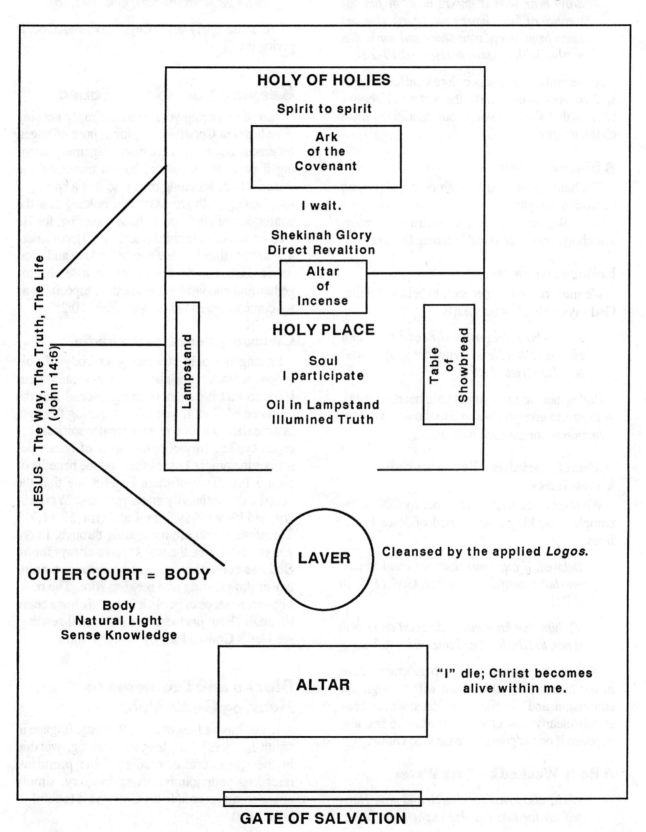

HOLY OF HOLIES

Spirit to spirit

Ark
of the
Covenant

I wait.

Shekinah Glory
Direct Revaltion

Altar
of
Incense

HOLY PLACE

Soul
I participate

Oil in Lampstand
Illumined Truth

Lampstand

Table
of
Showbread

JESUS - The Way, The Truth, The Life
(John 14:6)

LAVER

Cleansed by the applied *Logos*.

OUTER COURT = BODY

Body
Natural Light
Sense Knowledge

ALTAR

"I" die; Christ becomes
alive within me.

GATE OF SALVATION

a great priest over the house of God, let us draw near with a sincere heart in full assurance of faith, having our hearts sprinkled clean from an evil conscience and our bodies washed with pure water (Heb. 10:19-22).

As we come in stillness before God to hear His spoken work in our hearts, the writer of Hebrews tells us that the following four conditions must characterize our hearts.

A Sincere Heart

The heart must be true, with no hypocrisy, no deception, no lying.

Be wholehearted in love, praise, trust, returning, searching, crying unto and listening to God.

Fullness of Faith

We must come to a decision to believe all that God says with all of our hearts.

... he who comes to God must believe that He is and that He is a rewarder of those who seek Him (Heb. 11:6).

God is there to meet you in your heart, to speak with you, to give you life, and to show you things. *Immanuel* means God with us.

A Heart Sprinkled From an Evil Conscience

We must come to an acceptance by faith of the complete working of the blood of Jesus in our lives.

Beloved, if our heart does not condemn us, we have confidence before God (1 John 3:21).

To him that knoweth to do good and doeth it not, to Him it is sin (James 4:17, KJV).

We cannot approach God with unconfessed sin in our hearts. It must be dealt with through our confession and the blood of Jesus, which constantly cleanses us. One's heart must be free and at peace if one is going to sense God within.

A Body Washed by Pure Water

Christ also loved the church and gave Himself up for her; that He might sanctify her,

having cleansed her by the washing of water with the word [rhema] (Eph. 5:25,26).

We must apply and obey the *rhema* God is giving us.

Keeping Your Heart Tuned

Part of preparing your heart is simply keeping your heart in Christ — keeping it pure of anger, bitterness, negativism and discouragement; keeping it protected so others do not transfer these things into it; watching over it so it is a spring of life, issuing forth words of life; holding fast the confession of our hope without wavering, for He who promised is faithful (Heb. 10:23); considering how to stimulate one another to love and good deeds (Heb. 10:24); continuing to assemble together and encourage one another, especially as we come to the end of the age (Heb. 10:25).

Cleansing Your Heart's Radio

Fasting not only cleanses your body of poisonous wastes, but it also seems to cleanse your spirit so that it can more easily ascend into the presence of God. If you are not getting through, fasting should help you gain greater spiritual receptivity. The fifty-eighth chapter of Isaiah describes the proper kind of fast and the benefits of such a fast. Two of these benefits are that the "Lord will continually guide you" and "You will cry, and He will say,'Here I am' (Isa. 58:11,9)." Therefore, if you are not getting through, I urge you to fast to free the way. I have **always found God has come through as I have spent a number of days fasting and seeking Him. The most important steps of growth in my life have come through these periods.** For additional reading, see **God's Chosen Fast** by Arthur Wallis.

Blocks and Problems to Hearing God's Voice

1. You have a lack of faith. Remedy: Engage in "faith-builders" (i.e., tongue-speaking, worship in the spirit, praise, reading Bible promises, rereading your journal, using imagery, simply abandoning yourself to the God who is faithful — Heb. 11:6).

2. Your mind wanders. Remedy: Use a journal and use vision. Write down, pray through and confess things that are on your mind. Make sure your heart is not condemning you. If it is, purify it.

3. You feel God is not speaking. Remedy: Pour out your heart **fully and completely**. Begin writing down any words you receive, even if there are only one or two. Remember, the Spirit's impressions are slight and easily overcome by bringing up your thoughts.

4. God is not speaking. Remedy: It may be you are asking questions God does not want to answer. Maybe you need to fast to release His answer. Check for problems on the fine-tuning dial. Maybe you have wrong motives (James 4:3).

Even though Christ has opened the way before us into the Holy of Holies by rending the veil and sprinkling us with blood, many Christians do not enter frequently. The way is not burdensome or unduly complicated. Christ does the work ... Christ sprinkles us with His blood, Christ grants us faith, Christ gives us a clean heart. We simply need to be willing vessels to receive the finished work of Christ. Our love and attention must be set toward Him.

Yet, how often our love and attention are diverted to things other than Christ. We do not always earnestly seek His overcoming power because we enjoy a desire of the flesh. We are not always willing to lose our life in order to find His life.

Also, it takes **effort** to learn to walk in a new realm. I watched with amazement as my two children learned to walk. They tried so hard, stumbled and fell so many times. They hit their heads and hurt themselves so much for a period of **many months**, yet they would not give up. Walking just beats crawling, and the Holy of Holies just beats the Holy Place. I believe that for us to learn to walk in the Holy of Holies, it will take the same kind of attention and effort, involve the same kinds of falls and bruises, and take a **number of years** before we become skillful.

May we take up the challenge to come confidently before God and receive His life and love. May we put forth the attention and effort that is needed. May we be willing to fully lose our life in order to find it.

Checklist for Tuning to God

The checklist on the following page offers a review of the material in this chapter. God will speak into our hearts when our hearts are tuned to Him. Then, we will be able to engage in Spirit-led prayer.

Goal — cultivating the intuitive inner flow of the Spirit by training your senses to capture the spontaneous thoughts placed into your heart by the Lord.

A.   I Learn to Live the Tabernacle Experience (Exodus)

☐ 1. Altar — I am a living sacrifice.

☐ 2. Laver — I have washed myself by applying the Word.

☐ 3. Shewbread — My will is ground fine before God.

☐ 4. Lampstand — God illumines my mind, granting me revelation.

☐ 5. Incense — My continual offering of thanksgiving to God brings self and emotions under the control of God.

☐ 6. Ark — I have learned to walk into His immediate presence in silence and receive His words spoken into my heart.

   ☐ a. Rough-tuning Dial — becoming silent and focused on Jesus (Hab. 2:1,2).

      ☐ 1) I have a quiet place.

      ☐ 2) I silence my spirit by fixing my eyes on Jesus (Heb. 12:2).

      ☐ 3) I facilitate the flow by writing it down.

   ☐ b. Fine-tuning — remove inner blocks (Heb. 10:22).

      ☐ 1) My heart is sincere, honest and committed, and I harbor no reservations.

      ☐ 2) I approach God in full faith.

      ☐ 3) My conscience has been cleared through receiving Christ's cleansing.

      ☐ 4) I have been obedient to previous *rhema.*

B.   I overcome all evil by living out of the *rhema* God has spoken to me (Heb. 10:23-25).

☐ 1. I confess it with my mouth.

☐ 2. I consider ways to stimulate others to walk in the *rhema* God has given them.

☐ 3. I come together with others for mutual encouragement.

C.   I validate my *rhema* by submitting it to my spiritual authority (Heb. 13:17).

☐ 1. I am submitted to my spiritual elder, and he is willing for me to bring major decisions to him.

☐ 2. I submit major leadings to him, that is, leadings which have a major consequence in time or money.

My Personal Experience

I find God speaks to me from the Outer Court, the Holy Place, and the Holy of Holies. He has often directed me through the simple reading and application of the Bible. He has often illumined a passage of Scripture to my heart, lifting it right off the page, letting me know it was His *rhema* for me at that moment. He has often spoken with spontaneous thoughts, feelings and images directly into my heart as I have waited quietly before Him. Jesus has become my Way, my Truth and my Life.

Also, I have often found the Holy of Holies cut off to me because I did not adjust my fine-tuning dial. I have gone with a lack of faith or a condemning heart, and therefore, have not had the confidence to approach God.

Personal Journaling Application

Record what He says. Using vision, present yourself before each piece of tabernacle furniture. Fix your eyes upon Jesus and ask Him what He wants to speak to you about the placement of this experience in your life. Tune to spontaneity and record what He says. You may want to also ask Him about the fine-tuning dial.

Chapter 12

Yada Times — Sharing Love Together

Yada Times

Jesus said, "This is eternal life, that they might **know** Thee, the only true God and Jesus Christ whom Thou hast sent (John 17:3, emphasis added)." What a dynamic statement: eternal life is **knowing** God! But this is not the simple, casual "knowing" of an acquaintance, or even a close friend. The word used here for "know" is *ginosko*, and it means "to be involved in an intimate, growing relationship." In the Greek version of the Old Testament, this is the word used in Genesis 4:1, where it says, "Adam **knew** Eve and she bore a son (emphasis added)." This is the most intimate relationship possible. Jesus makes the fantastic statement that this is what eternal life is all about! This is the essence of eternal life: to be involved in an intimate, growing relationship with the God of all creation and His only Son, Jesus. What a magnificent destiny!

Paul had a hold on this precious truth. In Philippians 3:10,11, he said that his great desire was, "that I might **know** Him, and the power of His [inner] resurrection and the fellowship of His sufferings, being conformed to His death; in order that I may attain to the [outer] resurrection from the dead (emphasis added)." Can you hear the yearning of Paul's heart? That I might **know** Him! Out of that precious love relationship, we will sense His life flowing within us, putting the flesh to death and flowing out through us to others. This is the reason for our salvation! This is why we were born again!

The Hebrew counterpart of the Greek *ginosko* is *yada*, and we like to use that word to characterize our time of loving fellowship in prayer. Prayer is so much more that presenting our petitions to God. It is our "*Yada* time." Prayer is the link between lovers. It is communing with our lover, Jesus — being intimate, quietly sensing each other's presence, being totally available to one another. It is a treasuring of one another so much that we desire to be together constantly, to share everything with one another, and to walk through life together. It is a feasting on one another's love. It is communion between two lovers: a relationship, not rules. Do not make it rules; allow it to be a relationship. Lovers come together whenever they can to share what is on their hearts. Their relationship is characterized by joy and spontaneity, not legalistic bondage.

Romance With the King of Kings

It is so important that we learn to seek the Lord for Himself alone, and not for the things He can give us. He longs for us to abide in Him, to feast on His love. He wants us to enjoy fellowship with Him as our dearest friend. His heart yearns to be ministered to by our love.

We hurt Him so when we become too busy with our daily tasks to spend time enjoying His love or when we carelessly let sin slip into our lives, destroying our close communion. We must seek Him as our greatest treasure, seeing our time of sharing with Him as the highest priority in our lives.

As a result of our relationship with Him, we will begin to see His power flowing out from us, touching hearts, renewing life and strength, and working miracles. For out of relationship will come faith — simple faith, which is simply being close enough to Jesus to know what He wants to do in a situation and then doing whatever He instructs. But, the only way we will ever be able to know exactly what Jesus is thinking and saying is by spending much time with Him — living in His presence every moment of our lives. There are no shortcuts to this! But, oh, the fullness of joy we find in His presence.

"Come Wholly Unto Me"

The Lord speaks of coming wholeheartedly to Him so we can fully experience Him. The following are five aspects of the wholeheartedness that God requires in our approach to Him:

1. Make Me your **greatest treasure** so I can give Myself to you (Mark 12:30).

2. **Search** for Me with your whole heart so I can reveal Myself to you (Jer. 29:13).

3. **Trust** Me with your whole heart so I can guide your steps (Prov. 3:5).

4. **Praise** Me with your whole heart so I can gift you with My presence (Ps. 9:1).

5. **Return** to Me with your whole heart so I can be compassionate and bless you (Joel 2:12).

From My Journal

I will close this section by sharing two entries from my journal in regard to this. Notice how the *rhema* is grounded in *logos*, and though not really anything new to me, are still things I need to hear over and over so that I can believe them for each moment of each day.

"I am the Alpha and Omega, the beginning and the end. I am the first and the last, the light and the power. I am able to do exceedingly abundantly above all that you are able to think and ask. **Just come to Me**, and I will be your strength. I will be your lover. **You must simply come to Me.** It cannot be accomplished without time together, **so, come to Me often, continuously.** I am always here. I am always ready to listen and respond. I am a great and loving God, slow to anger and abounding in lovingkindness. I do forgive your sins. I do clothe you with righteousness. You must only seek Me with all your heart and turn from your ways, and **come to Me. Will you do that?"**

On another day:

"I enjoy just being with you, not doing anything special together, just being together. I enjoy the fragrance of your worship. Times of solitude are peaceful to Me. It is like a quiet brook, flowing on the mountainside. I desire your presence. It is refreshing to Me. It is the fulfillment of My purposes when you choose to be with Me. It brings Me great pleasure. Do it often. Do not think every time we come together it must be to accomplish something. Simply being together is the greatest accomplishment, just being with one another. Come let us enjoy one another."

Additional Reading on This Topic

The Gentle Breeze of Jesus by Mel Tari

Come Away, My Beloved by Frances J. Roberts

Talking With Jesus by Evelyn Klumpenhouwer

Documentation on the precise definitions of *ginosko* and *yada* may be found on pages 395-398 of **The Dictionary of New Testament Theology**, Vol. 2, by Colin Brown.

Personal Journaling Response

Spend some time journaling. Write a love letter to Jesus and let Him respond. Tell Him how much you appreciate Him, how special He is to you. Fix your eyes upon Him. Tune to spontaneity. Record what He says to you.

Chapter 13

Principles of the Spirit

In order to walk effectively in the spiritual world, one must understand the laws that operate in that realm. The most important laws to understand are those surrounding the working of the Holy Spirit. We have already studied how He speaks in our hearts. Now, we will study other ways in which He works.

PRINCIPLES	SCRIPTURES (fill in)
1. One moves mightily in prayer when led by the Holy Spirit.	Rom. 8:26
2. The Lord must reveal to us that our weakness in praying is perpetual so that we might learn to be perpetually dependent on the Holy Spirit. We must learn to "rest" in our weakness, not "strive" in it.	Rom. 8:26a — The Spirit helps (takes hold together with) us in our weakness. Ask the Spirit to help you overcome every weakness you encounter in praying — He will (Heb. 4:16). Laziness, apathy, bodily weakness, mental weakness, ad infinitum.
3. **All** our praying is to be **in** the Spirit (inspired, guided, energized and sustained by the Holy Spirit), otherwise, we are praying in the flesh.	1 Cor. 14:14

1 Cor. 14:15

Eph. 6:18

Jude 1:20

Rom. 8:9

---

4. We have the **right** to approach God   John 14:6
    through Jesus Christ. However, actual
    access (where we consciously ex-
    perience fellowship with God) is provided
    through the working of the Holy Spirit.

                                                   Eph. 2:18

---

5. We have **two** intercessors helping us to   Rom. 8:27
    pray.

                                                   Rom. 8:34

The Holy Spirit helps us form the prayers in our hearts and Christ stands before God, presenting our prayers
to Him.
Additional Reading: Pray in the Spirit by Arthur Wallis

Personal Response

Ask the Lord to speak to you about the truths of this chapter. Fix your gaze upon Him. Experience Him in a comfortable setting. Tune to spontaneity and record what flows within. Don't test it as you are receiving it. Test it later. Write in simple child-like faith what is flowing within your heart. Thank you, Lord, for what You speak.

Chapter 14

A Pattern for Praying in the Spirit

Prayer must flow from your heart, rather than from your head, if it is to be Spirit-born prayer. Prayer is begun, guided, sustained and ended according to the promptings of your heart. One begins by contacting God in his heart, uniting with His life, and then in faith, allowing His power to flow — speaking it forth into existence and praising Him for His accomplishments. Study now the chart on the following page for an expansion of this thought.

One now moves in prayer guided by *rhema*.

It is important to keep your heart open to the Lord, allowing yourself to receive the **burdens** He would like to share with you.

Use vision throughout to crystallize spiritual realities in faith. See God. See His power uniting with you or flowing toward another. Allow Him to establish the pictures. Do not paint them by yourself a stroke at a time. Do not see what you want to see. Instead, simply open the eyes of your heart. Ask Him to show you what He wants you to see. He will, in the same spontaneous way He gives you *rhema*.

Miscellaneous Reminders

- **Use thanks to maintain faith** through the rest of the day. Continually give thanks that His life is at work within you.

- **Use persistence and patience to complete more difficult healings** (morning, noon, evening). "Thank You, Lord, for what you have done and continue to do. Renew, now, that healing flow. Thank You."

- Your faith must be reborn by **the reeducation of your heart with the Word of God** (Josh. 1:8; Rom. 12:1,2).

Replacing	With
Every thought of fear	. . . .a thought of faith
Every thought of illness	. .a thought of healing
Every thought of death	. . .a thought of life

- **Love must be reborn by the reeducation of your heart in the love of God.** One must reeducate his heart so that its instinctive and natural reaction to every situation, every person and every animal may be one of love. It is easy because you are working in harmony with the laws of nature. When you find you have failed in some way, flogging yourself is self-defeating in that it pushes you back even farther. Instead, acknowledge the error, repent if necessary, and move on.

Praying in the Spirit

STAGE	SCRIPTURE	EXAMPLE
1. Relaxation — Become quiet, comfortable and relaxed physically so your mind is freed from thoughts of your body and can become totally immersed in the being of God and then the person for whom you are praying.	Ps. 46:10	Sit comfortably, head at rest, hands folded in lap, spine relaxed, yet erect. Encourage (do not command) the different parts of your body to relax. Visualize them relaxing.
2. Contact God in your spirit by meditation upon the reality of God. Do not strive. Just be still and know.	His nearness: Acts 17:28 Phil. 2:13 Gal. 2:20 Ps. 123:1	We overcome ourselves (our worries, cares, thoughts, efforts, etc.) by opening our spirits to receive the flowing life of God within (using whatever means that make Him most real to us). Rather than rushing to Him with our petitions and clamoring, we quietly come into His manifest presence. Use vision.
3. Unite with His life — Ask for the indwelling of God's life.	Luke 11:13 1 John 5:14,15	"Please increase in me now Your life-giving power, in Jesus' name." Unite your heart with His love by loving Him. See with your eye of faith the spiritual reality taking place.
4. Believe in faith that you have received His power and give thanks for it. Faith is the switch that turns on the power.	Mark 11:23,24	Do not keep saying, "Oh, please, Lord." Rather say, "Thank You, Lord, that Your power is making me well," as you look ahead with the eye of faith seeing that part of your body whole and functioning well. Forget about everything else and think of God and Jesus Christ and His light flowing through you. Do not work too hard at it. Get comfortable and relax.

A Pattern for Healing Prayer

Healing is not received only by the followers of Christ. It is the light and love of God reaching out to a darkened and hurting world. It is the goodness of God that leads men to repentance (Rom. 2:4). Out of ten lepers that Jesus healed, did nine accept Him as Savior? (Luke 17:12-19) Actually, those of the world often receive healing more easily than God's children. The world is receiving a taste of God's unmerited love and grace.

When beginning in healing prayer, choose a simple, tangible objective that you know is within God's will (for example, personal healing — Matt. 8:16; Acts 10:38). As Jesus would, lay your hands on the area of the body to be healed (when proper). You are transferring by touch the love and healing that resides in your spirit. The location of your hands and the tenderness of your touch should be guided by Jesus. Then, commune with Jesus until you receive His presence and authority within. Pray it forth as He directs.

If sickness persists, it is not due to a lack in God, but to a natural and understandable lack in ourselves. When our electric lights work partially or not at all, we should remember that Edison tried and failed 6000 times before he succeeded in making the electric light bulb.

Personal Prayer Response

Experiment with entering prayer by using the four stages given in this chapter. First relax. Then lift up your eyes to the heavens from whence cometh your strength. Begin to lift up the name of the Lord Jesus Christ. Declare His goodness and His glory and His greatness, His majesty and His wonder. See Him seated upon the throne, with the many thousands bowing down and worshiping before Him. Then thank Him that He can come to join His life with yours. Thank Him for uniting with your spirit. See the King as merging with you and all that He is beginning to flow out through you. Thank Him for the power that is flowing through you. Close in celebration and thankfulness. Use vision throughout.

Part 2

Maintaining the Rational Aspect of Prayer

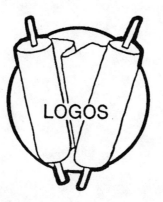

(Testing Spiritual Experience)

"Examine everything carefully.
Hold fast to that which is good."
1 Thes. 5:21

Chapter 15

Testing Spiritual Experiences Against the Bible

We have found that the inner world of the Spirit can be investigated in depth only when it is taken seriously and not subjected to logical sensory doubt. We found that we jam our receivers if we doubt and question incoming *rhema*. However, there is a place for using the mind to try every spirit. The testing of spiritual experiences against the Bible is one of the things that keeps us from error, and, although the mind is not the organ that receives revelation (the heart is), it is the organ that registers and compares revelation to Scripture to be sure it has come from God.

There are two ways you can use your mind to compare revelation to Scripture. One is to say, "Well, I've never been taught that or seen that in Scripture. Therefore, it must be wrong." The other is to eagerly search the Scriptures when something new appears in your journaling **to see if there are examples of it in Scripture.** I find that even though I may have never seen it before in Scripture, **once I have experienced it myself** I am then able to go back to Scripture and discover things that were there all the time. However, I was too blind to see them. Therefore, be careful to use your mind properly when you use it to evaluate the revelation you receive. You are to use it to compare your experiences to the Scriptures (not to

your theology), to see if others in the Bible have had similar experiences. While you compare, you are to be praying for a spirit of revelation as you study (Eph. 1:17,18).

I am convinced many people use their minds improperly when testing revelation. They test against their theology rather than against the teachings and experiences found in Scripture. Essentially most of our theology has been passed down for 300 years and has degenerated as it has been passed along. Most everything I was taught was in need of some major help.

The second major mistake people make in going to Scripture is they try to prove things wrong, rather than trying to prove things right. In this way, they use the Word unlawfully, as a club to beat and destroy, rather than as a rod that lifts and helps.

The lawful use of Scripture is to cause one to persevere and be encouraged to hope (Rom 15:4). I used Scripture unlawfully for years. I have repented and now teach about the wonder and marvel of the living Christ within the heart of the believer, rather than the believer striving hard to keep some laws. God made Galatians 3:3 so very real to me: "Having begun in the Spirit, are you now being made perfect by the flesh?" I had fallen back into encouraging people to struggle and strive with their flesh, instead of looking to the indwelling Christ. Not until I got over my own struggling and striving with my flesh and learned to simply come to the power of the indwelling Christ was I able to see this truth in Scripture. Then hundreds of Scriptures came alive that I had never noticed or understood before. (See **Abiding In Christ** or **Fused to Glory** by the same authors.)

Things Affecting Your Spirit

If you are a Christian, God's Spirit is in union with your spirit (1 Cor. 6:17). However, things other than God can affect and move your spirit. These are indicated in the following passages. Please look up the biblical references and write down the thing that affected the spirit in each of the following cases.

Circumstances of life (1 Sam. 1:1-15)

Physical, bodily circumstances (1 Sam. 30:12)

Satan (John 13:2)

Man (Prov. 16:32)

Therefore, spontaneous thoughts, ideas, etc. may not be coming from the indwelling Spirit of God, but from these other things. Discern when anything other than God is affecting your spirit, and call upon God's grace to overcome it.

As your mind goes to the work of purifying and testing *rhema*, it should:

1. Look for evidence of influences other than the Spirit of God.
2. Ask, "What is the essence of the *rhema*?" (The center is more likely to be pure than the periphery.)
3. Discern whether you were totally under the control of God as your received the *rhema*. Following are some questions that can help you decide:

- Had you presented your life as a living sacrifice?
- Were you washed by your obedience to His *logos*?
- Were you enlightened with His illumination?
- Were you totally committed to His will?
- Were you centered down through your offering of praise?
- Were you waiting quietly and expectantly with the eyes of your heart fixed upon Him?

These questions outline the requirements laid out by God for the Israelites as they approached Him through the six pieces of furniture in the tabernacle and received His *rhema* in the Holy of Holies. Another way of asking these six questions would be, "Were you living the tabernacle experience?"

Testing Whether a Thought Is From Self, Satan or God

The Bible tells us that we can test the spirit, the content and the fruit of a revelation to determine whether it is of God. The chart on the *following page* is an expansion. Read it now.

The fruit of inner spiritual experiences should be an increase in love, reconciliation, healing and wholeness. If, instead, you find the opposite happening, you should immediately discontinue your waiting for spiritual experience until you receive help from your spiritual counselor.

SELF	SATAN	GOD
	Find its origin — test the spirit (1 John 4:1).	
Born in meditation. A progressive building of ideas.	A flashing mental thought. Was mind empty, idle? Does thought seem obstructive?	Sensed in innermost being. Then formed in thoughts. Was mind focused on Jesus?
	Examine its content — test the words (1 John 4:5).	
A consideration of things I have learned.	Negative, destructive, pushy, fearful, accusative, Violates nature of God. Violates Word of God. Thought is afraid to be tested.	Instructive, upbuilding, comforting. Thought accepts testing.
	Inspect its fruit — test the fruit (Matt. 7:15,16).	
Variable	Fear, compulsion, bondage, anxiety, confusion.	Quickened faith, power, peace, good fruit, enlightenment, knowledge.

Knowing the *Logos*

It is **absolutely imperative** that you know and study the Bible so you have an absolute standard against which to test all spiritual experiences. The Bible is our absolute, infallible, unchanging standard of truth. Just as you learn to crawl before you learn to walk, so, too, before you learn to work with *rhema*, you should know the logos. You should, at least, have a working knowledge of the New Testament and be working on the rest of the Bible if you are going to investigate *rhema* in depth. Otherwise, you open yourself up for easy deception.

Commitment to a Body

God has given us one another, and together we are the Body of Christ. We find safety in our relationship to a Bible-believing fellowship. All *rhema* involving major decisions should be submitted to your spiritual overseer. Ephesians 5:21 states, "Submit yourselves one to another," and goes on to delineate the various areas of covering God has placed in our lives. Each is to lay down his *rhema* before his God-ordained covering, who provides safety from our tendency to rush off to do something that is not truly God's will. "In the multitude of counselors there is safety" (Prov. 11:14). Elders are the covering over a church, and those within the fellowship are to submit their rhema to them for confirmation or adjustment (Heb. 13:17). In an age of lawlessness, **order** is to characterize God's people. To whom are you submitted?

These	are to submit to	these
Children	Ex. 20:12; Col. 3:20	Parents
Wives	Eph. 5:22-24	Husbands
Husbands	1 Pet. 5:1-5; 1 Tim. 5:17; Heb. 13:17	Elders
Elders	Acts 14:23; Eph. 5:21	Each Other in Christ
Employees	Eph. 6:5-8; 1 Pet. 2:18-23	Employers
Employers	Eph. 6:9	God
Citizens	Rom. 13:1-7; 1 Pet. 2:13-15	Government
Government	Dan. 2:20,21; Prov. 21:1	God

Understanding the Principle of Authority

To properly relate to and respect authority in your life, you must realize several things.

1. God is responsible for placing the authority over you. (Rom. 13:1 — "There is no authority except from God, and those which exist are established by God." Ps. 75:6,7 — "Not from the east, or from the west, nor from the desert comes exaltation; but God is the Judge; He puts down one, and exalts another.")

2. God is bigger than the authority. Therefore, develop a confidence in God's working through the authority. (Prov. 21:1 — "The king's heart is like channels of water in the hand of the Lord; He turns it wherever He wishes.")

3. You should look for the reason God has placed the authority over you.

4. The hard-to-get-along-with characteristics of the authority over you represent an underlying purpose of God in your life.

5. Pray for God to work through the authority (1 Tim. 2:1-4). Our prayers determine the kind of authority under which we will work.

6. Realize that through prayer you will have influence over all authority in your life (Eph. 1:20-

22; 2:6). Therefore, pray for God to direct his heart, and obey any other commands of Scripture concerning the situation. Then, cheerfully accept the authority as from God (1 Pet. 4:12-14).

7. **The only exception** to obeying the authority over you is if he commands you to do that which is contrary to **a direct command** (not some fuzzy interpretation) of God in Scripture (Dan. 6; Acts 4:19,20).

8. Success comes from realizing that God works through the authority He has placed over your life, and that to resist that authority is to resist God. (Rom. 13:2 — "He who resists authority has opposed the ordinance of God; and they who have opposed will receive condemnation upon themselves.")

One who is going to operate successfully in *rhema* must know to whom he is submitted and lay down all major decisions before him. One who refuses to do that and walks off in the arrogance and pride of "God and I can do it alone" will inevitably fall and reap destruction.

Assignment: If by any chance you have not already established a spiritual covering in your life as you were instructed to in Chapter One, establish clearly in your heart and mind the one whom God has placed over you. Then go to him or her asking his acceptance of the submission of your *rhema* to him.

Steps of Action to Take When You Disagree With Authority

If you come to a point of disagreement with your spiritual authority, you are not to respond like a mindless, spiritless robot. There is specific action you can take.

1. Make sure your attitudes are all purified with tender love. Do not allow a condemning, resistant, impure spirit into your heart (i.e., Dan. 1:9).

2. Make sure your conscience is clear, that you have corrected your offending attitudes, and that you have sought forgiveness and made restitution as far as possible (Dan. 9:20). Lay aside your own wishes for the wishes of the one over you.

3. Discern the basic intention of the one over you. Is he looking out for your well-being? What is his frame of reference? (Dan. 1:10)

4. Then, with that information, design a creative alternative that satisfies each of you (Dan. 1:8).

5. Without condemning him, present that alternative to him as an appeal, emphasizing how it will meet his goals. Leave the final decision with him (Dan. 1:12,3).

6. Give God time to change his mind (Dan. 1:16). Know that God will be putting pressure on him; that he, therefore, will probably put pressure on you; and, that God can use that pressure to build Godly character in your life. Make sure you constantly respond in love and righteousness.

7. Finally, at times, you may have to suffer even though you have done nothing wrong (Dan. 6:12-16). God will be your strength.

Changing Authorities in Your Life

There are times when you will find yourself changing authorities in your life: when you move, change jobs, change churches, marry, etc. Whenever a change must occur, be sure to do everything possible to make it smooth and harmonious.

If possible, so far as it depends on you, be at peace with all men (Rom. 12:18).

If there has been tension in the relationship, work through the steps mentioned above. It is best that there be consensus between you and your authority concerning the upcoming change. However, regrettably, this is not always possible.

The important thing as you leave one relationship and enter another is that you be committed and established somewhere in the Body of Christ, under a protective covering. One's shepherd acts as an umbrella of protection providing safety and covering for you as you walk through life.

The "Principle of Authority" must be applied through the revelation of the Spirit in each individual's life. Thus we ask you to prayerfully apply these principles, through the manifold wisdom of the Spirit of Christ.

May "lawfulness" characterize the Church in an age of "lawlessness."

Personal Application

Remember that things other than God can affect your spirit; therefore, you must remain aware of and in touch with His Spirit within you.

Also, be aware that the essence of *rhema* is usually of greater purity than the periphery.

Select from your journal something God has given you and submit it to the following questions and tests:

1. What is its origin?
2. What is its content?
3. What is its fruit?
4. Compare it with Scripture.
5. Submit it to your spiritual overseer.

Self Evaluation: (circle one)

I have a good working knowledge of the Bible.	Yes No
I am submitted to my spiritual covering(s) and he/she is willing for me to bring major decisions to him.	Yes No

Personal Journaling Application

Prayer: "Lord, speak to me about being under authority. Do I have adequate spiritual covering in position over me? Do I have an attitude of submission? Am I walking in spiritual pride?"

Fix your eyes on Jesus and tune to spontaneity. Ask Him the questions listed above. Record what He says.

Chapter 16

Principles of Prayer

It has been found that in a fenced-off playground, children will play all the way to the edges of the grounds; whereas, in a non-fenced playground, children tend to huddle more towards the center and play there. I found that as I entered the world of spiritual experiences, I was wary because I did not know for sure where the edges were, and I did not want to fall into error. Therefore, I studied the biblical principles of prayer to help build a fence around me to keep me safe, as well as to provide definite steps or platforms on which I could stand as I walked in the sea of the Spirit. Following are the principles I discovered.

PRINCIPLE	SCRIPTURE (fill in)
1. Forgive **everything** against **everyone** so your prayers are not blocked. We are to live in Jesus' love, laying down our lives for one another.	Mark 11:25
At the end of this chapter you will find a section offering more help in the area of releasing forgiveness.	John 15:9
	John 15:12,13

1 John 4:7,8

1 John 4:12

1 John 4:18-21

---

2. Walk in **holiness**. This is required in   Ps. 66:18
    order to be heard by God.

                                                      Isa. 59:1,2

                                                      Heb. 5:7

                                                      Heb. 12:1

                                                      James 5:16

3. Prayer must flow together with *rhema.*   Mark 11:22,23
    Rhema gives **heart** faith, reveals God's
    will, and is to abide in you.

                                                   Rom. 10:10a,17

                                                   1 John 5:14,15

                                                   John 15:7

                                                   Heb. 11:1,6

                                                   James 1:6,7

---

4. Pray fervently and earnestly with your   James 5:17,18
    whole heart.

                                                   1 Kings 18:43

                                                   Ps. 19:58

                                                   2 Chron. 15:15b

---

5. Pray in Jesus' name.   John 14:13

                                                        Mark 16:17

---

6. Speak to the mountain   Mark 11:23
    (rather than simply praying to Jesus).
    Hold fast to your confession.
                                                        Matt. 8:26

                                                        Heb. 10:23

---

7. See it done. Believe that what you say is   Mark 11:23,24
    going to happen. (Letting God show you
    a vision of the completed action causes
    your heart to believe.)

---

8. Pray until you praise. A need is not   Phil. 4:6,7
    prayed for until it has been overcome in
    prayer by the power and promises of
    God, and you have entered into peace.

---

9. Pray persistently and   Luke 11:8-10
    exercise patience.

                                                        Luke 18:1,7

                                                        Heb. 6:12

---

10. Fortify prayer with fasting.   Matt. 9:15
    (Study Isaiah 58.)

                                                    Matt. 17:21

---

11. Pray with intensity, with compassion and   Matt. 20:34
    a sense of burden, with a broken heart,
    with agony, groaning and travail.

                                                    Ps. 62:8

                                                    Ps. 34:18

                                                    Heb. 5:7

                                                    Luke 22:44

                                                    Rom. 8:26

---

12. Pray when you need God's strength.   Heb. 4:16
    (Do not hide yourself in shame at your
    weakness.)
                                                    Ps. 50:15

---

13. Pray in secret.   Matt. 6:6

14. Pray specifically.   Acts 4:29-31

15. Resist satan's attack by calling upon God.   2 Cor. 10:3-5
    Do not fight satan yourself. You will lose.
    See the summary sheet "Satan's Tac-
    tics" for a delineation.

                                                 James 4:6-8

                                                 Eph. 6:10-13

16. Sow bountifully, for in so doing, you will   2 Cor. 9:6-8
    reap bountifully.

                                                 Phil. 4:16,17,19

17. Avoid vain repetition.   Matt. 6:7

                                                        Luke 20:47

**18. Do not seek your own
pleasure.**   James 4:3

Releasing Forgiveness

God is love (1 John 4:8), and His healing power will not flow apart from His love.

Forgive us our sins as we forgive those who transgress against us. If you forgive not ... your heavenly Father will not forgive (Matt. 6:12,14,15).

Forgiving and being forgiven are **essential** to effective prayer. If you are harboring guilt or condemnation toward yourself, or jealousy, resentment or some other critical attitude toward another, your digestion is upset, your muscles are weakened, your mind is confused, and when these negative attitudes are sustained, the body prepares for death (3 John 2).

1. Forgiving Yourself

God grants us forgiveness and cleansing as we confess our sins to Him (1 John 1:9). On several occasions after I have repented, the Lord has asked me if I will forgive myself, and I have realized that I had not, even though He had. To forgive myself, I find I have to fully accept my weakness and bent toward sinning, and realize that my righteousness is not something I obtain through my godly living, but something I receive

freely as I put on the robe of Christ's righteousness that has been prepared for me. In accepting this, I can accept my sinfulness, and God's grace and mercy that reaches down to me, picking me up and clothing me with Himself. Write out the following verses:
Eph. 2:8,9

Gal. 3:1-3

1 Cor. 1:30,31

God has also provided a picturesque means of receiving His forgiveness. When it is difficult to sense His forgiveness in your heart, you may go to the elders over you (or a close, spiritually mature friend) and confess your sins to them, allowing them to pray over you (James 5:14-16) and announce God's forgiveness for your sins (John 20:23). This actual demonstration of the invisible realities taking place will help make God's forgiveness more real to you. It can bring the healing of guilt and condemnation to your heart and soul that you so desperately need.

2. Forgiving Others

Those closest to us hurt us most, and it is these toward whom we will have buried anger and hurts. In turn, this unforgiveness will hinder our prayers (1 Pet. 3:7,8). We are to be understanding of one another's weaknesses, harmonious, sympathetic, brotherly, kindhearted and humble in spirit. (We, too, have no strength or good in ourselves.) We are to agree with our adversaries quickly (Matt. 5:15); do everything we can to be at peace with all men (Rom. 12:18); overcome evil with good, rather than be overcome by evil (Rom. 12:21); love our enemies, bless those who persecute us (Rom. 12:14); return a blessing for a curse (Matt. 5:39); use a gentle answer to turn away wrath and be blessed as a peacemaker (Matt. 5:9).

Following is a simple **drill on forgiveness:**

a. Use vision, seeing first the person, then Christ responding to that person in the way His love would cause Him to respond.

b. In prayer, forgive him in the name of Jesus Christ.

c. As Job (Job 42:10), pray God's blessing upon him.

It is only as we walk in the love and mercy of God toward ourselves and others that God's healing and power flow (Ps. 133:1-3).

Personal Journaling Application

If you sense you need to deepen your forgiveness toward someone, do so using the drill offered above. Otherwise, ask the Lord what He would like to speak to you about the principles discussed in this chapter. Using vision, fix your eyes on Jesus, tune to spontaneity and ask Him the question. Record below what He says.

Chapter 17

Areas of Prayer

As we examine the Lord's prayer and other prayers in the Bible, we find that there are various areas of prayer in which one can engage. Seven of these areas are listed below. They will not all be found in every prayer session, nor will they follow a legalistic order or a rigid time slot. They are to flow **as directed by the Holy Spirit**. We are always to "pray in the Spirit (Eph. 6:18)," meaning that all our prayers are to be inspired, guided, energized and sustained by the Holy Spirit. Through *logos*, we find what these seven prayer areas can encompass; through *rhema*, we find daily direction for our prayers.

As you pray, cultivate a constant openness to seeing and sensing the spiritual realm. Through dream, vision and imagery, you are able to see with the eye of faith what God is doing just as Jesus did (John 5:19-21; 8:38). Through sensing peace, burdens and other movings in your spirit, you are able to feel those things which God is feeling and impressing. By so doing, your prayer life will ascend above dry rationalism into the beauty and power of spiritual experiences. For prayer to be meaningful, it must be more than simple rationalism. Write in and prayerfully ponder the verses below.

Confession of Sin
1 John 1:7-10

Ps. 139:23,24

As we have already seen, our sins separate us from God, and He hides His presence from us (Isa. 59:1,2). You must deal with **all** your sin every day, or prayer becomes a meaningless, spiritless, fruitless, agonizing endeavor, rather than a meaningful, spiritual, fruitful, delightful encounter with God.

Praying in the Spirit
1 Cor. 14:2,4a,14a,18

Receiving: Waiting, Watching, Listening, Writing, Meditating
Ps. 46:10a

Eccl. 5:1,2

Hab.1:1; 2:2

Praying in the Spirit may permeate all areas of prayer life. It is one of the means given to us by God to ascend above rationalism. Praying in the Spirit is one avenue for opening up the spirit and is, therefore, a prerequisite to effective prayer.

Praise, Thanksgiving, Singing, Worship, Adoration
Ps. 100:1-4

Once you have quieted yourself (through Bible reading, praise, praying in the spirit, or any other means that is conducive to you) and contacted God in your spirit, you are to wait quietly before Him, looking to Him and recording what He says to you.

Personal Petitions
Matt. 6:11

1 Thess. 5:18

Matt. 7:7

Ps. 50:15

Your *"Yada* time" may likely come early in your prayer, as a time of getting your mind off yourself and becoming God-conscious (contacting God). Praise and thanks may also be used as the culmination of your petitions, to express your faith in God's overcoming power. A need has not been prayed for until you can praise God for His handling of it.

God wants us to be totally honest with Him so He can minister to all our needs. Only then, as we are touched with His power, will we become whole and full of His life.

Intercession For Others
1 Tim. 2:1-4

Record what First John 5:14,15 promises about prayer according to God's will:

We are constantly to pray for all men, and especially for all in authority. As we pray for others, let us recall that *paga*, the Hebrew word for "intercession," means "a chance encounter." Therefore, let us keep our hearts open and responsive to those whom God brings to us for prayer. See them as you pray for them, and allow Christ to contact them in vision and minister His grace to them.

As we pray, we need to know God's specific will, even as Jesus did. Then we can command it forth. Therefore, I begin my prayer by waiting for vision or *rhema* or a burden of how to pray. Then, I speak it forth as a command from the heart of God, and God performs it through the power of the Holy Spirit.

Following is a small list of items for which God wills us to pray. I suggest you extend this, making your own list. Then, as you pray, quiet yourself, receive His direction, and command it forth.

1 Tim. 2:1

Speaking to the Mountain
Mark 11:23

1 Tim. 2:2

In this passage we find that we are supposed to command things to happen. We are not to doubt, but are to believe that what we say is going to happen. Wow! We command things to happen! What awesome power God has placed in our hands. Jesus modeled this kind of behavior for us when He commanded sickness to depart. He said, "Arise, take up your pallet, and walk (John 5:8)." One area of our devotional time will be issuing forth commands for mountains to move.

Matt. 9:38

Matt. 6:11

Jesus did not normally pray "if it be Thy Will..." Instead He issued commands. The only time He prayed "if it be Thy will," He already knew what God's will was. He was wondering if there could be a way around it. So you see, Jesus knew the will of God and spoke it forth. We are to do likewise. A scriptural example is found in Acts 4:24-31. Read this passage in your Bible.

Matt. 6:12

Matt. 6:13

Notice: They began in unity (vs. 24). Then, they quoted Scriptures affirming God's will and control over their present situation (vs. 25,26). They affirmed their confidence in God's control (vs. 27,28). Finally, they asked for God's strength to be strong in and through them as they encountered the crisis at hand (vs. 29,30). The results of this prayer are astounding!

Phil. 4:6,7

Add your own to this list.

Personal Journaling Application

Prayer: "Lord, please speak to me about the balance between using a 'system' in prayer and flowing freely in prayer as You direct."

Fix your eyes upon Jesus in some comfortable setting. Tune to spontaneity, ask the above question and record what comes bubbling back into your heart and mind.

Chapter 18

Promises of Prayer

There are many promises concerning prayer. It is good to know them so they can be used as a source of encouragement. The following is a partial list. Once again, you will probably want to add other promises that the Lord reveals to you. Write out the verses below.

2 Chron. 16:9a

John 8:29

John 11:40

John 14:21

John 15:7,8

John 16:12

Heb. 6:24

Add others.

Chapter 19

Ways to Pray

There are many ways to pray for other people. Following are six of them. Write in the verses as you study.

1. Binding Evil Powers and Casting Them Down

Mark 3:27

Eph. 6:12

Before one can see effective results in prayer, it is often necessary to bind the power of satan so it is hindered from working in the situation. Binding is a temporary means of restraining satan's movements.

2. Loosing the Holy Spirit to Move in Their Hearts

Matt. 16:19

Pray for the moving of the Holy Spirit.

3. Building a Hedge of Thorns Around Them

Hos. 2:6,7

Building a hedge will: (1) cause them to lose their path toward evil; (2) cause evil influences to lose their power over them; and (3) cause their troubles to prompt them to return to righteous ways.

4. Praying That God Will Turn Their Hearts

Prov. 21:1

5. Praying That God Will Direct Their Mouths

Prov. 16:1

6. Praying for a Spirit of Revelation
Eph. 1:17,18

The Bible is the only book in the world that is alive (Heb. 4:12) and as such, should not be read simply as other books. Instead, you are to ask the Spirit who wrote it to reveal it to your heart. Then, read with your heart open to the illumination of the Holy Spirit. Without prayer (and obedience), the Bible becomes dead, and one receives head-knowledge rather than heart-knowledge.

Personal Application

Spend some time in prayer. Ask the Lord to burden you with the way(s) you should pray for any situations that He presents before you. Pray in these different ways.

Chapter 20

Interceding in Prayer

Note in the following verses the power that one (or a few) intercessors had in a situation. **You can** truly affect world situations by becoming an intercessor. Write out the following verses.
Gen. 18:32

Isa. 59:16a

Ezek. 22:30,31

Remembering that the Hebrew word for intercession is *paga*, meaning "to light upon by chance," we see that intercession begins with God laying a person on our heart for prayer. Not only will He give us the person, but He will also show us how to pray. I focus first on the person and then I bring Jesus into the picture, allowing Him to move as He wills. As I look at Jesus, I see that He is alive, seeking to touch the individual in a cer-

tain way. I then speak forth in prayer what I see Christ doing.

That is one form of Spirit-led intercession. No doubt, you will find your own. Some people are given the specific ministry of prayer and intercession. Record what the following verses teach.
1 Tim. 5:5

Luke 2:36,38

I have questioned whether I should use a prayer list. It is the problem of *rhema* versus legalism.

Each one will have to solve this question in the way that is best for them. I would recommend that if you decide to keep a prayer list, try not be married to it in a legalistic sense. When I first began to pray, I legalistically kept a prayer list. I found it deadening. After coming to an understanding of *paga*, I rejected all prayer lists. I then found there were things I wished I had prayed for more diligently, but I would forget about them for periods of time. I am currently seeking to work out a compromise, which would entail the use of a prayer list for prompting, but which would not require slavish obedience to it, or guilt and condemnation when I fail to perfectly keep it. I seek to pray for those things the Spirit wants prayed for that day. Each of you will have to establish your own balance.

From My Journal:

"Lord, what about prayer ...?"

"Pray for those I lay on your heart."

On another day, from my journal:

Having just finished studying the ways of praying, and the principles and areas of prayer, I felt like prayer had become a cumbersome burden.

6/17/80: "Good morning, Lord. I love you. I give You this day. I place it in Your hands. Are there things You would like to say to me?"

"Yes. Remember how simple it has been to come to Me? It still is. Do not make it difficult. I am here. I desire to answer you. The things you are learning are good and helpful, but do not let them become obstructive and block the simplicity of our relationship together. If you let Me help you keep them in proper perspective, they will be a real help and blessing. If they get out of balance, they will become meaningless legalism and bondage. I will help you keep them in proper balance. Just come to Me.

"Also, do not forget the specific actions that can be worked out through prayer. As one learns to come to Me, specifically in times of need, I am there to give the specific help they need — whether it be a word of wisdom or knowledge or discernment for the casting out of demons. All power and ability will flow out of our relationship, and that is the order. First, a love relationship. Out of that, the meeting of specific needs.

"I love you, Mark. Keep tuned to My Spirit."

"Thank you, Lord ..."

This reminded me of Psalm 105:4a: "Seek the Lord and His strength." It is so easy to overbalance one or the other, or to reverse the order altogether. But as we come to Him, He will help us keep it straight.

Personal Journaling Application

Ask the Lord whether He wants you to use a prayer list or not. Fix your eyes upon Him. You may want to begin with a time of praise and worship until you are caught up in His presence. Then tune to spontaneity and ask Him the question suggested above. Record below the effortless flow of thoughts within your heart.

Space for Journaling

Chapter 21

Prayer and Action

Fitting prayer and work together in proper understanding and balance can be trying at times. The following are four truths about the combination of prayer and action.

1. Prayer must precede action in order to have Spirit-born action.

Prayer paves the highway of accomplishment. Increasing work and decreasing prayer equals meaningless endeavor. It is the doing that flows out of prayer that is the mightiest in touching human hearts. "Unless the Lord builds the house, they labor in vain who build it (Ps. 127:1)." "That which is born of the flesh is flesh; and that which is born of the Spirit is spirit (John 3:6)." If you do not want action of the flesh, then you must pray and find what action the Spirit wants and move in that. How easy it is to decide what we will do and then pray and ask God to bless it. Later, we may wonder why the results were not what we had hoped. God wants us to come to Him first for direction. Then, He will pour out His blessing upon "our projects," for they will truly be "His work."

2. Prayer is to lead to action.

Write out James 2:17,22,26

When one has finished praying, he most likely will have received specific instructions that he is to obey. One may act and speak with **confidence**, knowing that God is performing the work according to the word that has been spoken.

3. Pray without ceasing while working at different tasks.

While working, your mind will often be attuned to the task before you. Your spirit (heart), however, is to remain open to being moved upon by God. One's work is not to enter his spirit. Only God is to be there. Anything else is idolatry. By keeping one's spirit open, relaxed and attuned to God, one is praying without ceasing (1 Thess. 5:17).

4. Separate yourself unto God so you can bring life to the world.

One can be totally immersed in God all the time, living in his little utopia, and not even be aware of the misery of the world around him. On the other hand, one can be overcome by the woes of the world and feel there is no hope for it. One must again achieve the balance of Jesus of

Nazareth, who spent enough time with God receiving His power that when He went to the world, He was able to overcome its darkness with His light. That is precisely what we are to do. We are to spend enough time with God in prayer that we are charged with His love and power; and then, guided and directed by the Holy Spirit, we are to go to a needy world and minister His grace. We flow with His power, not ours. We minister His thoughts, not ours. We are directed by our spirits rather than our minds. When we feel the power and life of God diminishing within us, we must again go to our quiet place of prayer to renew God's life within us.

Additional Reading

Poustinia by Catherine Doherty

Personal Journaling Application

Ask the Lord to speak to you about the balance of prayer and work in your life. Fix your eyes upon Him. Tune to spontaneity. Record below the flow that issues forth from your heart.

Chapter 22

The Word Become Flesh

Beginning to Pray

One really learns to pray **when he begins pray-ing**. We do not need people who think about prayer, who learn about prayer, or who preach about prayer. We need people who pray. Your prayer life is the proof of the pudding. It is where the rubber meets the road. Whether or not you have excelled in prayer will be determined by your prayer life and the results that flow from it.

Looking Intently

All of us have experienced the excitement of receiving a new teaching, only to experience some time later the discouragement of seeing that it has not been incorporated into our lives. James 1:25 not only describes this problem, but also tells how to over come it. Write out this verse:

The Place of the Bulletin Board

One way to look intently is to use a bulletin board. I actually have two — one entitled "Principles of Prayer," the other "Prayer Items." You, too, may want to use a bulletin board, reviewing those things you especially want to bring into your life.

A Place to Pray

Although one is to pray anywhere and at anytime, it is good for you to ask the Lord to help you find a place where you can go regularly to be alone and undistracted with Him. You will recall Habakkuk (2:1) had a special place to go and pray. Daniel had a roof chamber with a window toward Jerusalem (Dan. 6:10). Jesus went to a place of solitude to pray (Mark 1:35). ESTABLISH YOUR PLACE OF PRAYER. Record here where it is:

A Time of Prayer

One is to pray without ceasing. However, it is necessary for spiritual strength that one set aside time(s) specifically for prayer. Daniel went to his roof chamber three times a day to pray and give thanks (Dan. 6:10). David also prayed three times a day (Ps. 55:17). Jesus prayed at least morning and evening (Mark 1:35; 6:46).

Ask the Lord to help you establish your time(s) of prayer. At first, it will be difficult to keep your time of prayer because you will have to battle both the weakness of the flesh and the attacks of satan. Through persistence, you will shortly develop a habit of prayer. Once you establish something as a **habit**, it is much easier to maintain. So, expect a **battle** at first against both satan and your flesh.

Thought: If we spend sixteen hours daily of our waking life in thinking about the affairs of the world and five minutes in thinking about God, this world will seem 200 times more real to us, than God.

Chapter 23

Beyond Communion With God

Beyond Communion With God? How can that be? When Communion with God has brought us into such blessed communication with our Lord, what could possibly be beyond this? There are two errors that we are prone to when we come into new truth and new experience. The first is to fail to continue in that which we have learned. The second is to go no further than that which got us in.

Doors are nice. They get us inside where it is warm on a cold, snowy day. But spending the rest of the day just inside on the doormat clutching the key in our hand is not, for most of us, the ultimate in enjoying all the comforts of modern living. Communion with God is a doorway, a key that opens up a new stage of Christian experience. Paradoxically, the only thing wrong with any new step in Christ is to stay there and to refuse to move on.

What an idyllic existence for Elijah by the Brook Cherith! "The ravens brought him bread and meat in the morning and bread and meat in the evening and he drank from the brook. But it happened after a while that the brook dried up (1 Kings 17:6,7)." God wanted Elijah to move on. He had already provided a further experience in miraculous provision. At the Brook Cherith, it was "just Jesus and me." And it was a valid,

necessary, and blessed stage in Elijah's experience with God. But there was more.

God had spoken to a widow to provide for Elijah. This must have been a humbling experience for him. Did he not have a direct line to God? What was this business of depending on a widow — a widow, of all people? God was showing Elijah that the only thing better than a direct line to God was also enjoying God's provisions through other's direct line to God.

Truth is communal. None of us by ourselves has it all. This is true in our understanding of Scripture. It is also true in our communion with God. The only thing that could possibly be wrong with communion with God is if we thought that it was everything, that we had heard through personal journaling all that God wants to say to us and all that we need to hear from Him. But we know only in part. Hearing from God personally is only partial. We need the rest of the body of Christ. God speaks to me. But He also speaks to me through you.

Before **Communion with God**, we were at the mercy of only hearing from God "second hand," through what God had said to others in the Scriptures or what God said through older, wiser, more godly Christians. How tragic if, upon learning to hear God for ourselves, we should now "refuse Him that speaketh" through others.

How tragic, also, were we to limit ourselves to one method of hearing from God. What a blessing journaling has been! It broke us out of our shells of silence. It opened us up to "normal" Christian experience. It enabled us to bypass our hypercritical, left brain, trained in rationalistic philosophy, and tap into our God-given intuitive abilities. But what would we do if, desperately needing to hear from God, we were caught without pencil and paper? Could God speak to us without these means?

Of course He could. We learned in **Communion with God** to be open to dream and vision. We know God speaks to us in our spirits. Might not this in fact be the more normal way God speaks to His people? The Scriptures certainly seem to indicate this.

What a blessing it is to keep a journal, not only to journal in, but to record all that God speaks to us, through whatever means, be it:

- His voice in our spirits
- inspired writers
- dream and vision
- the Scriptures made *rhema* to us
- the prophetic word
- sermons
- the counsel of others
- the experiences of life ...
- however a God of infinite variety desires to speak to us.

When we come to listen to God, we listen to all of the above. We can be more certain God is speaking when all of the above line up. May we be those who hear God through the multiplicity of ways He speaks to us. In another book, **Experiencing God**, I go into much greater depth on these various other ways God speaks to us. Happy traveling![1]

---

1   Most of this chapter has been provided by my good friend and scholar, Rev. Maurice Fuller. Special thanks to him for his ongoing assistance.

For Your Personal Notes

For Your Personal Notes

For Your Personal Notes

For Your Personal Notes

For Your Personal Notes

For Your Personal Notes

For Your Personal Notes

<u>For Your Personal Notes</u>

Further Materials
for Your
Continuing Study

TESTIMONIES

Rev. Peter Lord — Park Avenue Baptist Church
"I have been an active Baptist pastor for thirty-seven years. As far as I am personally concerned, seminars like "Counseled by God" and "Communion With God" and "Abiding in Christ" are absolutely fundamental to the building up of the inner life. At this present time we have six ongoing classes in "Communion With God" using Mark's video series and one class on "Counseled by God." I highly recommend him and his ministry to you. I would be glad to talk with you on the telephone if you have any questions." 407-269-6702.

Dr. Richard Watson — Oral Roberts University
"**Communion With God** by Mark and Patti Virkler has dramatically changed my prayer life. I have found I can will to dialogue with Christ on a daily basis, and I do. I believe this inspired approach to be absolutely essential to the growth of every serious Christian. I further believe Communion With God is an excellent example of the uniquely powerful way God is reaching out to His people today."

Rev. Judson Cornwall, ThD.
"God has especially graced Brother Mark Virkler to help persons rediscover the art of communion with God. I have had the opportunity to observe this from a distance for a number of years, but I now have joined forces with this brother in seeking to get this teaching to an ever wider segment of the body of Christ.
"I would highly recommend Mark Virkler and his seminar "Communion With God" to all who still desire to do the will of the Father. His approach is both unique and God given. His integrity is well documented, and his value in bringing people into a depth of prayer cannot be overestimated."

Rev. Thomas Reid — Full Gospel Tabernacle
"The course **Communion With God** is GOING TO CHANGE THE NATION by building a new generation of people that hear God's voice and dream God's dreams."

COMMUNION WITH GOD — The Package of Materials

This is the most practical, down-to-earth training available today on how Christians can dialogue with God. Over 99 percent of all participants begin to use vision in their prayer lives and write down many pages of dialogue with Almighty God on a regular basis. If you are not completely satisfied with this material and do not personally begin to receive and record the things the Lord is speaking to you, you may return this material in resalable condition within 30 days for a full money back refund.

Communion With God Student's Workbook: A 224-page "write in" study manual. Mark Virkler teaches through this text on both the video and audio cassettes. $13.95

Communion With God Teacher's Guide: Twenty-two lesson outlines corresponding to the 22 video and audio sessions, laying the course out in detail for the leader/teacher. $11.95

Communion With God Video Tapes: Twenty-two half-hour sessions of Mark Virkler teaching in a classroom setting. Purchase $299. Rental $99.

Communion With God Audio Cassettes: Twenty-two half-hour sessions of Mark Virkler teaching Communion With God. This corresponds exactly to the video series, except for an additional tape with four quieting exercises on it. $42.00

Dialogue With God: A 250-page teaching testimonial sharing not only the teaching of **Communion With God,** but also many pages of inspiring stories and testimonies. Included are 30 pages of journaling from individuals across several nations — a great source of encouragement for those beginning to journal. $6.95

My Adventures with God: A Journal: More than merely a notebook of lined paper, this journal also includes a review of the four keys to hearing God's voice, what to do if your journaling is wrong, tips to overcoming stumbling blocks and a place for your own personal table of contents. In addition, there is a verse at the top of each journal page which provides instruction, support and encouragement in your spiritual walk. $7.95

Journal/Organizer: Bound in a rich brown padded loose-leaf binder with full color dividers, the Journal/Organizer contains the complete journal (above) as well as a daily appointment calendar, two-year planner, personal telephone directory, sermon and meeting notepad, and many other extras. Makes a wonderful gift for yourself or someone you love! (Available October 1990.)

Talking With Jesus: A 365-day devotional with Scripture and journaling for each day of the year. Evelyn Klumpenhouwer, the author, learned to hear God's voice in a Communion with God seminar in Canada in 1986. This book stands as a testimony of the power of the message of Communion With God to actually teach people to hear God's voice. Tremendously life-giving. $7.95

Our Father Speaks Through Hebrews: A devotional of Hebrews by Rev. Peter Lord. Each journal entry has a verse from Hebrews followed by what the Lord spoke to Rev. Lord concerning the truths in the verse. The first book of journaling written by a man. Excellent, inspiring and life-giving. $7.95

COUNSELED BY GOD — The Package of Materials

A revolutionary book showing you plainly how you can find healing for the basic emotional needs of your life by dialoguing through them with God. It deals with such topics as healing anger, fear, inferiority and condemnation; allowing Christ to heal deep hurts from the past; and learning to incubate only God's voice and vision. If you have found the deep healing that comes as this book has guided you into interaction with God, you may want to obtain other supporting materials for either your personal use or for group use.

Counseled by God Textbook: A 130-page stand alone trade paperback. Excellent for personal use. $6.95

Counseled By God Student's Workbook: A 130-page "write in" study manual. Excellent for group use. Mark Virkler teaches through this text on both the video and audio cassettes. $8.95

Counseled by God Teacher's Guide: Twenty-two lesson outlines corresponding to the 22 video and audio sessions, laying the course out in detail for the leader/teacher. $8.95

Counseled by God Video Tapes: Eleven hours of Mark Virkler teaching in a classroom setting. Purchase $299. Rental $99.

Counseled by God Audio Cassettes: Eleven hours of Mark Virkler teaching **Counseled by God.** This corresponds to the video series. $42.00

Mark Virkler is available as a seminar speaker. He travels full time conducting Communion With God and other seminars at churches worldwide. Contact him at 716-655-0647 to make arrangements to have him come to your church.

CULTIVATING INDIVIDUAL & CORPORATE CREATIVITY
— The Package of Materials

These texts restore the entrepreneur spirit to the Church of Jesus Christ. The goal of the Christian life is not simply death to the flesh, but a release of the resurrection power of Almighty God in every sphere and domain of life. This package of books deals with these themes.

Spirit Born Creativity: Releasing God's Creativity into Your World — The only book of its kind, teaching the process of releasing the creativity of God through the heart of the believer. Ideal for businessmen, parents and anyone who wants to become more creative. It shows step by step how one releases the creativity of Almighty God by filling all five senses of his spirit with God's spoken word and vision. This 238-page trade size paperback by Mark and Patti Virkler sells for $9.95. Teacher's guide available — $4.95.

What The Bible Says About Silver and Gold — Only two groups of people can control the world's wealth. One is the heathen. The other is the Christian. Which group do you feel should have control of the wealth of the world? Have you noticed that Abraham, Isaac, Jacob, David, Solomon and others were both spiritual leaders in their communities and multi-millionaires? Did you realize you could be both? Does God want to release the wealth of this world to His children? If so, what do we need to learn so we will be ready and able to handle it? How is it released? Does it float out of the sky or do we work and plan and pray and then see the fulfillment of our labors? This booklet by Mark and Patti Virkler covers several hundred verses from Scripture on these topics. $3.95

Twenty Biblical Principles for Christian Management

Whether you are responsible for the management of a church or a business, you need to conduct yourself according to God's principles. As Mark Virkler reached to set up his first corporation, he realized he had never studied biblical principles for management and therefore had no idea of what principles he was supposed to be obeying. If he obeyed only half of the key principles for management and didn't know about the rest, would the corporation survive and prosper? Can God's anointing rest upon a church or business that is breaking some of His principles for effective corporate management? This workbook contains 20 evaluation pages which allow you to evaluate your church or business according to key biblical principles. 110 pages, 8 1/2 by 11 by Mark and Patti Virkler — $9.95.

The above three books form the basis of a business seminar which Mark conducts entitled "Cultivating Individual and Corporate Creativity." You may schedule this seminar by contacting Mark at 716-655-0647.

Mark Virkler is available as a seminar speaker. He travels full time conducting Communion With God and other seminars at churches worldwide. Contact him at 716-655-0647 to make arrangements to have him come to your church.

Communion With God Ministries

Name _____ Phone _____

Adress _____

City _____ State _____ Zip _____

Quantity	Title	Price	Total

Communion With God

_____ Communion With God
Student's Workbook . . . $13.95 _____
_____ Communion With God
Teacher's Guide . . . . . $11.95 _____
_____ Communion With God
Audio Cassettes . . . . . . $42.00 _____
_____ Communion With God Video Tapes
VHS/Beta Purchase . $299.00 _____
VHS/Beta Rental . . . $99.00 _____
_____ Dialogue With God . . . $6.95 _____
_____ Talking With Jesus . . . $7.95 _____
_____ Our Father Speaks Through
Hebrews . . . . $7.95 _____

Counseled By God

_____ Counseled By God
Paperback Book . . . . . . $6.95 _____
_____ Counseled By God
Student's Workbook . . . . $8.95 _____
_____ Counseled By God
Teacher's Guide . . . . . . $9.95 _____
_____ Counseled by God
Audio Cassettes . . . . . . $42.00 _____
_____ Counseled by God Video Tapes
VHS/Beta Purchase . $299.00 _____
VHS/Beta Rental . . . $99.00 _____

Cultivating Individual and Corporate Creativity

_____ Spirit Born Creativity
Textbook . . . . $9.95 _____
_____ Spirit Born Creativity Teacher's
Guide . . . . $4.95 _____
_____ What the Bible Says About
Silver and Gold . . . . . . $3.95 _____
_____ Twenty Key Biblical Principles
for Christian Management $9.95 _____

Sub-total _____
Shipping & Handling Charges _____
TOTAL _____

Free in Every Order
A free ordering catalog describing over 50 guided self-discovery study manuals (many with cassettes and videos) which Mark and Patti have developed. These are ideal for personal, small group and large group use, including home cells, Sunday school, Bible school and Sunday and Wednesday evening church services. In addition to the above topics, this includes studies in the areas of abiding in Christ, Spirit born creativity, Christian dream interpretation, through the Bible series, creating and releasing wealth, worshipping with sign language, transmitting Spirit life and much more.

A free copy of **Communion With God Ministries Newsletter**, a magazine that keeps you informed of new materials and developments in Mark and Patti's ministry, Communion With God.

A free listing of 13 seminars by Mark Virkler, available to be hosted by your local church.

Money Back Guarantee: If you are not completely satisfied with these materials, you may return them within 30 days in resalable condition and receive a full refund on the cost of the book.

Make check payable in U.S. currency to:
Communion With God Publishers,
1431 Bullis Road,
Elma, NY 14059
716-655-0647

SHIPPING & HANDLING
minimum charge of $2.50 per order
or respective % of subtotal
U.S. 8%
Canada 12%
South America 16%
Europe, Africa, Asia & Australia . . 20%
Please allow 6-8 weeks for delivery to overseas countries. COD available in U.S. only.